The

EVERYTHING® Coin Collecting Book

Dear Reader,

Coin collecting is the hobby of kings, of young and old, of male and female, of husbands and wives. It can be an academic pursuit or a leisure-time activity, and it can be profitable. You can collect on a shoestring, or you can spend a significant amount of money on this hobby. Just don't lose perspective. With the exception of some commemorative coins as well as bank notes that are made for use in commerce, coins and bank notes are currency first and collectibles second.

This hobby can be all-absorbing. I began as a collector, eventually becoming a full-time coin dealer. There has been a tremendous learning curve along the way. Numismatics—the study or collecting of coin[...] is so vast that you never stop learnin[...]

I h[...]ctively participat[...]asure from coin [...]

The EVERYTHING® Series

Editorial

Publishing Director	Gary M. Krebs
Director of Product Development	Paula Munier
Associate Managing Editor	Laura M. Daly
Associate Copy Chief	Brett Palana-Shanahan
Acquisitions Editor	Lisa Laing
Development Editor	Jessica LaPointe
Associate Production Editor	Casey Ebert

Production

Director of Manufacturing	Susan Beale
Associate Director of Production	Michelle Roy Kelly
Cover Design	Paul Beatrice Matt LeBlanc Erick DaCosta
Design and Layout	Heather Barrett Brewster Brownville Colleen Cunningham Jennifer Oliveira
Series Cover Artist	Barry Littmann
Photo Research	Randy Thern

THE EVERYTHING® COIN COLLECTING BOOK

All you need to start your collection for fun or profit!

Richard Giedroyc

Adams Media
Avon, Massachusetts

This book is dedicated to my wife, Jewell, without whose support I would likely not be involved in this pursuit.

An Everything® Series Book.
Everything® and everything.com® are registered trademarks of F+W Publications, Inc.

Published by Adams Media, an F+W Publications Company
57 Littlefield Street, Avon, MA 02322 U.S.A.
www.adamsmedia.com

ISBN 10: 1-59337-568-9
ISBN 13: 978-1-59337-568-3

Printed in the United States of America.

J I H G F E D C B A

Library of Congress Cataloging-in-Publication Data

Giedroyc, Richard.
The everything coin collecting book / Richard Giedroyc.
p. cm. -- (An everything series book)
Includes bibliographical references.
ISBN-13: 978-1-59337-568-3
ISBN-10: 1-59337-568-9
1. Coins--Collectors and collecting--Handbooks, manuals, etc. I. Title.

CJ81.G54 2007
737.4--dc22

2006028186

Contents

Acknowledgments

This book would not have been written if it weren't for the patience of my wife, Jewell, and the encouragement of my editors David Harper at Krause Publications and Gina Chaimanis at Adams Media, as well as the countless number of coin collectors and coin dealers with whom I share this wonderful hobby on a daily basis. I would also like to thank Randy Thern at Krause for the many hours of research to locate the photos for this book.

Top Ten Ways to Get the Most Out of Coin Collecting

1. Get involved in the social aspects of the hobby.
2. Learn to grade and authenticate your coins.
3. Understand the ways to collect.
4. Learn the many avenues through which you can sell what you have collected.
5. Know the rarity and value of your coins.
6. Study the history behind what you are collecting.
7. The facts about coins as a possible investment are important—learn them!
8. Find where to go to learn more about numismatics.
9. Numismatics can become a full- or part-time profession. Consider it!
10. Treat coin collecting as a hobby first—have fun!

Introduction

▶ COIN COLLECTING HAS been around likely since someone invented the first coin. Collecting is one of the most popular pastimes people enjoy with their discretionary money. Coin collecting is a natural choice of hobby, since we see coins and bank notes virtually every day.

Among the spoils of war inventoried by Pompey the Great when he dragged the unfortunate Mithradates VI of Pontus through the streets of ancient Rome was a coin collection. Julius Caesar's nephew the Emperor Augustus was known to give what contemporary chroniclers call "ancient" coins to some of his colleagues. Since that time there have been the sophisticated and the unsophisticated, the rich and the poor, the elite of society and the commoner—all with one interest in common: the pleasure of collecting coins they value.

Coin collecting took root early in the history of the United States. By 1816, a major coin collection was in the makings, and the first acknowledged auction specializing in collectible coins took place in 1828. Nobody really knows just how many people collect coins today, in part due to a lack of reliable studies and in part due to a lack of an acceptable definition of where accumulating coins stops and true collecting coins begins. We know one thing for certain: There are innumerable people who have old coins they found, inherited, or simply accumu lated and are keeping the coins either for their collecting pleasure c because they hope those holdings may have significant value.

Coin collecting is a very organized hobby. There are local, regior and national organizations open to anyone with such an interest. Tl are hobby and trade publications, some of which are published weekly. The Internet has more numismatic-related sites than anyone could possibly read. There are a significant number of books on aspects of the subject published every year.

The nice thing about coin collecting is that it is for everyone. You can collect modestly by going through your change, or you can spend significant sums to own some of the almost legendary rarities of the hobby. There is an entry level for everyone.

The most important thing is to learn as much about what you are collecting as possible. By learning, you will avoid the many potential pitfalls and mistakes. Collecting should be a fun pursuit. By reading this book, I hope you, too, will enjoy coin collecting.

chapter 1

Welcome to Coin Collecting

Money in the form of coins has been around almost as long as there has been civilization, and almost as long as there have been coins there have been coin collectors. Coin collecting can be a solitary pastime, or it can be a social activity involving family and friends. It can also be an educational and a profitable undertaking. Coin collecting has been called the hobby of kings, but it is also the hobby of virtually anyone who takes an interest in studying and accumulating what we use as currency.

Defining Coin Collecting

Coin collecting is sometimes referred to as numanistics, which originates from the Greek word nummi, or "money." Coin collecting actually has three aspects. There are collectors seeking fun. There are coin dealers with profit as their sole motivation. Then there are scholars who find coins to be useful artifacts for studying human sociology and archaeology.

FACT

Julius Caesar was a coin collector. So was the Sun King, Louis XIV of France. Coins and people who collect them have been around for a long time. It is possibly one of the oldest hobbies in existence.

Coin collecting is more than just collecting coins. Considering the length of time that coins have been produced and the breadth of what has been issued to drive local economies, there is an almost unimaginable number of coin- and currency-related objects to collect. Most collectors begin with what is most available to them—their pocket change. Many collectors, for this reason, like to begin with the U.S. 1-cent coin.

What to Collect?

Along with coins, U.S. paper money is also a well-recognized part of the U.S. "coin" collecting hobby. U.S. paper money begins with colonial issues prior to the American Revolution, followed by a plethora of private bank issues, then with federal issues produced by various government agencies. The federal issues include Federal Reserve notes, U.S. or legal tender notes, compound interest treasury notes, interest bearing notes, refunding certificates, silver certificates, treasury notes, national bank notes, gold certificates, and military payment certificates.

Aside from U.S. coin and currency collectibles, there is an entire world out there to be considered. Today there are more than 300 coin and currency-issuing entities producing money around the world. This, of course, ignores all the earlier coin and currency-issuing entities that have existed during the past 2,600 years.

Some collectors choose a theme for their collection. However, not everyone wants to develop a theme by which they will collect. Some collectors like an eclectic collection—a collection of whatever piques their interest. There is no right way or wrong way to collect.

Where does a collector begin? Many people who collect foreign coins or bank notes select a country with which they can identify, such as the ancestral home of their family. Others may decide they like a particular theme appearing on coins, such as animals or buildings. Still others may decide they will collect a sample coin from every coin-issuing entity on earth. Medieval coins are yet another option. So are ancient coins. All it takes is imagination to develop a collecting theme.

A coin group.

Starting Your Collection

The most logical place to begin your coin collection is in your pockets. You will likely find the beginnings of a great coin collection—all sorts of coin denominations, designs, and dates. Perhaps you want to develop a type set (collecting an example of each coin currently used in circulation), a date set (for example collecting a nickel for each year they were produced), or a personal collection (such as coins of the years in which your children were born).

As you search through your pocket change each day, you may be fortunate to find some older coins that happen to be still in circulation. Building your collection in this way, from your pocket change, is the best way to begin. Later you can gradually advance to coins you purchase.

Get your feet wet at a modest price first. If you want to become a more ambitious collector, you should have an education base from which to cautiously move forward. It would be unwise to spend a lot of money on coins before you understand very much about the hobby.

As you collect, learn as much as you can about coins. Determine if the hobby is for you, then choose a level of sophistication and expense. Coin collecting can be complicated, and there is a learning curve. Keep your accumulation habits modest until you are comfortable that you know in what direction and at what financial cost you want to become involved. Take your time to develop a collection, not an accumulation.

The denomination side of a coin.

One important thing to learn as you begin collecting is the meaning of the word *rare*. It equates to simple economics: If there are fewer of a particular coin (supply) than are there people who want to buy that coin (demand), the likelihood of the coin selling for a favorable price is good. The opposite is also true: If there are more of a particular coin available than there are buyers, its value will likely remain unfavorable. In circumstances like these, the value of a coin may be in its precious metal content rather than due to its date.

Committing to Your Hobby

Anything you do in life includes an investment of your time, effort, and money. Don't be in a rush to spend them until you understand what you are buying. Shop around. Talk to collectors as well as to coin dealers. Buy something inexpensive, then resell it to find out how you really did. Here's how to conserve each of your precious resources—time, effort, and money.

Your Time

Coin collecting is a hobby, but it can take up as much time as you let it. You can spend very little time on coin collecting by simply accumulating coins from pocket change, then throwing them into a drawer. On the other hand, you can spend significant time studying each coin you collect, then assembling and housing your collection in some meaningful manner.

It's important to decide how you wish to spend your collecting time as well. You can spend your time in solitude, or you can spend it with others. This hobby can involve fellow collectors or family. (We'll talk more about the social aspects of coin collecting in Chapter 4.)

Your Effort

As with anything else in this world, the amount of effort you put into your coin collecting hobby will show in the results you reap. A very casual collector will generally assemble a modest collection, while a diligent collector who works to accumulate and study the coins he or she has acquired may assemble a more ambitious collection.

The best way to maximize your effort is to focus your collection, perhaps with a theme. Direction is important. You can try to collect everything, but a focused agenda will likely be more satisfying.

Your Money

There is no free lunch. This statement is just as true in coin collecting as it is in any other endeavor. Regardless of if your coin collection will be assembled entirely from your pocket change or if it will involve the purchase of expensive coins, there will be an outlay of cash involved. Just how much money you put into your hobby is up to you.

Bear in mind that just because you spend money purchasing coins is no guarantee you are buying something that will increase in value. Unless the demand for what you are acquiring outstrips the supply, you won't get rich quick. Most collectors buy coins with their discretionary money, not with their life savings. (We'll talk about investing in coins in Chapter 11.)

Here's one last important note about spending your resources: Regardless if you are a hobbyist or investor, purchase coins for quality, not quantity. Scratches and other detriments don't go away, and problem coins never realize the same value as problem-free coins do. If you buy, buy wisely. Along the same lines, if you collect coins from circulation, acquire the best examples you can find. In other words—spend your time, effort, and money wisely.

Educating Yourself

There's much to learn about the fascinating hobby of coin collecting. One thing many beginners find surprising is that the age of a coin has nothing to do with its value. People unfamiliar with the history of coins often think that anything older than themselves is ancient. Nothing could be farther from the truth; an ancient coin is any coin made through A.D. 476, the year of the fall of the Roman Empire. Coins made from A.D. 476 through about 1500 are called medieval coins. Both ancient and medieval coins were made completely by hand.

FACT

The obverse side of a coin is commonly known as "heads," and the reverse side is commonly called "tails."

Early modern coins, those made after about 1500, were struck by machines. However, these coins were made before the introduction of the coin collar—the part that holds the coinage blank when it is struck that ensures the coin remains round. Modern coins commence with the introduction of the collar.

A coin display.

Examining Coins Up Close

As you educate yourself about your new hobby, you'll need to know how to examine coins properly and to build a library. Even if you can't see something clearly on a coin, you shouldn't be surprised if later on you learn it was a problem coin. For this reason both magnification and proper illumination are important factors in coin collecting. Just how much magnification or illumination is necessary when examining a coin is in question, but some is necessary regardless. It is usually recommended that magnification of about ten times be used to examine collectible coins.

There are two reasons to use magnification to examine a coin. The first is to determine the amount of wear on the coin. The second is to determine if there are any surface problems or damage.

You don't necessarily need a halogen light bulb to view a coin properly, but typical household lighting is not sufficient. Instead, use natural sunlight or a nonfrosted light bulb. Rotate the coin to let all of its surfaces be caught in this lighting so you can see any problems such as scratches, dents, or wear. Only when these are recognized can you truly tell the condition of the coin you are considering collecting.

Building Your Library

You can go to a public library, visit a coin store, or even examine coin books in a museum. But there is still nothing like having a numismatic library of your own. It is at your fingertips, you can tailor it to your interests and needs, and you can add to it as you see fit.

Your own personal library is an extension of your collection. What museum has no research resources coupled to it? You can't live in a vacuum. Should you choose to ignore learning about what you are collecting, you will likely reap what you sowed when you go to sell your collection. Knowledge is power.

There is a downside to owning a numismatic library that collectors don't like to speak about: It costs money. Coin collectors like to collect coins. Why spend money on a book or magazine when you can use that same money to add more coins to your collection?

The astute collector understands that by gaining knowledge a collector can save money when buying coins and make money when selling them. This will justify any cost you invest in your personal reference library.

The content of your library is up to you. A person who specializes in U.S. national bank notes likely will need general references to paper money and also specialized books that identify the value and availability of the notes. A collector of ancient coins will likely want both general and specialized books on this field. For example, a collector of ancient Roman coins will likely want to own a copy of some general text covering the Roman Republic and Roman Empire, but he or she may also want a more specialized book on a specific coin denomination, a specific time period, or some specialized iconography appearing on his or her favorite coins. A counterfeit detection book might also be handy.

Especially if you decide to collect in a specialized area of coin collecting, you may find the books, just as your coins, are of value if you resell them.

(See Appendix B: References for Coin Collectors for a suggested list of the books you should have in your library.)

2

chapter 2

Important Coinage Vernacular

Coin collecting has its own language, like probably every other hobby. After reading this chapter, you, too, will know your pieforts from your proofs, and you'll know how to recognize green slime, to boot. Without fully understanding many of these words, collectors may make costly mistakes.

What Is a Numismatist?

A numismatist, using the strictest possible definition of the word, is a person who studies coins. This person draws conclusions about a society—including its technological and economic level, trade routes, and other social and political information—through the discovery and study of individual coins and hoards and the context in which they are found.

There are civilizations and rulers that are known today only through their surviving coins. Coins found in an archaeological context serve as index fossils; archaeological dig sites can often be dated by the coins found there. Coins are often the only artifact that can tell a tale since coins often include meaningful iconography, a legend (inscription) naming the local ruler, the issuing entity, and other information. Even the propaganda appearing on our current coinage may be studied thousands of years from now!

Our current coins will likely be studied generations from now. As an example, the Eisenhower dollar coin of 1971 to 1978 and the subsequent Susan B. Anthony dollar coin of 1979 to 1999 have an image of Tranquility Base—the landing of the first man on the moon—on the reverse. What better way to memorialize this event? The coins provide a record of this feat for posterity.

Our modern dollar coins leave a historical economic record. Before 1935, silver dollars contained silver. No dollar denomination coins were issued between 1936 and 1970. But the next silver dollar, the Eisenhower silver dollar coin of 1971 to 1978, does not contain silver. Nor does the Susan B. Anthony dollar coin. Interestingly, the Susan B. Anthony dollar coin is smaller in diameter than earlier dollar coins, but it has the same face value. All this will tell someone in the future about our economy during this period. This is true numismatics.

You don't have to be a scholar to be a numismatist in addition to being a collector. Even a coin found in your garden may tell something about the history of your property. You'll often hear stories about hoards of coins or bank notes found in old houses. The study of the "whys" surrounding these finds is also numismatic.

What Is a Coin?

It may sound silly to dwell on what constitutes a coin, but that understanding is key to collectors, and perhaps more important to investors. What we carry in our pockets and spend over the counter is typically coins, but not all coins are treated equally. In fact, not all coins are money! Here we'll talk about several types of coins—business strikes, commemoratives, noncirculated legal tender coins, proofs, mint sets, pieforts, bullion coins, medals, and tokens.

Business Strikes

Coins produced for the public to spend—which is known as "in circulation"—are called business strikes. They are mass produced on machines that typically stamp out (or "mint") more than 800 coins per minute. Modern coins bear the year in which they were issued, and many of them carry a mint mark identifying where they were made. The following is a list of mint marks appearing on U.S. coins:

- **C:** Charlotte, North Carolina, 1838 to 1861 (gold coins only)
- **CC:** Carson City, Nevada, 1870 to 1893
- **D:** Dahlonega, Georgia, 1838 to 1861 (gold coins only)
- **D:** Denver, Colorado, 1906 to date
- **O:** New Orleans, Louisiana, 1838 to 1909
- **P:** Philadelphia, Pennsylvania, 1793 to date
- **S:** San Francisco, California, 1854 to date
- **W:** West Point, New York, 1984 to date

Coins without a mint mark were also struck at Philadelphia. The concept of using an identifying mint mark dates from earlier times when quality control was poor and governments needed to identify where coins that were purposely made lightweight by unscrupulous mint masters were made.

All U.S. coins carry a date—the year that it was struck. Christian dated coins, with few exceptions, first appeared about 1501. The original function of the date, just as with the mint mark, was to identify problem coins being purposely struck too light by dishonest mint masters.

Commemoratives

Commemorative coins are made to honor a person, place, or event. Commemorative coins have been struck almost since coins were first introduced, however until recent history commemorative coins always circulated alongside their noncommemorative counterparts.

FACT

The Washington quarter was actually introduced as a circulating commemorative during 1932, on the 200th anniversary of George Washington's birth. But the design proved to be so popular that it has been continued ever since.

The first commemorative U.S. coins issued to be marketed at above face value were introduced in 1892 for the Columbian Exposition. This began a period of commemorative U.S. coins, known as the classic period, that lasted until 1954. Although the coins were meant to sell for a premium, many of them failed to sell, so they were dumped into circulation by the government and circulated as money.

A good example of a circulating commemorative coin is the U.S. statehood quarter series of 1999 to 2008.

Noncirculated Legal Tender Coins

Noncirculated legal tender coins, or NCLTs, are simply commemorative coins that are not meant to ever circulate. Most NCLTs are produced of precious metal, typically gold or silver, with an intrinsic value far exceeding the face value stamped on the coins. So these are coins, but they are not truly money.

NCLTs are struck strictly for collectors, and none of them will ever circulate unless someone breaks them out of their cases of issue and intentionally spends them. There is no logic to these coins circulating.

NCLTs have become increasingly popular with mints and governments strapped for cash worldwide. Collector interest for such coins is often modest, but the initial offering to the general public may be profitable if the public finds the subject commemorated on the coin to be of interest.

One problem with many of these world NCLT commemoratives is that there may be no secondary market of collectors into which the coins can later be resold. For this reason, they often sell for significantly less in the secondary collector markets than they did when first issued. There are also many world commemorative coins that are not legal tender in the country in whose name they were issued.

When a government-owned or private mint solicits a country that doesn't have its own mint to produce business strikes or commemorative coins, the mint will pay the government to which it has contracted for the right to choose the subject to be commemorated and market the coins wherever it chooses. As a result, many modern world commemorative coins have never been in the country in whose name they were issued.

Proofs

Proof coins are struck with great care rather than mass produced. They are specially packaged and sold to collectors. Modern proof coins are typically placed into special sets that are sold by the mint to the general public. Proof sets come out annually, offering examples of all the coins for that year in this special package.

The dies and the blanks from which proof coins are struck are superior to those from which business strikes (coins to be used as currency) will be produced. (We'll talk more about dies and blanks later in this chapter.) The presses from which such coins are made also operate more slowly to ensure a superior strike. The dies and blanks are hand polished, giving each coin a mirrorlike surface.

While some coins are designed to have a mirrorlike finish, other coins appear to be frosted. "Frosted" proof coins are normal on most modern proofs, however on proofs from before the 1960s they may command a premium value depending on the issue. There are specialized books in which such information is available for individual dates.

FACT

Specially packaged sets of coins—called mint sets, specimen sets, and uncirculated sets—are of the same quality as business strike coins. However, these sets of coins are hand selected, specially packaged, and sold to collectors.

Matte proofs are a special finish used on such strikes at the Philadelphia Mint prior to World War I. There is an attractive but grainy surface to such coins. When in doubt if a coin is a proof or not, examine the rims under magnification. The rims should be squared, not gently sloping as they are on business strike coins.

Sandblast proofs were made at the Philadelphia Mint between 1908 and 1915 by blowing sand across the surfaces. This is similar but yet slightly different from the matte proof, which does not use the sand to provide the finish.

Pieforts

Double-thickness coins, which are made for collectors, are called pieforts. Each of these is sold annually by the mint of their origin, with older date proof sets and other specially produced coins available through coin dealers. These are popular collectibles. Their prices vary in secondary collector markets depending on supply and demand.

A French piefort.

Bullion Coins

Bullion coins are true coins in that they have a legal tender minimum value denomination, year of issue, and country of issue on them, and in one sense they are treated as money. These coins became popular in the 1960s with the introduction of the South African gold Krugerrand. There is an advantage of bullion coins over other forms of platinum, gold, or silver bullion. In a coin format, the precious metal can simply be bought and sold, while ingots (a mass of metal cast into a convenient shape for storage) of these precious metals need to be assayed for authenticity and purity, a time-consuming, costly process.

Bullion coins, including the U.S. American Eagle series, typically trade at or near the spot price of their metal content; however they also have a guaranteed minimum face value in the unlikely scenario that the metals plunge in value. Bullion coins are typically struck of pure platinum, gold, or silver in convenient weights of one, half, quarter, and tenth ounce, making them easy to value and trade.

Collector versions of some bullion coins are struck in proof. Specially made collector versions are often worth a premium above the spot price of the intrinsic value of the metal involved.

Medals

What is the difference between a coin and a medal? Simply put, you can't spend a medal. A medal is not legal tender, nor is it a substitute for legal tender. It is a metallic object, not always round, that is produced to exhibit artwork and sometimes is produced to commemorate a person, place, or event.

It is important to know the difference between coins and medals since there are marketing promoters who purposely word advertising to make it appear as if they are selling a coin when in fact they a selling a medal. Some of the more unscrupulous marketers have assigned fictitious denominations that are actually words implying the weight of the medal in an effort to confuse potential buyers.

It is important to know the difference between coins and medals because few medals realize a premium above their precious metal content in secondary markets, while coins continue to be of interest to collectors and may for that reason be more saleable at better prices later.

The best protection for collectors is to know your coins and know the currency denominations that are legal tender in the country whose name appears on the object being offered. This will help you understand the difference between buying an ounce of silver at an exorbitant price above the spot price of its metal content and purchasing a legal tender coin.

There are also fantasy commemoratives, "coins" that are actually medals with the name of a possible coin issuing entity, denomination, and date on them but struck for nonexistent places. As an example, a place calling itself Sealand was actually a former oil rig platform near the mouth of the Thames River in Great Britain, but just outside the legal territorial limits of the country. The owner of the platform declared his independence and proceeded to produce fantasy coins and stamps meant strictly for sale to collectors. These have little value in collector markets today and have no value anywhere as money.

A medal.

Tokens

Tokens are substitutes for currency that are issued by companies, not governments. Tokens are typically vended into a receptacle device to receive a product (such as candy) or a service (such as subway transportation). Tokens are not legal tender, and they are often good for only a very specific item or place or for a limited period of time. Private companies issue tokens, not federal governments, however during periods of inflation tokens have sometimes become more popular than hard currency.

FACT

Inflation was a serious problem in Russia during the early 1990s. The purchasing power of coins and bank notes was quickly declining; however, a subway or telephone token could still be used, regardless of the increasing cost of the services. So people began bartering subway and telephone tokens for food, since these were the only objects with consistent purchasing power.

Company store tokens were issued to employees prior to when laws were changed to require employers to pay exclusively in U.S. currency. These

A token.

company store tokens were only redeemable at the company store, a place where goods could be purchased at prices determined by the company. If an employee left the company, his tokens were of no value anywhere else. The phrase in the song *Sixteen Tons*, "I owe my soul to the company store," originates from the forced use of coal company store tokens and ensuing debt when employees couldn't afford company dictated prices.

Token collecting is a popular and usually inexpensive area of coin collecting. Vending tokens and company store tokens are both popularly collected. Token collectors typically focus on a particular theme, or they collect tokens from a favorite town. There are specialty coin clubs and dealers that cater to token collectors.

What Is Currency?

Currency is a misunderstood and often misused term. In numismatics, the word currency refers to bank notes (commonly called paper money), but the general public uses currency to refer to both coins and bank notes, as a substitute for the word "money."

Within the coin collecting hobby, currency can also include paper scrip such as that issued by company stores and municipalities, various emergency issues, stocks, bonds, and checks.

Bank Notes

Paper money began as a receipt for specie (precious metal coins) that was stored at a banking facility. These receipts were occasionally traded in lieu of the gold or silver coins they represented, as long as the specie remained on deposit. Eventually this evolved into bank notes, notes drawn on banks as a substitute for the precious metal coins or bullion the receipt represented.

Abuses soon became rampant, with issuing authorities simply turning on the printing press and producing notes for which there was not real backing. It is easy to see how a run on a bank could easily exhaust what precious metal resources were really on hand, causing the bank to close.

U.S. and world bank notes are two major hobby collecting areas. Within the realm of U.S. bank notes, anything ranging from colonial period to modern notes can be collected. Bank notes of the world is an exciting and educational subject to collect without typically a lot of cost.

Scrip

Scrip is actually part of currency collecting, but it is worth discussing as a separate term since note collectors typically separate the two. Scrip is the currency equivalent of tokens. Scrip is often issued for redemption for a very specific item at a specific place, or for a limited time, but unlike bank notes scrip is not typically backed by any tangible asset such as gold or silver. The scrip collector may be interested in the local history surrounding the notes. Scrip often portrays vignettes and can also be collected by theme for this reason. Modern scrip is occasionally issued by municipalities to raise money by commemorating local events.

Several commercial companies have issued souvenir money more technically falling into the realm of scrip. The company "currency" is redeemable at specific stores and amusement parks, however a significant number of people will instead take the company scrip home as souvenirs, allowing the company to make a profit off the exchange. For example the Disney company issues its own Disney dollars. This scrip can be purchased by exchanging the same value in U.S. dollars at participating stores. The Disney dollars can then be spent as currency at Disney stores and theme parks.

What Is Odd and Curious Money?

Besides collecting coins and currency, some collectors collect what's known as odd and curious money. Another term for odd and curious money is primitive money. These terms are used interchangeably by collectors. This is a minor field of numismatics, however it can be entertaining and educational. Cowry shells, bricks of tea, "spade" money, the feathers of certain birds, and even the teeth of wild dogs are primitive money.

Spade money and other similar forms of odd and curious money typically resemble the farming or hunting implement at which they would be valued in trade as a substitute for the real thing. The teeth from wild dogs were used in trade in certain Oceana areas. When European traders arrived during the nineteenth century the enterprising Europeans soon learned they could trade manufactured replicas of these teeth as well, although the local natives discounted the value of these counterfeits.

All human societies began commerce by bartering. The value of items being bartered is not always easy to determine. Eventually as societies advance so does the method of monetary exchange due to the nebulous answer. It is at this point that money displaces the barter system.

The collecting of odd and curious or primitive money is more esoteric than are other areas of numismatics, however there are clubs specializing in this field and several books on the subject as well.

Coin Problems from A to Z

Collectors want quality, not quantity. Collectors don't ideally want coins with problems—bumps, blimps, damage, or those that have been cleaned. Condition is everything regardless of if a coin is rare or not. Even though coins are made of metal, there are many things that can damage them. Here are some problems you may encounter on coins.

- **Abrasions:** These are tiny marks appearing on coins due to friction, not wear or cleaning. Wear and cleaning will impact the condition of a coin, but the number of abrasions will determine the mint state grade of an uncirculated coin.
- **Adjustment marks:** These may appear as scrapes and wide scratches crossing a coinage blank. These scrapes were on the coinage blank prior to it being struck into a coin and were made to ensure the

blank met weight standards. Such marks are not detrimental to the value of a coin.

- **Bag marks:** Marks appearing on coins due to their contact with other coins when stored in a mint or bank bag (rather than due to circulation) are called bag marks. Bag marks will impact the condition and value of a coin.
- **Blemishes:** Blemishes are minor contact marks appearing on the surfaces of coins that impact the eye appeal and grade of the coin. Light wear on a coin that appears to be rub rather than circulation wear occurs from improper storage rather than from use in circulation. This is referred to as cabinet friction, based on the coin shifting within a drawer of a cabinet made especially to house coins.
- **Clippings:** Shavings taken from the edge of a precious metal coin in order to illegally collect a sufficient amount of that metal to produce further coins are called clippings. The initial coin is still circulated at its face value despite its now reduced weight. Clipped coins are problem coins.

A clipped coin.

- **Flyspecks:** Very undesirable flyspecks are small oxidation spots appearing on the surface of a coin. Avoid collecting coins with flyspecks where possible.
- **Hairlines:** These are light lines or scratches appearing on the surface of a coin due to the coin having been cleaned. This is one of many good reasons why coins should never be cleaned.

- **Retooling:** When a coin has been retooled, some of the worn details have been carefully reworked to artificially improve the grade of the coin. Careful scrutiny under good light with good magnification will detect such problems.
- **Strike quality:** The act of impressing coin designs on coinage blanks, or planchets, is the strike. The quality or lack of quality of the strike may determine the collector value of a coin regardless of if the coin is circulated or not.
- **Whizzing:** The artificial enhancement of a coin in an effort to make it more valuable is called whizzing. It can be detected under magnification. The surfaces may appear to be disturbed, natural flow lines may be missing or interrupted, and the surface color of the coin may not appear to be normal for the grade in which the coin appears. Avoid whizzed coins at all costs.

Toning means to assume a pleasing color or tint. The appeal or lack of appeal of a coin due to toning is called eye appeal. This is an intangible, since eye appeal is the taste of the individual collector, but if you consider the appearance of a coin to be ugly it likely will be ugly to someone to whom you might later want to resell it. Some collectors like toning on their coins, while others prefer white surfaces.

Beware green slime! Coins are often stored in clear plastic holders. Sometimes that plastic contains a chemical called polyvinyl chloride, or PVC, that is used to make plastic pliable rather than hard and brittle. Over time PVC will react with the surface of the coin, leaving an undesirable greasy green film known as PVC damage, or green slime. This is permanent and will diminish the value of the coin. There are chemicals that can remove the residue, however experienced collectors and dealers can detect the alteration.

chapter 3

Coin Handling and Storage

Take a few coins from your pocket and study them carefully. You may see coins that look as fresh as when they were released from the mint, as well as some dark, very worn coins that look like they've seen a lot of use. You want the best quality coins you can find for your collection, but here's what you have to remember: If you don't handle coins properly, despite the fact you've removed these coins from circulation, in time they will show the effects of having been handled.

Handling Your Coins

The two major threats to your coins are the oils from your hands and friction. Here are three general rules to safeguarding your coins:

- Hold all coins by their edges. Never hold coins by their surfaces.
- Do not use tweezers or other tools to grasp coins. These tools may scratch the coins.
- Wear cotton gloves, where possible, when handling collector coins to keep oils from your skin from being in contact with your coins.

Coins may be metal, but this doesn't make them indestructible, nor does it make them impervious to the environment. Protection of your collection is important. This includes how the coins are handled and how they are stored. In general, the less often a coin is handled the better it will be. Both the oils from your hands and the friction that comes from handling coins are damaging to a coin in a collection.

Oils

The oils from your hands react differently with different metals in coins. Although there are many metals of which coins are comprised, the most commonly encountered in U.S. coins are copper, nickel, silver, and gold.

Try this experiment. Pinch a new, bright penny between your fingers. Set the coin out on a surface open to the air for several days or weeks. Watch when the color of the surface of the coin begins to change. Does a fingerprint appear?

Copper

U.S. coins made of copper include the half cent, 1-cent, and 2-cent piece. Copper in particular will have a problem retaining its original surface color and mint luster if it is handled very much. It will also discolor if it is stored in a hostile environment, or if it is exposed to the elements.

Nickel and Silver

Nickel composition U.S. coins include the obsolete 3 cent and the current 5 cent, or "nickel." The obsolete 3 cent can also be made from silver. Other silver U.S. coins include the half dime, dime, 20-cent coin, quarter dollar, half dollar, and silver dollar. Silver and nickel composition coins will eventually tarnish from handling, but the color change is often more subtle and not always unattractive. Each may tone to a mild or darker gray, perhaps even to ebony. This is natural and may even enhance the eye appeal of some coins. It may also mask some undesirable abrasions.

Gold

U.S. gold coins range from the dollar to the $20 Double Eagle as well as the bullion American Eagle series. Gold is a more enduring metal than copper, nickel, or silver. It can in theory be buried in the ground or submerged in water for a long period of time, then be exposed once more to the environment without any deterioration or change in color. Handling gold coins carelessly may dull their original luster, but otherwise they will retain their sparkle better than copper, nickel, or silver.

FACT

Oxidation leaves discoloration as telltale signs. It doesn't have to be unattractive, although sometimes it appears in blotchy patches rather than in a pattern. Tarnish begins at the rims of the coin and work its way inward in attractive halo waves.

Friction

The greatest challenge to preserving a collector coin is to avoid subjecting it to wear by handling it. Handling causes friction that disturbs the surfaces and eventually wears away some of the design details. A coin is a metal blank on which a design has been impressed. This design is three dimensional; it has relief. The highest points of this relief will wear first. The more a coin is used in circulation, the more it is handled, and the more poorly it is stored, the more opportunity there is for this friction to gradually dull its surfaces and remove some of the high points of detail. This is known as circulation.

To protect your coins against friction follow the three rules mentioned previously: hold coins by their edges, never by their surfaces, and do not use tweezers or other tools to grasp coins.

Storing Your Coins

People have been known to put their collections in dresser drawers. But as a collection becomes more sophisticated, so do the lengths the collector takes to ensure the collection looks less like an accumulation and more like a collection.

You may simply want to store the coins, or you may want to examine them and someday even display them. But proper storage is also important to safeguard your collection. Beyond the friction your coins are exposed to when you're handling them, coins can also be exposed to friction when storing. You don't want your coins handled more than necessary, and you want to avoid exposing them to friction.

Storing coins properly will also keep them free from potential environmental damage. If you have any silver objects in your home, you may have noticed that over time they tarnish. Tarnish is environmental damage. Pollutants in the atmosphere are reacting with the metal. The metal is actually burning, although so very slowly that it is not detectable to the human eye. This is called oxidation.

There is no single best holder; there are many factors to consider. These include the diameter of the coins, the thickness of the coins, where you plan to store the coins, how and where you may want to display them at some time, and how you want to view or examine them.

Storage should be practical so the coins can be safely handled, and attractive so the coins can be pleasing to view. There are many holders in which a coin or a note may be placed. Some of these are available from commercial sources, while others may be devised by the collector. Common coin holders include 2×2s, flips, coin board, and coin cabinets.

2×2s

One of the most popular ways of storing a coin is in a 2" × 2" holder (usually referred to as a "2×2"), a cardboard square measuring two inches by two inches with an oval or a square cut-out center covered with clear plastic so once the coin is placed in it the coin can be safely viewed.

One advantage of using 2×2s is that you can view the coin without handling it. Another advantage is you can write information describing the coin on the holder.

The disadvantages are that you may not be able to view the edge of the coin, and that if the cardboard holder contains sulfur it may react with the metal composition of your specimen, causing the coin to tone. Also because these holders are not airtight, the coin can oxidize. Because 2×2s are typically held together by staples, if you remove a coin from such the holder, you have to fully remove the staples first to avoid scratching the coin.

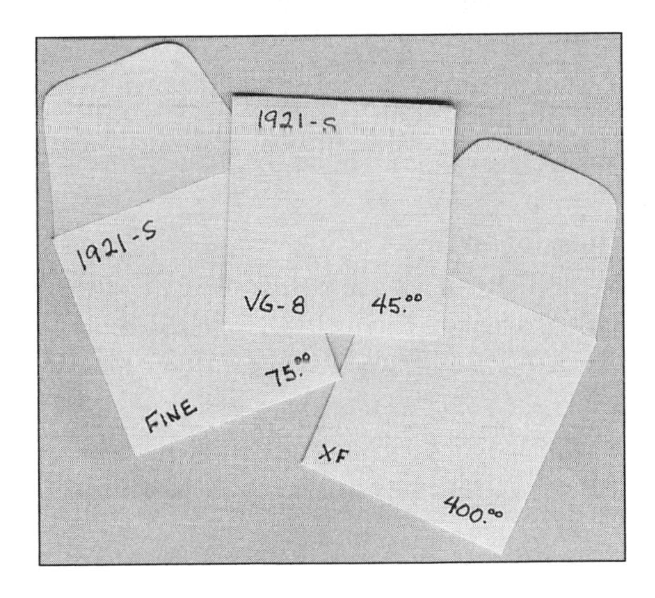

2×2s.

Flips

Another type of popular coin holder is called a flip. These are double-pocket hard plastic holders in which a coin is placed in one pocket, with a paper insert describing the coin in the other pocket.

An advantage of flips is they are more durable than 2×2s. Plus, flips do not contain any harmful sulfur as cardboard holders may. It is more difficult to write on these plastic holders, but you can use a felt tip marker.

FACT

The size and thickness of a coin are important to the holder in which you may want to place a specimen. A coin placed in a holder that is too big may rattle around in it, subjecting the coin to friction. Placing the coin in a holder too small is simply not an option. It won't fit. Bank notes have the same factors to consider.

A possible disadvantage of flips is that, because they are made of plastic, they commonly contain PVC, which can cause green slime to form on the coins. Look for flips that contain no PVC. If you find that the holders for your coins contain PVC, remove them as soon as possible. It will cost more to get better holders, but this cost is a better alternative than eventually learning that your collection is unsaleable. Another disadvantage of flips is that, like 2×2s, they aren't airtight.

Testing for PVC

A simple test can tell you if the holder in which you plan to place your coin or a bank note contains PVC. Heat the end of a copper coat hanger over an open flame on a stove. While the coat hanger is hot, touch the questionable plastic with the hanger to obtain a small sample of the plastic. Once again place the coat hanger over the flame. If the flame turns blue, the holder is safe. If the flame turns green, PVC is present.

2×2 and Flip Holders

You can buy specially made boxes to store either the cardboard 2×2s or the plastic flips, creating a sort of a filing system for your collection in the process. You can arrange the coins in any order, ensuring they are safe from friction and free to be examined. Then you can stash the entire box in a safe, strongbox, bank safe deposit box, or other security devise. This can be an easy way to store a large number of coins in a small space.

Coin Boards

Another time-honored way to store coins is mounting them on cardboard coin boards. These are typically commercially produced folders or books in which holes of the appropriate diameter to the diameter of a denomination of coin have been drilled into each page. Often the holes are covered with clear plastic so once the coin is placed in it the coin can be safely viewed.

These books can be purchased either with the dates of the coins in a series printed below each appropriate hole or without printing so a collection can be assembled as the collector pleases.

Once again there are advantages and disadvantages to coin boards. The advantages are that they are easy to store and that an entire collection can be viewed at once due to the simple presentation. The disadvantages are that once again the cardboard coin board may contain sulfur. Also, some boards only allow one side of a coin to be viewed. Other boards have holes drilled all the way through to allow both sides to be viewed, but when the clear plastic panels are removed, the surface of the coins are subjected to friction.

Coin Cabinets

There will always be innovative ways to store and display coins, but one of the more classical methods is a coin cabinet, a chest of drawers made specifically to hold coins. Many collectors in the United States consider coin cabinets to be old-fashioned, yet coin cabinets remain popular with collectors in Europe.

The composition of the cabinet is important: Choose plastic over wood. Most wood-composition cabinets will eventually react adversely with the metal of the coins, while modern plastic coin cabinets will not.

An advantage of coin cabinets is that they are an elegant way to store coins and a great way to view them—just open a drawer to see a larger number of coins at once.

A disadvantage of coin cabinets is that since coins are laid flat but loose in the drawers, they are subject to cabinet friction, which may affect their condition. Every time a drawer is opened, the coins may shift, subjecting them to minor friction.

It's interesting to note that museum-owned coin collections are often referred to as a "cabinet" because of this format of storage.

Bad Storage Ideas

There are some placess people store coins that are damaging and should be avoided at all costs. Among these are wallets, pouches, or anything else made of leather or plastic (except plastic coin cabinets); metal cans; and pots.

Coins and paper notes placed in leather wallets and other such items turn black from contact with the leather. Cleaning them isn't an option, since this will ruin the finish on the coin or note. The best suggestion is simply to keep them away from leather.

Wallets, pouches, and other similar currency carrying devices made of imitation leathers (plastic) typically contain chemicals, especially PVC, which will be harmful to coins or paper money if coins or notes are kept in these containers for long periods of time.

Cans and pots are problems in part because of the material the can or pot may be made from, and in part because the coins may be damaged by knocking against other coins in the same container. Storing coins in cloth sacks is also harmful, since the coins are subjected to contact with each other every time the sack is disturbed. People often tend to leave such sacks in places without climate control, further risking oxidation of the metal coins by their exposure to seasonal cold, heat, and humidity.

Taping coins or notes to boards or paper may make them look attractive for display purposes, but adhesive tapes will leave a sticky film on them that will likely leave permanent damage. Wood alcohol carefully applied may remove the sticky residue, but when applied by someone inexperienced with doing this the coin or note may be ruined. Rather than worry about cleaning sticky tape residue, don't use tape in the first place.

Handling Bank Notes

Paper money is susceptible to the same problems as are coins. Paper money wears out through use or circulation, how it is handled or mishandled, and the effect of its environment. The notes used in the United States are printed on specially made paper containing threads of other material both for durability and for security against counterfeiting. Bank notes issued in other countries are printed on various grades of cloth, paper, and even on leather. The latest technology uses polymer (plastic) substrates, which according to studies appears to be significantly more durable than traditional security "paper" on which bank notes are printed. No study, however, has been done to understand what the impact of direct sunlight on these polymer notes may be over a period of time.

Bank notes are made of organic materials, and for this reason will eventually begin to deteriorate, similar to how old books may deteriorate. But because many bank notes are made from superior grades of paper, some even from fabric, bank notes are generally more durable than books.

Coins, being metal, are more durable than are paper bank notes. Worldwide studies of coins versus circulating paper notes made by several foreign mints indicate a typical circulating coin may last between twenty and forty years, while a paper note of the same denomination may have a lifespan of between six and eighteen months. This is why in recent history a significant number of countries have replaced low denomination bank notes with coins.

If you collect bank notes, just as with their coin counterparts, handle them as little as possible. When bank notes require handling, ensure your hands are clean before picking up the note, or better yet wear gloves, to keep the oils from your hands from getting on the note. Hold the note by the edges. Avoid folding the note, even ever so slightly, or dog-earring the corners.

Storing Bank Notes

Like coins, it's best to store bank notes in protective plastic sleeves. Be sure that they do not contain PVC, which is as damaging to notes as it is to coins.

Humidity and sunlight must be considered when storing or displaying bank notes. Too little humidity may dry out a note, while too much may cause damage to the paper on which the note is printed. A bank note needs to "breathe." Protect your notes from particularly humid environments (such as a basement) and also from particularly dry environments (such as an attic). Common sense is necessary because there is no specific formula and exact humidity level at which it is recommended bank notes be stored.

Sunlight will make the images on notes fade with time, just as sunlight will fade the color of the spine on a book that is continuously exposed to light. Where possible, store your notes in a cool, dark place.

There are various plastic sleeves that are made specifically for storing paper money. Some of these are only large enough to hold a single note, while others hold three or four notes. Some holders have holes drilled into the page so they can be placed into a loose-leaf album.

Cleaning Coins and Bank Notes

One of the first questions an uninitiated collector usually asks regarding coins they acquire is, "How do I clean them?" The answer is simple: You don't. There is more to this than just the desire of advanced collectors to be purists, demanding that no one has ever retouched the surfaces of a coin. Any cleaning removes some of the surface, even if it is minute and nondetectable to the untrained eye. Furthermore, cleaning involves abrasive cleansers, regardless of how mild these cleansers may be. Cleansers do two adverse things to coins. First, they leave hairline scratches that are detectable under close examination. Second, they will strip the original luster from uncirculated coins.

Once a coin has been cleaned, it may be able to be artificially retoned, however the surfaces are never the same again. There is a difference in surface color that never goes away. This makes the difference between the coin being desirable or undesirable to collectors. Why would a collector purchase a cleaned coin when an uncleaned example is available?

Cleaning coins or notes will have an adverse impact on their desirability and value to collectors. Many a valuable coin or bank note has been ruined by the good intentions of someone who decided the surfaces were in their opinion too dark to be visible, not understanding that collectors would rather have this original color or finish, regardless of if the surface is bright or dark.

Bank notes should never be cleaned either. Washing a note; using an eraser to remove soiling, discoloration, or graffiti; adding tape to a tear; or ironing a note are noticeable and will impact the desirability of the note. A note that has been washed has a different consistency to the paper than before it was bathed, while a note that has been ironed lacks the intaglio relief that should be present because of the ink being ever-so-slightly raised on the paper. All of these efforts to enhance the appearance of a note can be detected and will decrease its value significantly.

In summary, there is no advantage to cleaning coins or notes. The novice may think a coin or note appears to look nicer once it has been cleaned, but to a collector this means the coin or note no longer has original surfaces and as such is of little interest to them.

chapter 4

Social Aspects of the Hobby

People who are not involved in coin collecting often view the pastime as a solitary hobby, that is, something for the "closet collector." The collector is viewed by uninitiated noncollectors as a quiet, private individual who is assembling a museum quality collection strictly for his personal pleasure, likely not sharing his hobby with anyone else. This stereotype is not always accurate!

A Solitary Activity?

There are no reliable statistics to prove that the majority of coin collectors are either introverts or extroverts, and perhaps many fit this description of an introvert, but there are social aspects to the hobby, and these social aspects can be quite exciting.

Among coin collectors have been such luminaries as Queen Elizabeth II of England, U.S. President John Quincy Adams, Francis Cardinal Spellman, and actor Buddy Ebsen. It could be argued that these well-known people would likely be considered to be extroverts. In more distant history, coin collectors have included such well-known persons as Julius Caesar, Lorenzo di Medici, and King Louis XIV of France. The social aspects of coin collecting are what you make of them!

Collecting and Your Family

Coin collecting can truly be a family affair. It's a great idea to involve your spouse, and also your children, in your hobby. Here's why.

Collecting and Your Spouse

There are many "widows" of active collectors, spouses who are pleased to see that their partner has a productive hobby, but allow the collector to keep the collecting activities to themselves. These nonparticipants in this all-encompassing interest of their spouses are not unlike football widows and the spouses of other sports fans; but coin collecting is not a seasonal sport. There are some collectors who may prefer this privacy, but where possible it is a great idea to share the hobby with someone you love. There are several good reasons to involve your spouse where possible:

- It promotes good relations between the two of you. This is an interest you can share.
- The nonparticipating spouse should know just how much family money the collector is dedicating to the collection, and if it is discretionary money or not.

- Your spouse might someday be burdened with selling off the family collection after the collector dies. Without understanding the collector's hobby, the coins your family collector acquired, and his contacts, this could become a problem.

Collecting and Your Children

Anytime parents can share in an activity that interests their children, this joint participation is going to be good for the nuclear family. Many parents become involved as coaches or as spectators to the sporting events in which their children participate. Why not involve your children in your coin collecting interests as well?

Just as coin collectors are sometimes referred to as numismatists, children who collect coins are sometimes referred to as young numismatists or simply YNs.

Surveys indicate that people who were introduced to coin collecting as young children often pursue the hobby until adolescence. These same surveys indicate that once these kids become adults, typically with a family and a stable income of their own, they may once more return to coin collecting.

The same care with which it is suggested an adult enter the hobby—slowly and inexpensively at first until they understand coin collecting more fully—is also the best way to get a child interested in coin collecting. Let them search through pocket change for coins to fill coin albums. They are too young to appreciate proof sets or something similar an adult simply purchases every year for them. Let them do their own collecting; don't do it for them.

Another reason to get your kids involved in your coin collecting hobby is that you can't take it with you. If you consider your coin collection to be your legacy, you need to get your kids interested in it now.

It takes more than an appreciation for what someone else has assembled to want to keep it. One of the foremost collections of U.S. coins ever assembled was resold by the collector's children, who had more interest in the value the collection represented than wanting to keep it intact to have something with which to remember their dad. This mentality is not uncommon.

A significant number of collectors hope in their subconscious minds that their coin collections will be retained and expanded upon by their family after they are gone. This may be wishful thinking, but one thing is certain. If you encourage your family to share in your collecting habit, there is a better chance that they will do just that. Too many times the family collector does not share what he is doing with others, yet incredibly this person still hopes his descendants will still want to retain what he views as his legacy.

As a minimum, you should at least educate your family about the value of your collection so that the surviving family may someday sell it for a fair price. Far too often, without a family being participants in a collection's assemblage, the collection will likely languish in a cabinet or drawer for a generation or two until the emotions surrounding the memory of the collector fade into history, or until some unappreciative finder encounters the collection and chooses to use it as handy "found" money that is very spendable at face value regardless of its value to collectors.

Coin Clubs and Organizations

Involving your family in your coin collecting hobby is important, but it is not the only social aspect of the hobby. Coin collecting is a highly organized hobby. There are clubs to join, learned societies to go to, shows and conventions to attend, and competitive displays to compete in.

Local Clubs

There may not necessarily be a coin collectors' club in your town, but unless you live in a very rural area, there is likely a club nearby somewhere. The problem isn't necessarily if a club exists, but in how to find it. Most clubs for coin collectors meet monthly or bi-weekly, often in libraries, churches, banks, or other public places.

You can usually find out about a local club through collector friends, by attending a local coin show, by contacting the chamber of commerce, or by contacting a nearby coin dealer.

FACT

Readership surveys conducted by a major coin hobby publication indicate that of collectors who consider themselves to be seriously involved in the more social aspects of the hobby, a majority do not travel more than about 50 miles from their home or workplace to participate in coin collecting activities.

Local clubs typically have a modest membership that may or may not include some dealers interested in buying and selling coins. Some clubs have meetings at which you have the opportunity to buy, sell, or trade, while other clubs may want only show and tell rather than commercial activity at their meetings. Some local clubs have their own hobby publications, too. If no club exists near you, why not start your own?

There may also be a local coin club for children who collect. Sometimes these are clubs that meet after school, while other times they may be a division of a local club for adults. Check with local schools for the whereabouts of these organizations.

Regional Clubs

States including California (California Numismatic Association), Pennsylvania (Pennsylvania Association of Numismatists), Florida (Florida United Numismatists), and others have statewide organizations for individuals, local clubs, and commercial coin dealers to belong. These statewide organizations typically have a large annual convention at which they hold their business meetings as well as conduct educational forums, facilitate buying and selling, hold banquets, and more. Some of these organizations also have their own hobby publications worth reading.

There are some even larger regional organizations, one of which is the Central States Numismatic Society. Such organizations draw an audience of both members and of nonmembers from a larger geographic area that want to attend their coin show events. An organization encompassing this large a geographic area also has the luxury of holding their conventions at different locations each time they meet. This can be an advantage first for the collector who doesn't want to travel too far from home, and second for the collector who wants to be in contact with collectors and dealers from a different region from where he lives. This gives the opportunity to obtain additional merchandise not necessarily available more locally.

Regional coin collecting organizations sometimes simply encompass a larger geographic area from which to draw their membership than do local clubs, while others are umbrella groups to which local clubs can belong.

National Organizations

In several countries in which coin collecting is particularly popular, there are national coin collector organizations. These include Belgium, Canada, Great Britain, and Japan. In the United States the national organization is the American Numismatic Association (ANA).

There are many advantages to belonging to a national organization. For example, ANA membership includes a subscription to the monthly magazine called *The Numismatist*, access to borrowing books by mail from its extensive library, connecting with other collectors with similar interests, opportunities to buy special insurance to cover the value of your coin collections, and participation in the organization on many different levels.

The ANA holds two weeklong conventions every year. The location of these conventions changes, which is good for collectors, because at one time or another the convention will be reasonably close to where the collectors live. ANA conventions are worth attending. There is a mammoth gathering of professional dealers selling everything from inexpensive coins to some of the world's most valuable coins and bank notes, educational forums, specialty and regional club meetings, competitive displays, social events, and activities for noncollecting spouses.

FACT

The ANA was founded in 1891. Its headquarters, research library, and museum are in Colorado Springs, Colorado, adjacent to Colorado College. There are several classes of membership in this organization. These include general membership with annual dues, club memberships for clubs that want to belong to the larger organization, and lifetime membership for very dedicated collectors.

Young Numismatists Organizations

Local, regional, and national organizations often have special activities for young numismatists. This is important if you want to encourage your children to participate in your hobby interests. It is also important if a young member of your family takes an early interest in coin collecting, even if none of the adults in the family do.

The ANA is among many coin collecting organizations that hold mock coin auctions and other activities for children during their conventions or meetings. These auctions involve real coins donated by collectors and coin dealers. The YNs purchase the coins by bidding with play money, and they get to keep what they have won.

Learned Societies

Another way to enjoy the social aspect of coin collecting is to join one of the many scholarly coin collecting societies. Coin collecting can be more than the assembling of a group of coins as a hobby pursuit, and it can be more than a way to make money as a business. Although coin collectors are often referred to as numismatists, a numismatist is actually a person who studies coins and currency to learn more about society.

You can learn a lot by studying coins, regardless of if they are ancient or modern. The images or iconography on them is important. It shows the skill level of the die engraver, the propaganda surrounding the images chosen, and more. The metal from which coins are produced, the quality of the minting process, and more can all be studied. Early trade routes, the economics of a region at a particular time in history, and even the likeness or name of some long forgotten king are sometimes brought to light through these studies. Some archaeological excavations and underwater wreck salvage operations include an on-site numismatist for this reason.

You do not have to be a member of a coin collecting organization to attend its conventions, but to get the most out of attending such events it is worth the modest annual dues most require.

This may appear to be highbrow or formidably academic to many collectors, but such studies and the organizations that focus on these studies are for the most part still dominated by collectors rather than by university professors and professional archaeologists. Many of the collectors that belong to such organizations are simply either advanced or extremely focused on the areas of coin collecting that may be emphasized by these societies.

The foremost such society in the United States is the American Numismatic Society (ANS) in New York. The ANS does not hold any conventions; however they do conduct symposiums periodically at which new discoveries or conclusions about specific areas of coins are presented, usually in a more consumer-friendly environment than may be imagined by many collectors who have never attended these events. The ANS has its own museum, museum curatorial staff, periodic publications, and research library. This is not a lending library such as is offered by the ANA, but the library is open to the public. There are two classes of membership: general membership and fellowship. A fellow of the ANS has voting rights on some of the internal workings of the organization.

Other scholarly national organizations exist in Great Britain, Canada, and other countries. There are also specialty organizations that are not national in scope yet offer a scholarly slant for people with an interest in particularly spe-

The American Numismatic Society Headquarters.

cialized areas of collecting. Most of these offer members excellent journals, meetings typically held at regional or national coin shows, and the opportunity to learn more about the specialty they want to collect.

There are also more localized clubs, such as the Chicago Coin Club, that are hybrids. The CCC, as an example, goes out of its way to have high caliber speakers at their monthly club meetings, holds meetings during nearby regional coin shows, publishes high quality journals, and holds social events including banquets at which spousal participation is encouraged.

Coin Shows and Conventions

Coin shows and conventions are owned and operated either by coin club organizations or by commercial promoters. Both can be worth attending. Just because a show is produced as a commercial event rather than to benefit a coin hobby organization doesn't mean the show can't have non-commercial events on its schedule, including educational forums, local club meetings, banquets, and other social events. One primary function, however, of all coin shows and conventions is the bourse.

The Bourse

The bourse is the area of a coin show where people rent table space as dealers in order to deal with other dealers and the collecting public. It is typically the most visited area of a coin show, and in many cases it may be the only thing offered at a show.

Anyone can rent bourse table space. You do not have to have a license or other credentials. Usually the people renting such space are full- or part-time coin dealers, however individuals and coin clubs sometimes rent bourse table space as well.

FACT

The word *bourse* is French in origin and is an area of a convention or show where buying and selling takes place. A majority of collectors, regardless of if they are members of the club conducting the show (if it is not a professionally promoted event), come to attend the bourse—buying, selling, and trading coins, bank notes, and anything else related to the hobby.

Auctioneers also use the bourse to show the lots to be offered prior to the auction. (This is helpful to you because it's important to examine coins in person rather than relying on catalog or Internet graphics.) Auctions are often held soon after the bourse closes for the day.

The bourse is typically open to dealers exclusively for a period of time to allow them to set up and to trade privately. The public is then allowed in. Some shows allow people without a bourse table to gain early entry for an additional fee, giving them an advantage over other collectors who wait for the official opening.

The bourse floor.

Vest Pocket Dealers

A vest pocket dealer is someone who comes to the coin show with the sole intention of buying and selling for a profit, but does not rent bourse table space. This person has no interest in taking anything home unless he cannot sell it, regardless of if he brought it with him or purchased it on the bourse floor.

The vest pocket dealer brings what he can carry in a vest pocket, or maybe his briefcase. Typically the vest pocket dealer is interested in purchasing coins for prices he perceives to be low enough that he can resell the item for a profit at another table across the room.

Vest pocket dealers hope to find coins for bargain prices or coins they believe to be too conservatively graded, either of which can (hopefully) be quickly resold for a profit.

Local Shows

Club-operated and commercial shows will primarily be local or regional. They are often one-day events held at public places such as a hotel or American Legion post. Both professional and part-time coin dealers rent tables at these events to buy and sell coins. Their objective is to make money, not to entertain. Keep this in mind when casually examining their merchandise.

Larger Shows

Most regional and national coin collector organizations conduct coin shows or conventions. The larger the organization, the wider in scope the selection of dealers on the bourse will be. The more sophisticated you become with your coin collecting, the more you may find the need to attend these larger events in order to find more challenging rare or expensive coins.

International Shows

A number of international shows are held each year, some conducted by major collector organizations while others are operated by commercial promoters. One of the most significant of these shows is the annual Basel International Coin Fair, held early each year in Basel, Switzerland. The vast scope of this convention gives collectors a glimpse into just how big business coins can be. The Basel show begins each year with a full day of meetings announcing new products, which is open only to the press and to mints. Following this event is a bourse open only to commercial dealers and the world mints. The objective of this part of the convention is to allow wholesale commercial transactions to be conducted. Finally, a bourse open to the general public begins. At this time antique as well as new coins are available through world mints and coin dealers. There are also social events including club meetings and educational forums.

Flea Markets

Clubs and other social organizations are one thing, but the bourse is the most important aspect of a show to most attending collectors—after all, collectors want to collect. In a way, a flea market is like a bourse—a strictly commercial event without any social organization by-products or educational events.

Uninitiated collectors often view flea markets as places where unknowledgeable dealers sell coins for bargain prices. Nothing could be further from the truth. In fact, coin dealers who rent table spaces at flea markets are typically mainstream regarding their knowledge of their wares and their connections among the many established coin-related organizations. They simply choose the flea market as the vehicle through which they wish to sell. There could be the occasional bargain found at a flea market, but don't go to one expecting to find an undiscovered gold mine.

When buying at flea markets, understand you will not have the benefit of clubs and other collectors as you would at a coin show. Remember that flea markets are not specialized. Don't expect a dealer at a flea market to exclusively sell expensive or rare coins. However, don't underestimate the knowledge of the flea market dealer either.

A well-known dealer in Islamic coins recently remarked that while years ago he could go to the bazaars in Turkey to buy collector coins at bargain prices, today virtually every dealer there selling such coins has a world coin catalog likely published in the United States tucked away somewhere at his booth. Times have changed! We now have a global economy.

Competitive and Noncompetitive Displays

You work hard to assemble your collection. You may spend some significant money in the process as well. You may spend some of this money on the coins or bank notes, but you may also have spent some significant money on the holders or display cabinets in which you house what you have assembled.

Some people, as was mentioned earlier, are very private "closet" collectors, treating the hobby as a solitary activity. These are the introverts. They will likely never have any interest in displaying their collection to anyone other than themselves. But hobbyists who are interested in the social aspects of the hobby may like to display their collections for others to enjoy as well.

QUESTION?

My collection is less than perfect. Can I still display it?
Absolutely! You don't have to have a world-class coin collection to display it. If you want to display your collection competitively, you will need a high quality collection that is reasonably complete, but many people will simply join a local coin club in displaying their collections at a local library or other public place.

Becoming involved in such public displays can be rewarding, although for security reasons, don't have your name and address associated with the display. Use good taste in your presentation. Use some creative artwork, and involve your family in preparing the display. This should be part of the fun of collecting. Once more it gets you involved on a social level.

People who feel they can win display awards should focus more on the regional and national coin shows, but displaying your collection or parts of it can be for virtually anyone. Be proud of what you collect.

chapter 5

Buying and Collecting Coins

As you begin your coin collection, ask yourself if you would like to purchase coins for your collection or would you rather collect them from circulation. Perhaps a mix from each source will work best. It really depends on the availability of what you plan to collect. Once you decide what, and how, you'd like to collect, you might consider buying your coins in several different places, including at coin shows, through mail order catalogs, off of television shows, at coin stores, at auctions, and online.

Assessing Your Ambitions

If your goal is to collect Lincoln cents beginning in 1959, the year in which the Lincoln Memorial first appears on the reverse, you can likely find all the dates, mint marks, and scarcer varieties from circulation. But if you insist all your coins be uncirculated, you will likely have to purchase some of the older dates simply because uncirculated examples are unlikely to be found in change. If you become even more ambitious and want to collect the Lincoln cents of 1909 to 1958, on which two wheat ears appear on the reverse, you'll need to purchase some of them due to a lack of availability; several rare dates will not likely be found in change. The extent to which you want to advance your collection and your budget will dictate if you solely collect coins from circulation or if you purchase some of them.

If you are collecting a set of coins by denomination, date, and mint mark, you will likely have your hands full, however you may notice that while one date appears to be very available perhaps another date is not. Any of the many books published listing coin values will also indicate how many coins were produced for each year and at each participating mint (called "mintage"). Although this is not an indication of how many examples have survived, this information is usually helpful in identifying which dates are harder to find than others.

There has to be sufficient coinage produced (paper money as well) annually to drive the economy. There will periodically be a low production date or mint mark for some economic reason. This lower mintage date is the scarcer and likely more valuable coin to find. The age of a coin has nothing to do with its value. Rarity and condition drive values.

Set realistic goals for yourself if you plan to collect most or all of your coins from circulation. Regardless of if your source of coins is going to be strictly what you receive in commerce, if you are going to check other peoples' change as well, or if you are going to get rolls of coins from a bank to search, you should anticipate finding current coinage, not some great rarity dating from 100 years ago. Should you decide to seek these more challenging to find coins, you will likely have to either purchase or trade to get them.

Quality, Not Quantity

It doesn't matter if you have a collection of common coins or of rare coins. The quality, not the quantity, is what is important. Coin collectors seek the nicest examples they can afford. Even a modest collection of Lincoln/Lincoln Memorial cents in uncirculated condition is more desirable than is a collection of well-circulated examples. Your goal should be to keep the collection at least one step ahead of being average. There should be something special about it, something that makes it stand out, be more desirable, more collectible.

Grade Rarity

Rare coins, those produced in smaller quantities than are most others from the same series, were just discussed. There is also something called "grade rarity," a very important factor even regarding very modern coins you can expect to find jingling in your pocket.

Even a very common date coin may have been produced poorly. There may have been little interest among people to put aside uncirculated coins of a particular date when they were first released to the public. A really choice example of such a coin, even if it is a common date, may be very challenging to find.

FACT

A rare coin that is damaged or very worn will never command the premium a nicer example will command. Since the primary reason coins are produced is to satisfy the demands of the local economy, even older coins and those with discontinued designs will typically be found in well-circulated grades. The nicer the condition, the more desirable the coin will be to collectors.

The Jefferson nickel is a good example of this. No truly rare dates have been produced since 1950 (1950-D is a scarcer date in the series), however even among the uncirculated examples few dates can be easily collected on which all six steps on Monticello on the reverse have been sufficiently struck to be able to count them. Jefferson "Full Step" nickels, as these are called by collectors, of certain dates are grade rarities, commanding a significant premium.

Upgrading Your Collection

If you upgrade the coins in your collection you will eventually build a collection that will be more desirable than that assembled by somebody else. Many collectors take the first coin of a particular date and mint mark that they find and simply plug it into the appropriate hole in their coin board. Then they forget about that date and move on to others they don't have.

It is rewarding to continually watch for better quality coins to replace what you have already collected in order to constantly improve your collection. It doesn't matter if you are collecting simply for your own personal pleasure, if you are looking to exhibit your coins competitively, or if you are trying to build significant value into your collection. Upgrading, where possible, is always going to be a positive.

Impulse Purchases

Beware the emotions surrounding the purchase of a coin, bank note, or medal, especially when the item is offered through a mass media outlet. Ordering a coin, bank note, or medal marking a celebration, mourning the passing of a prominent person, or commemorating a current event is an impulse purchase based on emotion. In time, the memory of all such events fades. So does the interest of collectors in purchasing such items, often resulting in depreciation of the resale value of such items. Be careful what you are willing to pay for such items when they are first issued.

The same can be said about purchasing treasure coins recovered from shipwrecks, buried hoards, and the like. If a shipwreck containing $1 million in gold or silver coins of some sort is salvaged there are two problems: First, there will be a glut of the coins on the market, where they may have previously been scarce. Second, since these coins were in the water or soil for a significant period of time, the coins will have environmental damage.

Despite these two glaring points, due to the magic marketing word "treasure" unsophisticated buyers will rush to purchase the coins at prices that typically are significantly higher than they will be when these coins are later resold into secondary markets, where collectors rather than the general public buy. Common sense tells you that unless you are being offered rare date coins from this hoard, and that the hoard has been sufficiently studied that it is already known only a few coins of this date were within the hoard, you may be paying a hefty price due to slick marketing rather than due to the price that will be determined by supply and demand later.

Buying at Coin Shows

One of the best ways to collect coins is with the help of others. Family is the best place to start, especially if what you collect are coins from circulation. Anyone who becomes more ambitious, seeking to collect coins that will be unlikely to be found in circulation, will need to consider trading with other collectors, or purchasing them. For example, it doesn't make much sense to try to collect nineteenth-century U.S. silver dollars from circulation. To collect coins like these, your best bet is a coin show.

How do I know which coin shows to attend?
If you want to buy or sell coins, you may want to look at how many tables have been rented for the show, and if the names of those dealers renting these tables are people with whom you may have an interest in dealing. There is no point attending a show to buy silver dollars if the show is advertised as being for world coin or paper money collectors.

The Bourse

The bourse, the place at coin shows where dealers set up tables to buy and sell coins, is usually the most widely attended place at such conventions. Although many coin shows include educational forums, competitive exhibits, and social events, the primary reason most people attend is either to buy or to sell coins.

At a coin show, you can shop around for competitive prices and speak to knowledgeable people when you have a question.

Due to the competition, coin shows are good places either to sell your coins and to purchase coins for your collection. You may also find collectors who are willing to trade. Dealers attending for commercial reasons are less likely to be interested in trading.

You'll find two main types of shows—commercially sponsored shows and club sponsored shows. There is no advantage of attending one type over the other. Some clubs have excellent reputations for running good shows, while others do not. Commercial promoters have either good or poor reputations for the quality of the show they operate as well. It is more important to give thought to what you want to accomplish by attending a show and then get advanced information about the show to see if you will be able to accomplish your goals there.

FACT

Not all shows, especially some of the more localized commercially sponsored shows, offer anything beyond a dealer bourse. If you want to fraternize with other collectors in a meeting-type environment, or if you are seeking educational meetings, you should first check to see if these will be offered at the show. All shows are not of equal size or quality.

This is a reason to consider attending a mix of local, regional, and perhaps even national shows. A majority of dealers who attend a one-day local show will likely be part-time dealers whose dealings are an extension of their hobby. Their stock will likely be more limited in scope than will be that of dealers who depend on buying and selling for their livelihood. These full-time dealers are more likely to attend the more major shows, yet these same dealers are less likely to bring the more common or inexpensive coins and bank notes with them than might be expected from the part-time dealers who rent bourse table space at the more localized show.

Buying Through the Mail

One time-honored way to purchase merchandise is through the mail. There are businesses that sell coins and bank notes this way, selling them just like any other merchandise. Purchasing coins through the mail can be convenient, especially if you don't have the time or inclination to attend coin club meetings or shows. It is also an excellent way to purchase otherwise hard to find coins or to deal with someone who is otherwise too far away to make a face-to-face visit practical.

Where can I learn about mail order coin companies?
You might find them in coin hobby publications. (Check if those publications screen their advertisers.) Sometimes they advertise in Sunday newspapers or other non–coin-related publications. You might see their coin catalog at a coin club meeting or at a doctor's office or receive it unsolicited through the mail.

It does matter with whom you deal by mail. Since this is not a face-to-face encounter, you want to ensure you are dealing with someone reputable. You can't always find out if the company with which you are considering dealing is reputable or not through your contacts. You could test the waters by first buying something inexpensive to ensure you are getting what you pay for.

Full Disclosure

Mail order coin and bank note dealers publish fixed price catalogs. These catalogs should include a reasonably full description of each item offered, a specifically assigned grade or condition for each item (not a nebulous description such as "nicely circulated"), and where practical illustrations of what is available.

There is no point to describing every Lincoln cent someone has on a fixed price list, however the dates and mint marks need to be present, as does the specific grade in which the coin is for sale. You shouldn't expect an illustration of every Lincoln cent being offered, but it would be nice to have an illustration of a rare date coin being offered for a significant price.

Return Policies

Return policies should be spelled out on mail order catalogs. Usually a coin dealer can be expected to offer a time period in which the coin or bank note can be returned if it is not satisfactory, although the dealer might require that the item to be returned hasn't been removed from the holder in which it was shipped to you.

FACT

A mail order company should agree that if at some later date a coin is determined to be counterfeit, the dealer will refund your money. There's likely a time limit on this guarantee, though, typically between ten and thirty days.

The policy that a coin must remain in the packaging in which it was shipped to be considered returnable is important to protect the dealer from someone switching coins or damaging them. It isn't the dealer's fault if you fail to remove staples holding a coin in place, than scratch the coin when removing it from its 2" × 2" holder.

Buy Backs

Any reputable dealer should be willing to buy back anything he sold you at some later date. All coin dealers need stock. They can't simply telephone a manufacturer to get more. A dealer should be willing to repurchase coins he sold you in the same grade in which they were sold. The price may not be the same, however. If market conditions are good, the dealer may pay you more than you paid for the coin or note. If retail prices are about the same as when you made the purchase, however, you must take into consideration the dealer needs to discount the value by some modest amount in order to make a profit later. However, modest means modest, not some ludicrous discount. Dealers make their profit more in turnover than in markup.

Buying on Television

The shopping networks on television have become popular since cable and satellite television came into being. Among the many things they sell are collector coins, bank notes, and medals. Announcers on these programs often create a sense of urgency regarding the purchase. They may emphasize that prices are increasing rapidly, that supplies are limited, or that these coins are no longer being made. Ask yourself this question: If prices are rising rapidly, why aren't they keeping the coins until prices get higher, then selling them?

Caution is the watchword when it comes to making purchases through a television network dedicated to selling products rather than a network on which advertising sponsors the entertainment programming. Since these shopping networks have no entertainment programming, someone has to pay for this advertising. That's the person purchasing the merchandise they are selling.

Products, including collectible coins, sold on shopping networks may be a good buy, but don't make purchases based on some announcer's sales pitch. Study the products offered first, then make your purchases if you are satisfied that the price being asked (including shipping and handling charges) is what you are willing to pay. If you are not knowledgeable about the collectibles being offered, you may be better off not making the purchase. Remember that anytime someone is selling merchandise, regardless if it is collectibles or something else, through a mass media such as television they have to have sufficient inventory to satisfy the large numbers of buyers they are anticipating. They are not going to sell rare coins that are difficult to stock in large quantities. They are selling collectibles, not rare collectibles.

This same situation is true of newspaper advertising to sell coins, bank notes, or medals. The advertiser needs to have sufficient stock to justify the cost of the advertising and to fill anticipated orders.

One other note of importance regarding buying on TV and newspapers is that medals rather than coins may be advertised. Watch the wording either through the announcer if you are watching television, or read the ad carefully if it is in a hard copy publication. If the word "coins" is not used, you are likely purchasing medals. Medals seldom have the same value as do coins when being resold.

Buying at Coin Stores

Coin stores were a traditional place to buy and sell coins in the past. However, there are fewer coin stores today than there were during the mid to late twentieth century, mainly due to the increasing overhead such stores must absorb. Yet coin stores are still a good place to do business.

How do I find a good coin store?
You can locate coin stores in your area through the telephone book or via the Internet. Many of them advertise in hobby publications as well. Make sure to shop around. Most dealers buy and sell coins within a narrow range that is very similar to that of competing dealers, but you may find that you can purchase or sell something slightly more favorably at one store than at another.

Coin stores are a good place in which to build a working relationship while dealing with someone face to face rather than by telephone, mail, or e-mail. A good relationship with a local dealer can become important if you are building a meaningful collection. It will also become important if either you or your heirs sell the collection at a later date.

Buying at Auctions

There are two types of auctions, public and private. Private auctions are by invitation only, but they are seldom conducted in the United States. Public auctions are more popular since the additional people who might attend may encourage competitive bidding. This is good news if you are selling, but it could require you to bid higher in order to win.

Auctions are held for local, regional, and national audiences depending on the size of the auction house and the scope of the merchandise offered. Coins and collectible paper money are sold by local auctioneers also selling household goods, and they are sold by major auction houses that specialize in selling rare coins. These larger auction houses seeking a national audience typically publish illustrated auction catalogs and may in addition publish lists of coins and money to be offered on the Internet.

You must attend the auction to bid at a local sale. An auction house seeking a wider audience may allow bidding by telephone, mail, and via the Internet. Local auctions tend to offer common collectibles, however an occasional rare coin may also be offered. Auction houses seeking a national audience are likely catering to collectors anticipating paying significant amounts for significant collector coins.

Auctions are conducted relatively consistently nationwide. A person consigns items to an auctioneer, and the auctioneer receives a percentage of the price as his fee. The consignor may want to set a minimum bid at which the item can be sold (called a reserve price), however auctioneers typically charge for this additional service in case the item fails to sell.

When planning to bid at an auction, you need to first determine if you are seeking common or rare material, then choose the auctions appropriate to your needs. You also need to set a limit you are willing to bid for a specific lot. If the lot continues to be bid higher, stay with your plan and stop bidding. Auction fever occurs when bidders get carried away by the excitement and bid far beyond what they had planned to pay, likely paying more than fair market value in the process. Self control is important when bidding at an auction.

Auctions should not be confused with mail bid sales. Mail bid sales are conducted the same way a public auction is conducted, with people placing bids on the items. However unlike at a regular auction, at a mail bid sale, the coins cannot be viewed in person, nor can the event be attended. Bidders must rely on descriptions and illustrations provided. Be certain you understand return privileges before bidding in mail bid sales in case you later learn what you purchased is less than what was described. Also unlike with auctions, people conducting mail bid sales either by mail or on the Internet don't need to have auction licenses.

Buying Online

There are many excellent Internet sites at which to purchase coins, but make certain you are dealing with an established company that offers full disclosure regarding what they are selling and doesn't retouch images of their merchandise.

If you go digging for treasure, make sure you can legally keep coins and other items you find on property you don't own. In Great Britain, for instance, there are treasure trove laws under which finders may receive either a reward or keep what they found, depending on whether the find was buried intentionally or lost. In Turkey, Italy, and Greece, however, it is illegal to excavate anything.

A word of caution regarding the Internet: Don't determine the value of your coins from what you see on the Internet. You don't know for certain the coin listed on the Internet is the same date, mint mark, and in the same condition as what you have. You also don't know if the price realized someone posts on the Internet is real or if it is a bid they themselves placed in an effort to get someone else to buy the item at an inflated price.

6

chapter 6

How Coins Are Made

Coins are such an integral part of our lives. They're so commonplace, few of us probably ever stop to think how they were made in the first place. But like so many other products, making coins is a fascinating process.

Government-Owned Versus Private Mints

In an ideal situation, a government owns and operates its own mints. Due to economic conditions, not every nation has this luxury; some nonissuing entities find it necessary to contract with outside sources for their coins and bank notes. These governments can contract with another government's mint, or they may contract with a private firm that produces coins to order.

FACT

In 1650, the Spanish king sent a new viceroy to the Potosi Mint in what is today Bolivia to investigate the debased silver coinage being minted there. Several mint officials were executed and the designs on all Spanish coinage of the New World was changed from a design showing two hemispheres to that of the portrait of the king to indicate the newer coinage was now of proper weight and purity.

One example of a private mint was owned by Matthew Boulton in eighteenth-century England. Boulton went so far as to try to convince the United States to close its mint and contract with him to produce U.S. coinage. Although this proposal was rejected, some of the contemporary coinage blanks on which U.S. coins were struck were purchased from Boulton.

In modern history, the best known private mint is likely the Pobjoy Mint based in the United Kingdom. The Pobjoy Mint competes against such government-owned mints as the British Royal Mint and the Royal Canadian Mint for foreign coin contracts.

Private and government-owned mints compete for business strike coinage contracts. The country requiring the coins prepares the coins' specifications, including their metal content, weight, diameter, magnetic properties, designs, and the number or mintage required. The lowest bidder typically receives the contract. Not all government-owned mints solicit foreign contracts, though. Some only strike coins for their own country.

Modern Coin Production

A mint is simply a factory at which coined money is made. The processes through which a coin is made are in many ways very similar to how many other products are produced. Here's how it works.

From Design to Hub

The designs for coins are first sketched by an artist, then made into a modeling wax or plasticene bas-relief model, typically by a mint employee called an engraver. This model will be about three to twelve times larger than the diameter of the proposed coin. A plaster negative is cast from this model, and then the design on the model is retouched to refine the details as necessary, with appropriate legends (inscriptions) added. A plaster positive model is then made from the plaster negative.

A coin galvano.

What is a coin galvano?
A galvano is the model for a coin design that serves as a lathe before the design is transferred to a coin-size hub.

Once this hard plaster model is approved by the appropriate authorities, a hard epoxy composition model is made from this same plaster model. The epoxy model is mounted on a Janvier transfer engraving machine, a machine that reduces the design to the appropriate size for the coin as it transfers the image onto a master model for the proposed coin called a hub.

From Hub to Coinage Dies

The hub is heated to harden it, then it is placed in a hydraulic press. The hub is hydraulically pressed into a blank piece of soft die steel until a negative duplicate image appears on the soft die steel. This is called a master die. Working hubs are made from the master die by again using a hydraulic press to transfer the coinage image. Working coinage dies are produced from the working hub. These dies will be used to strike coins until they wear out, at which time new working coinage dies will replace them. In theory the finished coins should be identical regardless of which coinage die is used, since all coinage dies originate from the same working hub. (In fact, on occasion a collectible coin variety may inadvertently be made when something alters the features on an individual working coinage die or on the working hub from which the working coinage dies are made.)

Coinage Blank Production

The appropriate metal for the individual coinage denomination is assayed for purity, melted, and formed into ingots. The ingots are rolled into long strips of the appropriate coinage thickness. The strip is coiled for storage until needed. The strip is fed into a blanking press to punch out coinage blanks of the appropriate weight and diameter. The blanks are sifted through a bedplate with holes of the correct diameter for quality assurance. Burrs are removed from the edges of each coinage blank in an additional quality assurance operation.

Coining Operations

The approved coinage blanks are heated, or annealed, to about 1,400 degrees Fahrenheit, then given a water bath to keep their crystal structure consistent to this softened state caused by the annealing process. The coinage blanks are given a chemical bath to remove any discoloration caused by the annealing process. Then the coinage blanks are blow dried. The coinage blanks are given a slightly raised edge rim by passing through an upsetting mill. Obverse and reverse coinage dies, and an appropriate diameter collar to hold the blanks are set up in a coinage striking machine. Coinage blanks are fed individually by gravity from an overhead hopper into the coinage striking machine. The coins go through a final quality control inspection, and then they are bagged for shipping to Federal Reserve banking centers.

Die sinker working on a die.

Blank production.

Other Mint Functions

The primary mission of any mint is to produce coins. Typically minting business strike coins is this primary mission, however collector coins may also be made, or in a few rare instances collector coins may be the only product made by a privately owned mint. Other mint products may include bullion (precious metal) composition trade coins, refined metal, and bank notes and security paper products such as stocks and bonds.

Ancient and Medieval Coin Production

Coins were made quite differently prior to the introduction of modern machinery and techniques. Mints were divided into individual mint shops, each supervised by a mint master. Minting was seldom centralized, with many locally located mints striking coins as needed for the local community. A mint issuing authority insured that the coins were all consistent in design, metal purity, and weight.

In ancient times, the coinage dies were all individually engraved by hand by a person called a *celator*. The reverse design was engraved into an anvil, with the obverse design engraved onto a hammer. Once a coinage blank had been forged by hand, it was held over the anvil with a long pair of tongs. A mint worker would then strike the blank with the hammer, leaving the coinage impressions on each side of the blank. No collar was used, commonly resulting in misshapen or off-center coins.

FACT

Medieval coins were still struck without the use of a collar, so medieval coins are almost never perfectly round and are often slightly off center. Not surprisingly, higher quality coins of these periods are in greater demand by collectors.

During medieval times in Europe little changed, except that the typical coinage became paper thin in composition. The metal blanks during this time were made by pounding the metal into sheets from which coinage blanks were cut by hand. These required weighing, with adjustments made to blanks that were initially too heavy.

Coin Errors

As with any product, there is margin for error. Errors are educational because they graphically show what can go wrong at a mint. But because error coins are the exception rather than the rule, they can be quite collectable. People who collect error coins are called error collectors. Error coins can be collected as error type sets, date sets, or even what one collector calls a "looks cool" set.

Here is a list of coinage errors you might encounter.

- **Broadstrike:** A broadstrike is a coin struck without a collar around the coinage blank, resulting in a coin that is not perfectly round. This coin will typically lack good centering and detail.

- **Brockage:** A brockage is similar to an indent (when two coinage blanks get into the coining machine at the same time, causing one to overlap the other), however with a brockage a struck coin is struck onto the blank, leaving a distorted but mirror image impression.
- **Caps or die caps:** Coin blanks occasionally stick to the coinage die when they are struck. When the die slams down on the next blank ejected into the coinage machine, the metal flows up around the die and the resulting coin looks more like a bottle cap. These are typically caught by mint quality control and for that reason are desirable among error collectors.
- **Capped die strike:** If the coin press continues to operate despite a coin now being stuck to one of the coinage dies, as further coin blanks enter the machine the additional blanks will either be produced blank or with only varying degrees of mush-like detail until the capped die coin finally either falls off or disintegrates.
- **Clashed dies:** A coinage blank is supposed to enter the coining machine every time the obverse and reverse dies come together to produce the desired coin images on both sides of that blank. When a blank fails to enter the mechanism and the coining machine continues to operate, the two dies will clash, leaving a partial image of the opposite side on each of the coining dies. When coinage blanks now enter the machine, this clashed image will be transferred to the coins that are produced.
- **Die break:** A die break is a flaw in the coinage die in which a piece of the coinage die is missing. The blob of raised metal appearing on the resulting coin is called a "cud" or "die break."
- **Die crack:** If a coinage die begins to wear and develops a crack, that crack will be transferred to coins struck from that die. This will appear on such coins as a thin, raised line. As the die continues to disintegrate, the die crack will extend further on coins the die strikes later during this degeneration.
- **Double denomination:** When a finished coin of a particular denomination for some reason goes back into the coining machinery and is struck a second time by dies producing a different denomination, a double denomination error will occur. The image of both denominations must be partially visible.

- **Doubled die:** This is one of the more celebrated errors, especially regarding the 1955 Lincoln cent. This error occurs when the hub from which the working coinage dies rotates or shifts so that the doubling is transferred on to the coinage die. Coins struck from this die will have the same doubling.
- **Indent:** When two blanks get into the coining machinery at the same time, one overlaps the other. This causes a partial strike with an indented blank area on the bottom coin.
- **Lamination:** If the coinage blank begins to peal or crack after it has been struck to become a coin, this is because of defects in the host blank. This pealing or cracking is called lamination.
- **Mechanical doubling:** While this type of error is often confused with the doubled die error, it is not a rare doubling effect. Mechanical doubling is caused by a loose die that twists slightly at the moment of striking the coinage blank. A flat shelf-like doubling results. A coinage die that has been overused until it is significantly worn will also result in mechanical or machine doubling, likely with weakly defined detail.
- **Off-center:** An off-center error is a coin struck without a collar, causing part of the detail to be off the coin. Off-center strikes are more desirable when the surviving image includes the date, since there are collectors of these who seek them by date.

An off-center coin.

- **Off-metal strike:** This is one of the more heralded coin errors. If a coinage blank meant for a different coin somehow gets into the hopper from which coinage blanks are being fed into the coin striking machine an off-metal strike occurs. The most famous of these is likely the 1943 copper composition Lincoln cent, a coin that was supposed to be produced of zinc and steel that year during World War II.
- **Partial collar:** A coin struck with only part of the collar holding the blank will result in an area of the edge of the coin expanding out of shape. On coins with reeded edges this will give the appearance of a two-level railroad wheel, known to collectors as a "railroad rim."
- **Split planchet:** A split planchet error is a progression experienced by a severe lamination problem. The defect in the blank causes the coin to split into two halves.
- **Struck through error:** A foreign object such as a piece of cloth, string, or even machinery grease may get between the die and the coinage blank, leaving an impression or causing the finished coin to lack part of the intended impression.
- **Uniface:** When the image of only one side is struck onto a coin, the coin is uniface. This error is typically caused by an obstruction blocking one of the dies from striking the coinage blank.
- **Weak strike:** This is a coin lacking detail due to insufficient pressure having been applied to the coinage blank by the coining machine. Do not confuse wear with weak striking quality.

Coinage blanks, or planchets, are made by punching blanks from a metal sheet of the appropriate thickness. There are three types of clipped planchets—curved, straight, and ragged. If the sheet is not properly advanced, the punch may overlap a hole, producing a blank with a circular clipped edge. This is called a clipped planchet. Beware that this type of error can be artificially created outside of the mint. Genuine errors of this nature do not have a raised edge of metal bordering the missing metal, and the coin image detail bordering the area of missing metal will not be sharply defined.

The second type of clipped planchet is the straight clipped planchet. This happens if the missing part of the coinage blank is the result of the sheet shifting toward its edge when the blank was to be punched. The third type of clipped planchet is the ragged clipped planchet. This happens if the blank was cut from a ragged edge of the sheet from which the blanks were being punched.

As with any coins, the collector value of error coins is determined by supply, demand, and the eye appeal of the error. The more graphic the error, the more valuable it typically will be.

Coin Alterations

Even with many fail-safes and quality control checks in place, mints aren't perfect, as you might imagine by the many error types just described. But sometimes, mints are able to fix their mistakes by altering the coins. These coins are called alterations. For example, when a letter in the legends on a coin, a mint mark, or the date is impressed incorrectly into a coinage die, a mint engraver may repunch that letter or numeral over that mistake to make a correction.

If you think about it, any alterations are technically errors, but coin collectors treat them as desirable varieties within a series rather than as error coins. Many date and mint mark sets of particular U.S. coin denominations are not considered to be complete unless the "overdates" are included. As an example, the Standing Liberty quarter series of 1916 to 1930 includes a 1918-S quarter in which the coinage die originally carried the date 1917. Since no one at the mint wanted to have to destroy a perfectly good unused die, the last digit was simply repunched into the die so it could be used to mint coins during 1918. This is expressed as "1918/7-S" in coinage vernacular. This overdate variety sells for many times more than does the normal 1918-S quarter.

Repunches and Overdates to Look For

There have been many repunched and overdated U.S. coin variations since U.S. coinage began in 1793, however a casual collector has a much better opportunity to encounter such variations struck during the twentieth and twenty-first centuries than from earlier periods. If you'd like to identify all the overdates and repunches in the entire U. S. coinage series, check out a coin catalog on the subject.

Here are some repunches and overdates that you might find in family collections and accumulations:

20th and 21st Century Repunches and Overdates

Repunch or Overdate	What to Look For
1909-S Over Horizontal S Lincoln Cent	The mint mark appearing below the date was initially added sideways to a coinage die, then corrected.
1922 No Mint Mark Lincoln Cent	Excessive die polishing wore the mint mark (appearing below the date) off three coinage dies to varying extents. Varieties of this coin exist with only a partial or no mint mark as well as the normal 1922-D coin. The most valuable variety is that in which the mint mark is entirely missing. Beware of counterfeits.
1922-D	Cents where the mint mark has been artificially removed.
1943-D/D Lincoln Cent	The mint mark appearing below the date was punched twice onto the coinage die from which this variety was made.
1944-D/S Lincoln Cent	The wrong mint mark was added to a working die, followed by repunching the correct mint mark over it.
1946-S/D Lincoln Cent	Once again the wrong mint mark was first punched into a working coinage die, followed by an easy-to-see correction.

Repunch or Overdate	What to Look For
1914/3 Buffalo Nickel	During 1914 a 1913 coinage die was used, with the digit 4 punched prominently over the 3.
1918/7-D Buffalo Nickel	The lower portion of the 7 weaves through the lower loop of the 8 on this interesting repunch. The mint mark appears below the denomination on the reverse. This is an expensive coin.
1937-D Three-Legged Buffalo Nickel	This is an almost legendary error in coin collecting. The front leg was accidentally polished off a working coinage die. Be aware of counterfeits! Genuine examples show a stream of raised dots between the buffalo's belly and the ground.
1938-D/S Buffalo Nickel	You'll need to look closely at the mint mark below the denomination to find this variety. The S mint mark is very light, while the D is bold.
1942-D/Horizontal D Jefferson Nickel	This is the copper-nickel variety nickel of this year, not the "war" nickel with silver content. The mint mark was first punched sideways into the working die. The mint mark appears at the right side of Monticello on the reverse.
1943/2-P Jefferson Nickel	This is not a well-known variety and can be seen only under strong magnification since the underlying 2 is not well defined.
1949-D/S Jefferson Nickel	It is unusual to find a mid to late twentieth-century repunched U.S. coin. Use magnification to examine this mint mark. This is a coin that might still be found in circulation.

Repunch or Overdate	What to Look For
1954-S/D Jefferson Nickel	The lower loop of the S will appear to be doubled under close examination, but it is actually part of the underlying D you will see.
1955-D/S Jefferson Nickel	Watch for what appears to be a doubling to the top of the D. It is actually part of the underlying S.
1942/1 Mercury Dime	The date will appear to read "19412" on this grossly messed up overdate. Someone was particularly careless at the mint when correcting a 1941-dated coinage die for use during 1942.
1942/1-D Mercury Dime	This is the only case in U.S. coinage history in which two mints struck overdated coins of the same denomination in the same year. The 4 will appear to have an extra lower leg on this overdate.
1950-S/D Roosevelt Dime	Although several doubled die coins exist within the Roosevelt dime series, this is the only repunched mint mark. Unlike on modern nonsilver composition Roosevelt dimes struck beginning in 1965, the mint mark appears at the left of the lower portion of the torch on this coin.
1918/7-D Standing Liberty Quarter	This is a very popular coin since it is the only overdate in this particular series. The 7 appears to run right through the loops of the 8 on high grade examples.
1950-D/S Washington Quarter	Close examination is necessary to see the underlying repunched mint mark on this variety.

Repunch or Overdate	What to Look For
1950-S/D Washington Quarter	Whoever added mint mark punches to the working coinage dies for this coin made a mistake twice, as there is both a D over S and an S over D variety to collect. Once again, magnification should be used when looking for this variety.
1900-O/CC Morgan Silver Dollar	This is the only such twentieth century or twenty-first century repunch found on any dollar coin. Leftover Carson City Mint reverse dies from 1893 (1893 is the final year in which silver dollars were struck in Carson City) had been shipped to New Orleans for use, but the old mint mark was not entirely effaced. A shadow of the original CC mint mark appears below the O.
1901/0-S Coronet $5 Gold Half Eagle	Repunching and overdate varieties are extremely rare in the U.S. gold coin series. Ironically this overdate does not command much of a premium value over that of the normal 1901-S coin.
1909/8 Saint Gaudens $20 Gold Double Eagle	The only way to see the underlying 8 on this coin is by examining the area of the lower hook of the overlying 9.

Mules

In coin collecting terminology, a mule is when two mismatched dies were used to strike a coin. An example would be a 1-cent coinage obverse with a 5-cent coin reverse, although this has never happened. Collectors should be aware that obverse and reverse dies mount differently into mint coinage striking machines. For this reason it would be easy to determine if two obverse or two reverse dies had improperly been set up together. In other words, there is no such thing as a "two-headed" coin.

A U.S. "mule" coin has in fact been legitimately minted. The so-called "transition" 1859 and 1860 half dimes and 1859 dime lack the legend "United States of America." The variety of 1856 to 1859 carries this legend on the reverse, while the variety of 1860 to 1873 transferred it to the obverse. Because of mismatching the dies, this legend is missing from each of these mint mistakes.

In fact, two-headed coins are occasionally found in circulation. These are novelty or magician pieces produced outside the mint as trick coins. Either two coins have been cut in half and fixed together (in which case a tell-tale groove will appear on the edge) or one side of a host coin has been carefully machined out inside the grooved edge, with the complementary side of a second coin carefully machined to fit into this void. Close examination of the inner side of the raised edge of a coin will reveal a tiny gap in such a nicely made piece.

Two-headed fantasy pieces are typically available through novelty mail order catalogs. The coins occasionally enter circulation, where noncollectors often mistake them for being fantastic rarities.

chapter 7

Coin Rarity and Values

Nobody ever said every coin (or bank note) that is collected has to have a value over its face value. Collectors collect. They can be coins or notes merely of face value, but even when someone is collecting from pocket change the question always arises, "How much is it worth?" The other half of this question is the rather naïve, "When will my coin become valuable?" The mechanics of this intangible value will be addressed in this chapter.

Defining a Rare Coin

The words rare, scarce, and desirable are probably the most abused terms not only in coin collecting, but within antiques and collectibles in general. How can you truly define these rather intangible terms? Each of these terms is relative. Each is a perception. When each of these terms is used in advertising, it is meant to project a sense of urgency to the potential buyer. The message each of these terms is meant to send is that you can't put off that purchase until tomorrow, because either the coin will no longer be available, or it will have increased in value. These are psychological terms. Be watchful for when each of them is overused or abused. And understand that two things that help to make a coin rare are publicity and notoriety.

Publicity

It might surprise the average collector to learn that there are many coins that are known from only a few examples, either because of low mintages or because of a low survival rate. But why does a silver coin dated 1492 from Brabant in the Low Countries sell for perhaps $100 to $200, while a U.S. Liberty Head or "V" nickel sell for millions of dollars? Both are "rare."

Does the value of a coin increase with age?
No, age has nothing to do with the value of a coin, bank note, antique, or of anything else. If this were true there would be a lot more valuable old things then there actually are.

One coin will become valuable while another will not simply because of the attention drawn to it. This is an emotional rather than a rational response, but because coin collecting is a hobby, all collectible coin purchases are based on spontaneity rather than on logic. If logic was used, and age was truly a factor in the value of a coin, the Brabant coin should logically be more valuable than the U.S. Liberty Head nickel.

As an interesting note, the 1913 Liberty Head nickels were not an official issue of the U.S. Mint. It is generally believed that they were made after hours

A 1913 Liberty Head nickel

by a mint employee using unused coinage dies and mint equipment. The only nickels officially made in 1913 are those with an Indian and buffalo on them. All five of the 1913 Liberty Head nickels were clandestinely sold to a local coin dealer and were disbursed from there. Today they are sold for very high prices despite the fact technically the U.S. Secret Service could seize them as being illegal to own. No such attempt has ever been made because there is too much publicity surrounding these famous coins.

FACT

During the 1930s, Fort Worth, Texas, coin dealer B. Max Mehl, realizing the whereabouts of all five examples of this nickel were known, advertised nationwide that he would pay a very high price for any the public could offer him. The ad worked. It drew attention both to coins as a collectible, and to Mehl as a merchant.

While the 1913 Liberty Head nickels continue to make headlines every time one of them sells, no one has ever heard of the 1492 coins of Brabant. The publicity, or lack of it, surrounding the two coins makes all the difference in their perceived value. Realistically neither will ever be spent as money. Under such a circumstance the amount someone is willing to pay for either of them is truly based on desire, not on logic.

Notoriety

The notoriety surrounding the 1913 Liberty Head nickels also triggers excitement. The very idea the coins were not legally made, yet the government has never made any effort to confiscate them, adds almost folklore status to the coins, as well as to the desire of those collectors who have deep pockets to covet owning them. Yet the Brabant coins are almost as rare, and they are definitely less often encountered in collector circles! But the Brabant coins are far from notorious.

The bottom line is that you can have the best coin in the world, but if little or no interest is drawn to that coin no knowledgeable collector will pay a premium for it.

Sleepers

In collectible terminology a "sleeper" is an item that is known from only a modest number of examples, yet despite this scarcity the item has not shown any value appreciation. There is little difference between a coin that is considered by some people to be a sleeper and a stock an investor perceives as being undervalued. This perception could be correct, or it could be wrong. There will likely be logic applied to justify that the item, be it an investment stock or a collectible, is truly undervalued. But logic does not drive values. Emotion does. Sleepers should be approached, especially when considering purchasing collectible coins, with caution. It could be an opportunity, but is it an opportunity for you as the purchaser, or for the person selling it to unload a dinosaur?

Supply and demand are the basic fundamentals of economics. Together they determine prices for virtually everything. Supply is a fact. There is simply a specific population of every item. If this is a fixed supply, it means the population will not increase or decrease. If the item is consumable, potentially the supply will eventually diminish. If the supply is able to be replenished then it is not a fixed supply either. Regarding older coins or bank notes, an identifiable fixed supply was produced. If they were produced for circulation, logically some of them eventually wore out and are gone. The surviving supply or population can be further broken down by the condition in which each coin has survived. If only a limited number of the surviving population is in a very high grade, some people may perceive these better examples to be more desirable grade rarities.

Tastes in collectibles change continuously, just as the value of real estate changes based on the community that surrounds it. A coin is perceived as a sleeper when statistics indicate that there are fewer of this coin (in a specific condition) available than the number of collectors who will want to purchase it. Should this statistic later be proved the price will rise.

Publicity is often the key. What is rare today will always be rare, and what is common today will more than likely always remain common. Unless someone draws attention to what is perceived to be the scarce item, and people not only pay attention but also act on that publicity, even a coin known from a single example may not necessarily increase in value.

This is particularly true in what people perceive as grade rarity coins, coins that are difficult to find in especially high conditions. Will anyone at some later date care enough to pay an additional premium for the right to own such a coin? If there is a solid collector base collecting this particular series then perhaps this will happen. If it is an area of collecting that is only mediocre in popularity the awakening of such a sleeper becomes less likely regardless of any statistics to give logic to its greater desirability.

Factoring in Condition

Basic economics tells us that the value of anything is determined by supply and demand. A third factor, condition, should be applied regarding coins and bank notes. Because our modern money is mass produced by machine, in theory all coins of a specific date, mint mark, and denomination should be identical. But in fact, due to the quality of manufacture and the amount of circulation to which an individual coin has been subjected, there will be differences in just about all coins that may otherwise be perceived as identical.

In other words, all 1950-D Jefferson nickels are not truly identical coins. Some may be in good condition, while others might look mint-new. This will make a difference in their individual values.

It is to the advantage of the government issuing coins to try to make them as identical as is physically possible. Their acceptance as money by the general public depends on the public being able to rely on each coin having a standard weight, diameter, and ease of identification. If our coinage was not standardized, it would be incapable of being accepted by coin vending receptacles. If there are variations in coins, many of them may also fail to circulate because people will hold onto them as collectibles.

FACT

The bottom line is that coinage is produced to be used as money, not to be collected. Coins struck in special sets are marketed as collectibles, but the coins made for circulation become counterproductive to a government if they fail to be used. Consistency in production becomes important for this reason.

If there are error coins in circulation due to a lack of consistency in production that are attractive to collectors, the general public may begin to hoard these coins as well. This is counterproductive to the very reason the coins were made. Collectors will remove some coins from circulation regardless of whether there are rare varieties or not. The number typically held by collectors is miniscule compared to the vast numbers usually produced. Different marks and signs of wear make each coin unique unto itself even when quality assurance assures production is consistent. This is why no two coins are truly identical.

Understanding the Values of Coins

You learned about several different types of coins in Chapter 2, including NCLTs and proofs. But here you'll learn about the values of these types of coins.

Treasure Coins

One type of coin that has a high perceived value to the general public is treasure coins. Treasure coins are a marketing agent's dream come true. There are stories about their origination to be told, the coins typically receive a lot of attention from the mass media, and the public loves the word "treasure." Treasure coins are found in either of two places—in the ground or under water. Treasure coins are often well publicized without a lot of cost to the organization selling them. Since the general public rather than experienced collectors are the primary market, such coins typically sell for more than what experienced collectors would be willing to pay for them. Here are the facts of life regarding treasure coins:

- Coins found in the ground or under water are likely to have some damage. Cleaning them may remove some of this, but cleaned coins are not welcomed by collectors.
- If a coin was relatively scarce and a hoard of that coin is suddenly discovered the additional supply should drive down the value of the coins. Once the excitement of the disbursal of the treasure find subsides, it is often discovered there is now a glut of these coins on the market, but with little secondary collector market into which they can be sold. Prices at this time typically decline dramatically.
- Due to the excitement surrounding the find, the general public typically buys on emotion, paying more for these coins than collectors will. Even when not implied in advertising, the public often perceives these coins as an investment.

Treat treasure coins the same as you would any other coins you're considering purchasing for your collection. Use logic, not emotion.

Noncirculating Legal Tender Commemoratives

Noncirculating Legal Tender commemorative coins or NCLTs have been issued with increasing frequency since the beginning of the second half of the twentieth century. Governments have since that time realized there is money to be made by selling commemorative coins with emotional appeal due to a person, place, or thing, or the anniversary of a person, place, or thing.

In recent years, the issue of NCLTs has reached the point where a mint or marketing organization will contract with a government for the rights to use the name of that country on coins chosen by the mint or marketing organization. The results have included coins commemorating the sinking of the ship Titanic commemorated by African nations with no connection to the disaster or countries issuing Olympic commemoratives while the country of issue never participated in the Games.

An NCLT is just what the wording says. It is a coin because it identifies the country of issue and a coinage denomination, however the coin is not meant to circulate even though it is technically legal tender. In several situations it has been later proved the coins were not legal tender. NCLTs are coins, but are they money?

NCLT commemorative coins are typically limited issues. But before buying them, ask yourself if these "limited editions" are limited to a specific number to be produced regardless of demand, or are they merely limited to the number of orders that can be filled. The answer to that question will influence the coin's value.

The true value of collector coins and bank notes is determined by the demand for them in the secondary market, not in their initial offering. If a government issues one million commemorative coins but only sells 750,000, it then melts the unsold pieces or sells them to a bulk distributor. Everyone who initially wanted this coin already bought it, so there is no secondary market demand.

Several astute governments have ensured supply does not outstrip demand on the initial issue of their commemorative coins in order to ensure a stronger secondary market demand for their products. These coin issuing entities understand that initial sales eventually will decline significantly once people learn they can never recover what they spent to buy such NCLTs.

U.S. Commemorative Coins

In 1892 Congress authorized the first true U.S. commemorative coin, a silver half dollar meant to help raise money for the Columbian Exposition the following year in Chicago. Through this issue two things were established. First, Congress rather than the U.S. Mint would determine what commemoratives would be issued. Second, commemorative coins would be issued to raise money for private interests. Both of these facts would invite abuses into the system that have remained to this day.

Between 1892 and 1954 an almost ever-increasing number of commemoratives were issued in both gold and silver. By 1954 interest had waned and what today is considered to be the first U.S. commemorative coin series ended unceremoniously.

In 1982 what is generally regarded among collectors to be a second series of NCLT commemorative coins began, once again the subject and where the profits were to go being mandated by Congress. Each of these funded some private enterprise lobbied before Congress.

One significant difference between the early and modern U.S. commemoratives is that the early series was typically struck in uncirculated and occasionally circulated as money. The modern series are specially encapsulated and virtually never enter circulation.

Regarding value, the earlier commemoratives through 1954 command a premium above their issue price. The more modern commemoratives (beginning in 1982) in general have such high authorized mintages that most have depreciated in value in the secondary collector markets.

FACT

In 1975 the United States issued circulating commemorative quarters, half dollars, and dollars to mark the U.S. bicentenary. Since that time the United States has issued additional circulating commemorative coins in addition to the specially made examples specially packaged for collectors.

World Commemorative Coins

Although commemorative coins have been struck since ancient times, it is the early modern German silver taler coins that are usually though of as the earliest commemorative world coins. In more modern history, it was Finland who in 1951 and 1952 issued a commemorative coin to mark the Olympic Games that initiated the many issues now offered.

Commemorative Bank Notes

Commemorative bank notes are now gaining popularity. Although commemorative bank notes first appeared during the 1890s, it wasn't until recent years that governments realized it doesn't cost very much to print a commemorative bank note, yet commemorative bank notes may either appreciate in value in collector markets or the public may choose to hoard the notes. This will make a profit for the government of issue through *siegniorage*. Siegniorage is the difference between the cost of producing a coin or bank note and its face value. This is recorded as profit by the government of issue. If the coin or bank note is not eventually redeemed, this profit remains as an accounting profit, however if the coin or note is redeemed this profit must be offset.

The U.S $2 Federal Reserve bank note issued in 1976 with a vignette of the signing of the Declaration of Independence on the back was not meant to be issued as a commemorative, but, because of its timing to the Bicentenary celebration and the three circulating commemorative coins, it has since been treated by the public as our only domestic commemorative bank note.

Proof and Uncirculated Sets

Proof coins are specially made, using higher quality coinage blanks, better coinage dies, and special handling. They are meant to be pristine examples of coins. Proof sets are date sets that show proof examples of one of each coinage denomination that will be released into circulation during that year.

Uncirculated or mint coin sets are also examples of the coins that will be released into circulation, however these are business strike coins, not specially made and handled coins as are the proofs. Coins found in uncirculated coin sets are usually of a higher quality than are uncirculated examples released into circulation.

Collectors purchasing proof sets, mint or uncirculated sets, and commemorative coins in the secondary market will insist all the original packaging and the certificates of authenticity remain, and that this packaging is undamaged. Dealers will deeply discount the price they are willing to pay for stock sets and commemoratives if the packaging is incomplete or damaged.

Modern U.S. Mint sets include examples of all coins planned to appear in circulation during that year, including examples from each mint issuing these coins. These mint sets have in recent years been packed in two clear plastic flat packs, one with a blue stripe representing coins struck at Philadelphia, and the other with a red stripe representing coins struck at Denver. Both of these flat packs together make one complete mint set.

Pre-1960 Proof and Mint Sets

Individual proof coins have been made for collectors with connections to the mint almost since U.S. coinage began. Proof sets consisting of an example of each denomination struck for a particular year were first offered in 1936. Production was interrupted following 1942 due to World War II, then resumed in 1950. All proof sets prior to 1960 are in demand from collectors and command good premiums.

Mint sets were first offered by the U.S. Mint in 1947. Each set consists of coins of each denomination issued by each mint facility during the year. Again, the sets prior to 1960 are challenging to find and command good value.

Post-1959 Proof and Mint Sets

Due to the increasing popularity in coin collecting, the number of proof and mint sets sold each year increased dramatically beginning in 1960. Some years are better than are others, but in general most of the post-1959 proof and mint sets do not bring the values that are realized by these earlier sets.

No proof sets were made between 1965 and 1968; special mint sets for these years took their place. No mint sets were made during 1982 and 1983, however souvenir sets of these two years are also available.

2004 U.S. proof set.

Prestige proof sets including commemorative coins were introduced in 1983, with silver composition proof sets first introduced in 1992. Each of these sets are made annually in addition to the standard annual proof set.

Beginning in 1999, the number of coins included in both the proof and mint sets grew because of the statehood quarter circulating commemorative coins. This will continue until the series ends in 2008.

World Coin Sets

Proof and mint sets of coins of the realm are issued annually by many countries around the world as well as by the United States. Since coins are often produced for a country that doesn't own its own mint by a mint in another country, it is not unusual to find such sets marketed by the mint where they were made.

Specimen sets are similar to prooflike coins and have been issued in addition to proof and mint (or uncirculated) sets by Canada. Other set variations can be expected depending on the mint producing the coins. Due to the foreign languages used in some of these coin issuing entities, you might encounter proof and mint sets described by other names.

The 1780-dated Austrian silver Maria Theresia taler depicting the Empress Maria Theresia became so popular that for more than a century it served as an international trade coin of good silver content. The coins were often counterstruck in the Levant to ensure they were legal tender. They have continued to be struck right through the present still bearing the original date.

Bullion Issue

The original intent of coins was that they ensured a specific weight and precious metal purity to a lump of metal. Coins that are composed of precious metal content and circulate at the value of that precious metal content are known as specie. Beginning in 1933, the United States abandoned gold in its circulating coinage, followed by abandoning silver in its circulating coinage after 1964 (with the exception of the half dollar, which has some silver through 1970).

It may sound like a logical way to run the economy by including appropriate precious metal in all circulating coinage, but what happens when the value of that precious metal fluctuates? This has happened several times in U.S. economic history.

Arrows appear at the date on most silver content U.S. coins dated 1853. The value of silver became sufficiently high enough by that date that there was greater silver value in U.S. coins than was the face value of those coins. People began to melt the coins to exploit this additional value. The government decreased the amount of silver in the coins, adding arrows at the date to identify the new, lower silver content coins.

The same situation occurred regarding gold coins. If the price of gold reached a certain level, the intrinsic value surpassed the face value of these coins. The large quantities that were melted at that time accounts for why some gold coins of certain dates are particularly rare today despite relatively generous mintage figures for that time.

Precious metal coins are still made today; however due to the current world economy these coins serve the purpose of holding precious metal without having to have the metal assayed when it is resold. A coin can be easily identified as being either genuine or not on sight, while an ingot must be subjected to destructive testing to determine its true content. Assaying takes time and costs money, while trading a coin of the same weight and purity can be done without a time lag or overhead.

The United States produces bullion platinum, gold, and silver coins on an annual basis called American Eagles. Each of these coins has a legal tender value below which the coin cannot be valued regardless of the value of their precious metal content.

There are bullion composition medallions issued by private organizations. There is nothing wrong with holding platinum, gold, or silver in medallion form, but ensure the weight and purity of the metal appears on the medal. Do not pay a premium above the precious metal content of a medallion under the assumption these are collectibles or coins.

The Gold American Eagle.

The Silver American Eagle.

The South African Krugerrand.

The Platinum American Eagle coins are issued in denominations of $100 (one troy ounce), $50 (half ounce), $25 (quarter ounce), and $10 (tenth ounce). The **Gold American Eagle** coins are issued in denominations of $50 (one troy ounce), $25 (half ounce), $10 (quarter ounce), and $5 (tenth ounce). The **Silver American Eagle** has a face value of $1 and is a one troy ounce coin. Proof versions of each are made for collectors. The **South African Krugerrand** was the first of the modern gold bullion coins. The coin fell out of favor with gold traders during a period in which the South African government practiced the racial separation policy of apartheid. This policy has since been abandoned, but the Krugerrand has never regained its position of prominence with coin collectors who wish to own gold coins. When the Krugerrand fell out of favor, other world mints were quick to fill the void. Today popular gold bullion coins are produced annually by other countries, including Canada (Maple Leaf), Great Britain (Britannia), Austria (Philharmonic), Australia (Kangaroo Nugget), and the United States (American Eagle).

NCLT commemorative coins are often available in precious metals, however the price of the initial offering of such coins is usually significantly higher than is their intrinsic value. Do not confuse these coins with bullion issues, although they may trade as bullion issues once they reach the secondary collector markets.

Pricing Sources

Coin collecting is different from many other collectible fields in that pricing information is readily available, in some cases almost too available. During the 1960s, the primary source of coinage values were coin handbooks by Richard Yeoman known by their cover colors as the "Blue Book" and "Red Book." By the 1970s, several hobby tabloids were publishing weekly values.

Today you can get pricing information from auction prices realized and Internet sources. Take Internet sources with caution since the person posting the price may be able to manipulate it. You can also get U.S. and world coins as well as paper money prices in a series of books published annually by Krause Publications in Iola, Wisconsin.

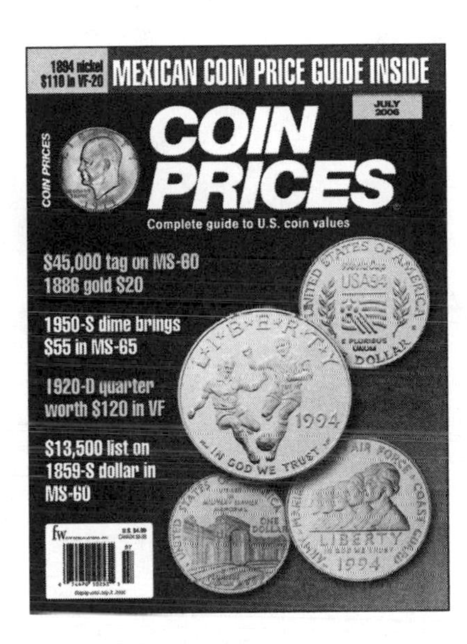

Krause price list.

chapter 8

Grading Coins

8

The single most important thing affect the value of a collectible coin or bank note is its grade, or condition. The date and mint mark are also of importance, but even a rare coin or note in a low grade will never command the interest or the price a better grade coin or note will command.

Learning How to Grade

It is important to learn how to grade, since the quality and value of the coins or bank notes in your collection depend on it. Problem coins and notes—those that have been cleaned, whizzed, repaired, or otherwise artificially enhanced—do not merit the prices coins and notes that have been left in their natural state will bring. Damaged coins are typically "net graded" a full grade or more lower than the appearance of the surviving design details.

Because coins are three dimensional, it is the amount of the relief that has been worn away that determines the grade. The best way to learn to grade is by first determining the high point of wear for a particular type of coin and examining that spot first.

Regarding paper money, the grade is based primarily on the wear of the paper, the surviving color of the inks, and on the centering of the note on that paper. Severely off-center notes were likely cut this way in error and bring a value determined by that error.

The American Numismatic Association and other groups periodically offer seminars on grading. It is well worth your time and money to attend at least one seminar. Considering the costly mistakes you will likely make if you have not learned grading properly, it is time and money well spent.

For both coins and bank notes, the grade is affected by the eye appeal as well. This is a very difficult factor to explain since eye appeal can vary from coin to coin or from note to note. In general the more attractive the coin or note, the better value it may have. For coins, mint luster is important, as is the appeal of toning when present. One person may like the eye appeal of one coin, while someone else does not.

Another factor that is difficult to identify until you become familiar with grading is differentiating between weakly struck coin detail and wear. A coin with weakly struck detail can still qualify for a grade higher than a coin on which the same details are worn. Some series of coins are known for poorly produced detail. Check out one of the specialized coin books that can assist in determining when weak detail may become a factor in determining a grade. Experience in handling a particular type of coin is also important in determining when detail is weak or simply worn away.

Coin Grades

Grading isn't an easy process. The following descriptions of the accepted coin grades are general guidelines. But because so many different designs have appeared on U.S. coins, you should study a specialized book on grading prior to attempting to grade coins.

Coins are graded according to their conditions into ten categories: uncirculated or mint state, about uncirculated, extremely fine, very fine, fine, very good, good, about good, fair, and poor. Yet these descriptions are merely words. As you delve more deeply into coin collecting, you'll encounter the Sheldon scale. This numerical grading system, which was developed by Dr. William H. Sheldon in 1949, is a more sophisticated modern grading system that grades coins between a low grade of 1 to a high grade of 70.

QUESTION?

How was the Sheldon numerical grading system established?
Dr. William H. Sheldon was a collector of large cents (1-cent coins of 1793 to 1857) who in 1949 published the book *Early American Cents.* Later editions of this book are titled *Penny Whimsy.* Sheldon attempted to assign numerical grades to large cents in an effort to determine a logical mathematical relationship between the numerical grade and the value of each coin.

Sheldon intended to have his "quantitative grading of condition" system applied exclusively to large cents. The problem was that he used the 1794 cent as the basis for his system, applying a mid-twentieth-century value of $1 for an identifiable and unmutilated coin, assigning the appropriate grade poor 1. Since the same coin sold in good for $4, he assigned the grade G4. In very good, it sold for between $8 and $10, thus he assigned the intermediate grades VG8 and VG10. Extrapolating the numbers, Sheldon determined that a perfect coin would sell for $70, so his scale ended at 70.

During the 1970s a decision was made by the ANA to adopt this numerical system for the entire U.S. series. It became widely used in the 1980s. Unfortunately, in an age of decimalization it doesn't make as much sense to have the system based on 70 points instead of 100 points. Nevertheless the Sheldon scale is the system currently in use despite discussions regarding changing to a 100-point system someday.

It's important to note that the Sheldon scale is more often applied to higher grade than to common circulation grade coins, unless the coin in question is a rare date.

Here you'll see how the more traditional verbal coin descriptions equate to the Sheldon scale numbers.

Uncirculated or Mint State Coins

An uncirculated, or mint state, coin has never been used in circulation. It is often abbreviated MS. An MS coin is as fresh as the day it was released from the mint. It likely displays "mint luster," that fresh brightness that radiates from the surfaces of a newly struck coin. Even if the coin has toned significantly, that luster should still be present, though perhaps subdued. (A lack of mint luster is usually an indication the coin has been cleaned.)

What separates the best uncirculated coins from the less perfect examples are bag marks and abrasion marks. Also, a weakly struck coin on which some of the details are mushy may also be assigned a grade on the lower end of the scale.

The quality of mint state coins can be further broken down into a numerical system of mint state 70 to mint state 60:

- **Mint state 70:** An MS70 coin is a theoretically perfect strike with full detail that is free of all contact marks. It is completely uncirculated, as struck. This coin is perfect!
- **Mint state 69:** Only miniscule imperfections such as a disturbance in the design element frosting are present.
- **Mint state 68:** Slight imperfections with possible strike detail weakness are present.

- **Mint state 67:** This coin is well struck, but with minor imperfections and lack of detail.
- **Mint state 66:** This is an excellent coin, but with minor contact marks or hairlines detectable.
- **Mint state 65/gem uncirculated:** This is an above average uncirculated coin, with minor marks or hairlines, but none are present in more obvious areas of the design elements. MS65 is normally the highest grade available for any particular coin other than those made specially for collectors.
- **Mint state 64:** An above average uncirculated coin, however this coin has trivial marks present in more obvious areas of the design elements.
- **Mint state 63/choice uncirculated:** This is an excellent coin, but not necessarily a full strike, with moderate contact marks or hairlines visible.
- **Mint state 62:** An excellent but not necessarily full strike coin, this has a few more contact marks or hairlines than appear on an MS63 coin.
- **Mint state 61:** Although this is an uncirculated coin, it was possibly weakly struck and displays significant contact marks.
- **Mint state 60/brilliant uncirculated:** No signs of wear may be present, however detail may be weak from the strike. Significant contact marks will be present. An MS60 coin is usually called "baggy" because of the numerous small contact marks appearing on the surfaces despite the fact there is no indication of any wear to the relief details.

U.S. silver dollars of the period 1878 to 1935 are popularly collected. They are particularly prone to contact marks on the cheek of Liberty's face and in the fields due to the large diameter of those coins. Under close examination, these marks can be seen on an uncirculated example. In general the number of these marks will determine the coin's MS grade.

For another example, the New Orleans silver dollar issues are notorious for lacking full breast detail on the eagle on the reverse. Because of this, the quality of New Orleans–issued silver dollars is rarely as good as are silver dollars produced at other mints during the same period. This detail weakness must be taken into account when assigning a grade to these coins.

Due to the amount of polishing of the dies from which certain coins were struck, some uncirculated coins may display mirrorlike surfaces similar to what may be expected on proof coins. This mirrorlike surface is referred to as Deep Mirror Prooflike or DMPL (pronounced "dimple" by coin collectors). Morgan silver dollars issued between 1878 and 1921 particularly are known for DMPL surfaces, which command a premium above that of an uncirculated example in the same MS grade. DMPL surfaces may appear on coins other than Morgan silver dollars, but they seldom command a premium other than for this series.

FACT

The grades for paper money are similar to those for coins, however rather than calling a never circulated note mint state, the term applied to perfect notes is crisp uncirculated. Proof has a different meaning also. For coins, "proof" is a special way a coin was produced, whereas for a bank note a "proof" is a test note rather than a condition.

You should be able to see your reflection in a DMPL surface. In the past, collectors measured the depth of a DMPL surface with a ruler to determine its quality. A prooflike coin will also display some of these mirrorlike surfaces, causing it to be confused with proofs by collectors not familiar with the difference. The mirrorlike surface, especially if the design devices appear to be frosty, can command a premium in value above that of other uncirculated coins, but it is important to understand that proof coins have squared rather than gently sloping rims.

A Morgan silver dollar.

About Uncirculated Coins

About uncirculated, often abbreviated AU, is an intermediate grade that was first introduced when grading was becoming more refined. This is not a recognized grade for many world and ancient coins, in which case those coins are either uncirculated or in extremely fine condition. But for U.S. and Canadian coins, the about uncirculated grade is important because it represents a very desirable coin on which only the most modest wear can be detected on the highest points of the relief. The difference in price, should you plan to purchase an AU versus an uncirculated grade coin, can sometimes be substantial, yet the AU coin is usually just as attractive until it is examined under magnification.

There are no general rules regarding the high points of wear on coins, however since the Seated Liberty and various Liberty Head designs dominate the obverse of nineteenth-century U.S. coins, there are several points of reference that may be useful. Among these, on the various Liberty Head designs, is the area between the eye and either the first curls at the forehead area or the cap that Liberty wears, depending on the design. Any lack of detail may appear to be trivial, but to coin collectors these are major points.

It is very important to understand both where the highest points of wear will be on a coin as well as when these points show wear rather than a lack of detail regarding strike quality when grading an about uncirculated coin.

Another important general point regarding AU coins is mint luster. Mint luster should normally still be present on AU coins, however it may not necessarily be as continuous across the entire surfaces without some interruption as it would be on an uncirculated coin. Lack of original luster may indicate the coin is actually in a lower condition or that the coin has been cleaned. Artificially added luster is never the same as the original mint luster and can be detected by experienced collectors.

About uncirculated coins are graded on the Sheldon scale between AU58 and AU50.

- **About uncirculated 58:** Only a slight loss of detail from friction on the high points of wear are permissible for this grade. "Sliders" are coins of this grade that are sold to inexperienced collectors as mint state coins. Always examine borderline grade coins (coins at the top end of a grade, such as this one) with magnification at the high points of wear.
- **About uncirculated 55:** For this grade, wear must be isolated to the highest points of relief, while the coin retains almost full detail.
- **About uncirculated 53:** At this level, rub or wear may appear on as much as half the surface, however detail must remain on more than half of the highest points of design relief.
- **About uncirculated 50:** Indications of wear are more widespread than on higher AU coins, but the wear remains isolated to the very highest points of the design elements.

Extremely Fine Coins

The best way to be able to grade circulated coins is to familiarize yourself first with what an uncirculated coin of this design looks like. From there, once you have learned to identify the high points of wear, you can visualize stripping away those high points and understanding better what the first, then the second level of wear should be.

Extremely fine, typically abbreviated either as XF or as EF, is the first level when wear becomes somewhat obvious without the aid of magnification or better lighting.

Design detail must remain sharp for a coin to be designated XF. Original mint luster will likely still remain in some protected areas surrounding higher relief design elements. Due to production techniques, many nineteenth-century U.S. coins have stronger reverse than obverse detail. For this reason, many inexperienced collectors may find it easier to look for signs of wear on the obverse when dealing with XF to MS coins. The eagle and other design elements typically appearing on the reverse of U.S. coins begin to show more obvious signs of minor wear in XF grade.

If you're examining a U.S. coin on which a wreath design appears on the reverse, look closely for missing detail especially on the high points of the bow at six o'clock and on the leaf details. This will tell you how circulated a particular coin may be. XF coins are graded on the Sheldon scale from XF45 to XF40.

- **Extremely fine 45:** Modest wear now appears on areas other than the very highest point of relief for the first time. This is still a very attractive coin.
- **Extremely fine 40:** On coins of this grade, design detail is still complete, however minor overall wear is now becoming obvious.

Make sure to familiarize yourself with the highest relief points at which wear will appear first on any coin or coin series you plan to collect. Learn to distinguish wear from weak strike and pay close attention to even the most minor contact blemishes. Discoloration is another factor that may impact the condition of a coin.

Very Fine Coins

This is still a very presentable grade, but by the time a coin has worn to the point of being very fine (VF), some of the finer points of design details are gone. All lettering and major design details should still be present, though, unless the coin was weakly struck.

- **Very fine 35:** The high point detail is now gone, with modest wear appearing on some of the lower areas of relief.
- **Very fine 30:** Design detail remains complete, but flat areas now appear within the overall designs.
- **Very fine 20:** A loss of overall design detail is obvious on VF20 coins, but lettering, dates, and mint marks remain sharp and very easy to read.

Fine Coins

A coin designated as fine still retains some of the detail on the obverse bust as well as on the reverse, but about half of the finer portions of the design details are by now gone on both sides of the coin.

On coins, especially nineteenth-century U.S. coins, where the word "Liberty" is featured either on the headband or on a shield, this word should still be complete in coins in fine grade, however the lines defining the ribbon or band on which it is displayed are by now interrupted.

In Fine 12, only the more deeply recessed areas retain detail, but the lettering, dates, and mint marks must remain well detailed and easy to read.

Very Good Coins

The major design elements such as the obverse bust and the reverse eagle commonly found on most U.S. coins are still present in this grade, but most of the details of hair, feathers, and leaves are gone. The rims about the edge of both the obverse and reverse must remain present, however if the coin was weakly struck some of this rim detail may begin to become interrupted.

FACT

Proof coins are a separate case than other coins. Proof coins are generally graded between proof 60 and proof 70, using the same standard as is applied to MS60 to MS70 coins. A proof coin with a designation less than 60 has been severely mishandled.

On U.S. coins in which the word "Liberty" is featured either on the headband or on the shield only the first three letters of this word remain visible. The ribbon or band on which the word was placed is likely entirely worn away.

- **Very good 10:** Only slight detail remains, otherwise the profile of the major design elements is all that survives.
- **Very good 8:** Slight detail is still present, but the outline of the elements, date, mint mark, and other lettering are no longer well defined.

Good Coins

Coins surviving in good condition must still have full definition of the rim on both the obverse and the reverse, however little more than the outline of the obverse bust, the reverse eagle, wreath, or other major design element remains. Any stars and legends near the rims are beginning to disappear, but they must still be present. A coin on which the date or mint mark is no longer visible is not in good condition.

The word "Liberty" is now entirely worn away on U.S. coins on which this word was featured on either a headband or on a shield, especially nineteenth-century examples.

Since good is a low grade coin, a coin designated as such may be bent or otherwise damaged. However, such a coin should be net graded as an about good or fair coin. Good is not a particularly desirable grade, but it is the grade in which a majority of nineteenth-century and older U.S. coins will be encountered. Such coins are excellent for filling in date sets if the collector is on a budget, but such a collection should not be expected to appreciate much in value since most of the dates in such a set will be readily available.

- **Good 6:** Design detail is flat, and the rims on both sides are now interrupted, with lettering remaining full in peripheral areas.
- **Good 4:** Dates, mint marks, and lettering must remain readable, but rim detail is now gone, as are all details of the design elements.

About Good, Fair, and Poor Coins

A coin graded *about good* or AG is a very worn coin. The date and mint mark must still be readable, but the rims on each side of the coin are partially or fully gone, as well as is much of the detail of any design elements near the rims. The major design elements are by now a mere outline, and the obverse bust looks more like a faceless mannequin.

- **About good 3:** Dates, mint marks, and lettering must remain readable, but rim detail is now gone, as are all details of the design elements.
- **Fair 2:** Wear is significant, but some detail survives.
- **Poor 1:** The coin design and date can be identified, but not much more than that.

Low grade Morgan dollar.

High grade Morgan dollar.

Collectors and dealers call AG coins fillers; they are used to inexpensively fill out the coin boards of a date set. Even the rarest dates of most U.S. coins sought for such date sets are inexpensive on a coin this low in condition.

Grading Bank Notes

In some respects, bank notes are easier to grade than are coins since it is the quality of the paper on which they are printed rather than the relief that dictates the grade in which the note will be identified. Bank notes are graded utilizing a similar grading system to that used for coins. Like coins, U.S. bank notes are often graded using a combination of the traditional verbal grade accompanied by a Sheldon number, with 70 representing a perfect note.

Uncirculated Notes

In general, the term *uncirculated* regarding paper money is interchangeable with the word "new," however note collectors prefer the term "uncirculated." Mint state and the numerical grades that go with it, often used interchangeably for coins, appears associated with notes that have been examined and assigned a grade by third-party grading services.

The ultimate grade for a bank note is gem crisp uncirculated, a note that is as fresh as when it was first printed at the Bureau of Engraving and Printing. The note is well centered, with all printing being fresh and unfaded, and being free of smudges, wrinkles, or virtually any problems.

One step down from a gem note is a choice crisp uncirculated note; the only real difference is that aging or minute wrinkles may be apparent under careful examination. It is all right for the printing of a choice CU note to be ever-so-slightly off center.

A note still as new in appearance as when it was first printed is called crisp uncirculated. There is room for minor problems such as a smudge mark when a banker counted the note within a stack or "brick" of notes received from the Federal Reserve. Again, centering does not have to be absolutely perfect, and a very minor foxed corner is also permissible.

- **Superb crisp uncirculated 67:** A nearly flawless note with perfect centering. Full wide margins all around. Colors are totally bright, crisp, and vibrant. Quality is outstanding.
- **Gem crisp uncirculated 65:** An almost perfect note. Better than average margins. No aging or fading.
- **Very choice crisp uncirculated 64:** A bright note that's slightly below gem quality. Margins and color are above average. A note that may have slight centering problems.
- **Choice crisp uncirculated 63:** A nice new note but not quite gem. Centering may be a little off. May show some aging or light counting smudges or wrinkles.
- **Crisp uncirculated 60:** No trace of circulation. Can have centering problems, pin holes, counting smudges, wrinkles, close margins, or a corner tip fold (not into the design).

About Uncirculated Notes

Minor imperfections, a foxed corner, or a wrinkle able to be seen under close examination is permissible for a note in AU condition, however nothing more than this. Fading or damage to a note is not permissible on an AU note.

A grade of almost uncirculated 50 refers to a note that is almost new. These will be much the same as a "new" note except for a single fold or several corner folds.

Extremely Fine Notes

An XF or EF note still retains crisp paper qualities, however the note now shows indications it has been used to some minor extent. Folds should not be apparent. Watch for notes that have been ironed to disguise such folds. Folds are usually visible when a note is placed in front of a light. Ironing or other alteration of a note is usually detected by a lack of raised intaglio inks on the paper surface.

A note graded extra fine 40 has been circulated and may have some folds, but still has some crispness.

According to the well-respected *Currency Dealer Newsletter* the numbered grades following are the accepted grades for bank notes. Intermediate numerical grades such as AU55 or XF45 can expect to be encountered, just as within the standards usually accepted for U.S. coins.

Very Fine Notes

This is still an attractive bank note, but it has been folded. Soiling, tears, paper clip rust marks, stains, and other problems are not permissible on a note designated at this grade. The paper must still be crisp, and the ink color must still be good.

A note graded very fine 20 has seen some circulation. It may show several folds, and will have lost some of its crispness and color.

Fine Notes

For notes graded fine, the paper no longer is crisp, but it retains some body (in other words, it is not limp). A fine note has likely been folded many times and may display signs of wear from having been retained in a wallet. The edges of a fine note do not need to be perfect, however all paper material must be present, even if slightly torn.

A grade of fine 12 denotes a well-circulated note, with little crispness remaining; the edges may be rough.

Very Good Notes

Soiling and wear are present and obvious on a VG note. The paper no longer has much fibrous substance left to it, and light stains or discoloration are possibly present. Corners may be rounded rather than squared, but the paper must not be missing any pieces or damaged.

A note graded very good 8 will be fairly well-soiled, may be significantly worn, and might have roughness around the edges with only minute problems.

Good Notes

This is a well-worn note with rounded corners, minor tears, stains, and other problems from significant use in circulation. It is not attractive and usually serves only as a filler when no better note is available for your collection.

The newsletter does not list grades below VG8, however scarcer notes in lower grades can expect to bring a premium above their face value. Some bank notes are known from so few surviving examples that even an about good note with pinholes, tears, stains, or writing on it may be surprisingly expensive to acquire.

Grading Ancient Coins

Ancient and medieval coins were struck by hand rather than by machine. Each of the dies from which the images were transferred to the coinage blanks were also made by hand by a person called a *celator.* If the celator had a good day, the quality of his workmanship was superior and coins made from those dies often command a better price than otherwise like coins.

The centering of ancient and medieval coins is important since so many of them are off center due to the repetitious work of the moneyers who produced them. Quality control, so important to modern coins, was usually not a factor regarding ancient and medieval coins. So the things to look for when buying ancient coins are the quality of the workmanship, centering of the coin, and the quality of the strike.

Split grading, that is when the obverse and the reverse are assigned two different grades, is not unusual, especially with ancient Roman coins. The method of strike has something to do with this, with the obverse often appearing to be more attractive and having more design details than the reverse.

Collectors from all over the world seek coins of ancient Greece, ancient Rome, India, and China. This is a worldwide market of conservative collectors, so it's not surprising that grading ancient coins is also conservative. The numerical grading system used for U.S. coins is not acceptable to these collectors. Instead, they are only graded into the following categories: fleur de coin, uncirculated, extremely fine, very fine, fine, very good, and good.

FACT

Modern coins are generally considered to be coins struck by a machine rather than by hand. When modern coinage begins differs from country to country depending on when modern presses were first introduced. Some grading terms are different for ancient and medieval than from modern coins in part due to the technique of their manufacture and partially due to time-honored collector preferences.

Fleur de Coin

A *fleur de coin* (FDC) ancient or medieval coin is a perfect coin. The coin has full strike detail, is well centered, and has no indication of any wear. Even ancient coins often retain mint luster if they are composed of gold or silver, although copper, bronze, and brass (orichalcum, a type of zinc-rich brass) coins should not be expected to have survived with this surface quality. FDC coins do exist, but they are challenging to find.

Uncirculated

An uncirculated ancient or medieval coin shows no wear, however it may have less than perfect centering or indications of a lack of design detail due to the poor quality of the strike. Fully struck and well-centered uncirculated ancient and medieval coins do exist, but are very uncommon.

Extremely Fine

This is the first grade usually assigned to an ancient or a medieval coin on which any indication of wear appears on the high points of the design elements. Such wear must be minor and almost undetectable. American coin collectors would likely designate such a coin, if it was a modern coin struck by the United States, to grade AU. Centering does not need to be perfect, but poor centering may relegate a coin with XF details to a VF grade designation.

Very Fine

This is still a very desirable coin on which only minor wear appears on the high points. This is often the highest grade encountered when shopping for ancient and medieval coins.

Fine

Significant wear is now visible for the first time on a coin that is graded fine. Fine is a commonly encountered grade for medieval coins, in part due to the crude methods of manufacture and in part because the coinage blanks on which the coin image has been impressed are almost always paper thin, making it very difficult to get a really superior image onto the coin regardless of the amount of wear the coin later encounters.

Very Good

Design detail is lacking on a VG ancient or medieval coin, although the coin should still be identifiable. Inexperienced collectors may not understand that ancient and medieval coins should still be able to be identified by any legends or images appearing on them regardless of their grade. A VG coin can still be identified, yet the wear is extensive and the centering of the design elements may be inferior.

Good

This is not a nice coin, but it is still identifiable from its design elements or through the surviving portions of the legends on the coin. This is not a rusty looking round disk, as is sometimes offered to inexperienced collectors. The profile of the obverse and the reverse legends must still be present, as will be any identifying legends and magistrate marks.

Grading Foreign Coins

Be careful when purchasing foreign coins assigned grades based on the Sheldon numerical grading system. The foreign coin market has a different set of standards for grading. This standard is more conservative and often resists change. The numerical grades assigned to U.S. coins are seldom used on foreign coins other than those of Canada.

It's important to remember that foreign coins may have a strong home market in the country from which they originate, especially if that country has an economy through which potential collectors have discretionary money.

chapter 9

Authenticating Coins

There is a grading problem in coin collecting. It is a long-standing problem that is unlikely to go away. There are books on how to grade coins, but regardless of how much information is available, grading continues to be misunderstood and even abused.

Grading Challenges

You learn how to grade by doing it, but without first learning how to grade, you will be at a distinct disadvantage regardless of how much experience you may have. This lack of knowledge can lead to abuses if a person overgrades and overprices coins.

But grading can be a problem for even the more experienced collectors, since it is only natural for someone to have a high opinion of something he owns. As you'll learn in this chapter, coins and notes are authenticated and certified to help combat this grading problem.

Part of the problem with grading coins is disagreement on how much wear a coin has received, but the other part of the problem is overlooking edge damage, surface scratches, and other problems on a coin. When acquiring a coin, you must consider the amount of wear and these other potential detractions as well. The person selling you the coin may have conveniently ignored these problems! Or sometimes dark surface toning may hide some of these problems if a coin is not examined properly.

When it comes to grading, take the slogan "buyer beware" seriously. A coin with problems in addition to wear must be net graded, in other words, it must be categorized one or more grades lower than would be warranted when considering the amount of wear alone. The price of such a coin must be adjusted accordingly as well.

Another problem with grading coins is that despite the information available, people don't always grade consistently. Two dealers might grade two coins with identical wear differently. Perhaps one dealer isn't grading coins as accurately as he should. Unfortunately, some people purchase coins at one grade, only to offer them for sale at higher grades. Neither collectors nor dealers should do this; it is dishonest.

ANA Certification Service

Grading abuses became rampant by the early 1970s, leading the American Numismatic Association to decide to do something about it. Their solution was to introduce a service through which a coin would be certified as genuine, then assign a numerical grade to the individual coin based on standards established by the ANA. The new service was called the American Numismatic Association Certification Service (ANACS). It was the first of what's called third-party certification services.

FACT

The ANA eventually adopted a grading system based on 65 points. (This system was later extended to 70 points.) The numerical system made grading more accurate, and it also removed the grading abuses by the loose use of such descriptions as gem, brilliant, and choice. Dealers could no longer choose whatever words they wanted to describe their coins. There was finally a consistent system.

ANACS grew in steps. For the first seven years of its existence, the service only authenticated coins. Beginning in March 1979, ANACS also began to render an opinion on the grade of a coin, issuing a certificate with a photograph of the coin in an effort to avoid having the certificates switched to other coins. The black and white photographs on the certificate were not an exacting science, but it was a good beginning. An ANA grading guide was published about the same time, this serving to identify the standards ANACS would use to ensure consistency in their grading.

ANACS grading began during a coin bull market, however when a bear market began during the 1980s the same collectors and dealers who had complained the service had been too conservative with its grading now began to complain the service was overgrading coins. What the dealers wanted was a double standard. It was to their advantage if a coin previously graded mint state 65 in a bull market was now graded MS63 in a bear market. Confidence in ANACS dropped, threatening to make third-party certification services an experiment that didn't work.

Other Grading Services

In 1985, Professional Coin Grading Service (PCGS) was founded. This new service filled the vacuum created by the lack of acceptance of ANACS. PCGS introduced new innovations as well. Once they authenticated and graded coins, they sonically sealed them in tamperproof, hard, clear plastic holders nicknamed "slabs." (A coin that has been encapsulated in these holders is called "slabbed," and a coin that is not in a holder is called "raw.") A large national network of coin dealers agreed that they would accept the PCGS grades assigned to the slabbed coins.

This established what is called the "sight unseen" market. A collector or dealer can trust that a coin has been properly graded without actually seeing it, if the coin is encapsulated in a PCGS slab.

PCGS also established something called consensus grading. This means that a team of examiners agree on the grade to be assigned a coin, rather than the grade being assigned by a single examiner. Also, PCGS promised that coins would be graded consistently regardless of the economic state of the rare coin market.

PCGS slabs.

Today there are more than a dozen third-party coin certification and grading services, however only three are generally recognized throughout the hobby: ANACS, PCGS, and a company called Numismatic Guaranty Corporation of America. In addition there are now at least five services certifying and grading bank notes. Once again, dealers and collectors will likely favor one service more than another.

Soon after PCGS, entrepreneurs established other commercially owned grading services. Some of these services flourished while others did not. Some perished because they could not grade consistently, others failed because they lacked the acceptance of dealers and collectors, while still others failed because of conflict of interest or blatant dishonesty regarding their activities.

Buyer Beware

Understand that not all third-party services are equal. This is not to suggest you only should buy, sell, and trade with slabs from the three companies just named, but you should be aware of the acceptance or lack of acceptance of the service in which a coin offered to you has been encapsulated. There may not be anything wrong with the coin or the grade assigned to it, however if the slabbing service is not well recognized within the coin hobby community, you may find the price of that coin may be discounted from like coins slabbed by a more recognized service.

Guarantees

Whichever service you choose, make sure that its work is guaranteed. Guarantees are important. Ask these questions: Will the service guarantee that if they made a mistake they will buy the coin to cover your costs? Will the company grade a coin with problems such as scratches or having been cleaned at one time? If so, will they identify these problems? Is the slab truly tamperproof?

Third-party authentications are very helpful. But it's important to buy the coin, not the holder. Use the third-party assurance as a tool, not as an absolute. Since people rather than machines still grade coins, there is still margin of error involved.

Are all the competing third-party authentication services of equal value?

There are many third-party coin certification and grading services, besides PCGS, Numismatic Guaranty Corporation of America, and ANACS. These others are simply not well enough known to have the full acceptance of the hobby. Some third-party authentication services were established to service the telemarketing industry, and their grading standards are considerably more liberal than the services dealers and serious collectors generally use.

Breakouts

"Breakout" is coin collecting slang for a coin that has been removed from its slab. This is usually done for one of three reasons:

- The collector intends to resubmit the coin in hopes of receiving a higher grade.
- The collector believes he can sell the coin unslabbed (also known as "raw") for more than it will sell if it is left in its encapsulation.
- The coin was encapsulated by a service that is not well accepted in the hobby market, and the collector wants to have the coin regraded by a more accepted service.

Breaking out a coin from its encapsulation is a gamble. The person doing this is assuming that despite all the efforts of the third-party services to remain consistent they may grade the same coin in a higher grade if it is resubmitted. On occasion this may happen, but make sure you fully understand grading before you take such a chance.

Population Reports

A number of major third-party grading and authentication services now offer population reports, or "pops." These reports are tallies of the number of coins submitted of a specific denomination, date, and mint and the grades assigned for each coin. These statistics give a better view in what grades coins are commonly submitted, how they compare to the numbers of other dates that are submitted, and where the grade rarities exist. Such data can identify that a seemingly common date coin in an uncommon condition may be rare, perhaps even rarer than a coin of a significantly lower mintage.

There is a downside to these population reports. These reports cannot identify when a coin has been broken out and resubmitted, nor can they be compared to pop reports published by competing third-party services. Furthermore there is no way to tell when a coin has become a "crossover," broken out of the slab of one company to be submitted to a different company for grading. Population report statistics are handy, but for these reasons, they should be used with some caution.

Paper Money

Just as coins can be authenticated, so can bank notes. And the third-party authentication services create pop reports for them as well. Because each individual U.S. bank note has its own serial number, it doesn't skew the pop report if it is resubmitted for examination to the same or another service. With the serial numbers, bank notes can be tracked as they travel through the hands of dealers and collectors. The reality is that most bank notes are not tracked, however some of the more classic notes, particularly the National Bank Note series, are followed.

Since collectors like to handle their notes directly, there was resistance to having paper money slabbed when the services were first offered. But today, with the number of companies offering these services expanded, it is more common to encounter encapsulated high value notes.

Foreign Coins

Encapsulated foreign coins have met with the same resistance as have other slabbed materials, with U.S. collectors preferring coins they can physically handle until encapsulation became more popular.

Foreign collectors, however, with the exception of those in Canada, view third-party certification as an American hobby idea. Dealers who buy and sell coins overseas often find that if they purchase a certified foreign coin in the United States, they may have to first remove the coin from the slab before selling it overseas.

The Importance of Authentication

This may sound like a sales pitch from a real estate agent, but there are three words that are of adamant importance in coin collecting. These words are price, price, and price. The emphasis in coin collecting is on buying and selling, not collecting from pocket change. Collecting from pocket change is a beginning spot from which to advance to more ambitious collecting.

Considering the first question typically asked whenever someone, collector or not, first is shown a coin is, "How much is it worth?" the value of a coin is paramount within the hobby. For this reason grading is extremely important. So is counterfeit detection. The third-party services now in business are expected to first authenticate a coin, then assign a grade.

Third-party certification and grading services have taken much of the concern out of both the authenticity of coins and the grade or condition in which collectors agree to accept the individual pieces. The question remains, however, as to when a coin (or a bank note) needs to be "slabbed" by one of these services, and when it isn't necessary.

Coin dealers will agree that any coin that has been slabbed, regardless of its value, is easier to sell. Collectors, however, need to look at the value of the coin "raw" (without being slabbed) as compared to the cost of having the coin encapsulated and its true value after this service has been used.

If a coin has a value of $100 without such services, and costs about $30 for the service, but will likely grade to a value of perhaps $110 once the coin has been examined, having the coin slabbed isn't worth the trouble. However, if the coin has a potential value differential of several hundred dollars between each grade increment, it is more likely worth the investment to have a third-party service examine the coin.

A coin that has been certified by encapsulation does not necessarily have greater value than another similar coin. Ensure the coin has been encapsulated by a well-accepted third-party service within the hobby. Coins encapsulated by lesser-known or less popular services command lower prices.

Another time it is likely worth the investment to have a coin slabbed is when the difference in value between one grade and the next may be significant. Then it becomes particularly important to be certain the coin you are purchasing or selling is correctly graded. This is where these third-party services become particularly important to the collector.

Certificates of authenticity often accompany modern issues of coins. These certificates may be attractive additions to the fancy packaging, but you can't trust a coin to be authentic and in the grade stated unless it has been slabbed. Certificates of authenticity can be switched or printed on any available computer.

chapter 10

Counterfeiting and Altering Coins

Counterfeiting may be one of the oldest professions in the world. The counterfeiter has been around almost as long as there have been coins to counterfeit. Considering that the coin was invented in Asia Minor likely in the early seventh century B.C. (possibly even earlier in China), forgers have had a lot of time to hone their skills. Bogus paper money was added to the products of the forgery trade almost as quickly as the first bank notes were printed. Modern counterfeiting has its roots in the Middle Ages.

A History of Counterfeiting

Counterfeiting techniques have changed as technology has changed. Governments continuously try to keep one step ahead of forgers. Collectors need to understand what types of forgery techniques existed for the period in which they collect in order to avoid purchasing bogus coins or bank notes.

Counterfeiting Medieval Coins—Clipping

Although clipping isn't technically counterfeiting, it was an unsavory practice, so we'll talk about it here. Medieval coins were produced by hammering a sheet of gold or silver until it was paper thin, then cutting out coinage blanks from the sheet. The coin images were then impressed onto these blanks with a hammer and anvil. Due to the crude designs and the thin material of these coins, it was commonplace to clip a minor shaving of metal from the edge of a coin, then pass the coin at full value despite it now being underweight. Technically these coins were meant to trade at the precious metal value of their content, which also equaled the denomination assigned to each coin. After the clipper clipped enough metal, he took the metal to the local mint, where it could be made into more coins. The underweight original coin might continue to circulate unless the clipping was very obvious.

When does medieval coinage end and modern coinage begin?
This varies from country to country depending on when machine manufactured coins replaced the thinner hand hammered coinage. In general this begins about 1500, however in countries such as Russia modern coinage began two centuries later.

Governments attempted to foil clippers by extending the design of a coin all the way to the edge on both sides. English silver penny coins, as an example, first bore a reverse design known today to collectors as the "short cross" design. The crossbars of the cross did not extend across the entire coin surface, leaving plenty of room to shave metal off the edges without detection. The crossbars of the cross were later extended all the way to the edge of the coin, known as the "long cross" design, to discourage clipping since it would interrupt the design on the coin.

Once modern coinage presses began to replace the earlier hand-manufactured process, coins became more sophisticated both in design and in fabric. Another way clipping was discouraged was adding vertical serrations called "reeding" to the edge of a coin. Clipping would be obvious because it interrupted both the more perfect shape of the coin and the reeding.

Counterfeit coins and bank notes were traditionally made to deceive people in commerce. Today specific coins are targets of counterfeiters because of the high price they may realize if they are undetected as being bogus. Collectors should be aware of which coins are more likely to be counterfeited or altered.

Clipping is rare today due to the fabric and thickness of our modern machine-produced coins, but it is common to find clipped medieval and early modern hand-manufactured coins. These clipped coins are still acceptable to collectors, but they may command lesser prices if the clipping is particularly noticeable. Clipping should be expected to be present on some English colonial period coins struck in what later became the thirteen original states of the Union.

Counterfeiting in China

China is generally credited with introducing paper money to the modern world about A.D. 806. Marco Polo brought the concept of paper money to Europe after visiting China approximately 400 years later. Merchants deposited specie (precious metal) with the government, who in turn gave the merchants paper receipts marked to a specific value. These paper receipts could be traded in lieu of coins, and they were significantly lighter in weight to carry. The government had the actual deposit on hand if the paper was redeemed.

It didn't take counterfeiters long to realize the opportunity this new currency concept presented. In 1207, the Jin dynasty in China recognized counterfeit "flying kite" or paper money as being dangerous in the Bank Note Law Treaty. Paper money has been counterfeited ever since. In 1368, paper notes printed by the Ming dynasty carried a warning that counterfeiters would be beheaded.

QUESTION?

What does the term flying kite money mean?
Flying kite money is a reference to the early paper money of China, which dates from the thirteenth century. Since paper is light, it could blow in the wind just like a Chinese kite.

Counterfeiting in Merry Old England

Counterfeiting of English coins is documented at least as far back as in 1150 when the *Anglo-Saxon Chronicle* records that the right hand and other unmentionable parts of a counterfeiter were to be removed as the penalty for this crime. In 1533, counterfeiting of any foreign coins that circulated in England was added to the list of treasonable offenses.

Only a few years later, in 1578, Eloye Mestrelle, a former Royal Mint employee, was hanged as a counterfeiter. In 1696, master counterfeiter William Challoner advised the English Chancellor of the Exchequer on how to improve the nation's coinage. But then the laws were changed, making counterfeiting a hanging offense, and Challoner was hanged.

England thought it had the ultimate way to deal with counterfeiters, however. In 1770, the English shipped convicted counterfeiters off to Maryland. But there, the forgers continued their illicit profession without having to worry any further about the local constable. England's plan didn't work, and during the 1820s the country withdrew and reissued 1- and 2-pound bank notes because of rampant counterfeiting.

About a century later, in 1928, England began employing color and machine engraving techniques to its paper money in an effort to keep ahead of the forgers. This worked to an extent, but it couldn't hold the counterfeiters off forever. The German government counterfeited British currency during World War II.

Counterfeiting in France

King Louis IV of France earned his dubious title as *le faux-monnayeur* ("the false moneyer") due to his less-than-honest activities about 1285. His successors learned from this king. In 1350, King Phillippe VI ordered the coinage of the realm secretly debased for economic reasons. The value of all circulating money at that time was based on its precious metal content, not on the denomination assigned to each coin.

In 1422, the Countess Jeanne le Boulogne et Auvergne was convicted of counterfeiting the coins of France. Perhaps there haven't been any French counterfeiters of such prominence since, but forgers still ply their trade in that nation nonetheless. In 1993, France added innovative security devices to its paper money on short notice in an effort to combat spurious bank note production.

Counterfeiting in America

In what would become the United States, the Maryland Assembly passed an act in 1638 making it treason to counterfeit the king's coin. Only a few years later, in 1645, the English colony of Virginia made it a death penalty offense to counterfeit Spanish silver coins, Spanish colonial American coins being the currency primarily found in local circulation at that time.

Nothing was sacred regarding forging of currency. In 1647, the General Court of Rhode Island ordered fake wampum confiscated. (Wampum are beads made from shells that were traded with Native Americans as a form of odd and curious money.) Pennsylvania prosecuted its first counterfeiting case as early as 1683.

FACT

During the 1990s the New Jersey State Police made a major arrest regarding a counterfeiter producing his own casino tokens! Although some of these bogus tokens were used in gaming machines, the intention was to cash them in at unsuspecting casinos in exchange for hard cash.

The British colonies in America had just as many problems with counterfeit paper money as did their Chinese predecessors. In 1735, the Virginia House of Burgesses warned that the Virginia colony's economy might be ruined due to the vast amount of counterfeit paper money that was circulating there. In 1835, Massachusetts offered money to any organization willing to help stop the rampant local counterfeiting. Emanuel "Bill the Penman" Ninger was arrested in 1891 in New York after one of his masterfully hand-drawn bank notes didn't hold up well when it became wet following his payment of a bar tab (for which he received change in genuine gold and silver coins).

One of the more notorious counterfeiting rings in American history operated from Cave-in-Rock in the Ohio Valley. It began in around 1790 and continued until "Bloody Jack" Sturdevant and his gang shot it out unsuccessfully with government authorities in 1831.

In 1865, just as the American Civil War was concluding, the U.S. Secret Service was established with two major missions. One major mission was to protect the president of the United States, his family, and other important government politicians. The other major mission was to prevent counterfeiting. This was followed in 1923 by the establishment of the International Criminal Police Organization, better known today as Interpol.

The list of counterfeiting stories is endless, and counterfeiters are unfortunately here to stay. Despite all the efforts made by the U.S. and foreign governments to eradicate counterfeiting, counterfeiters continue to ply their trade by keeping up with the technological advances in coins and bank notes. As soon as an innovative anti-counterfeiting device is used, forgers quickly work to copy the new device, in turn encouraging governments to seek further technological advances.

Government-Sanctioned Counterfeiting

Counterfeiters have likely operated in every country in the world, but most of them have been in business for themselves. A significant number of times in history, however, governments have sponsored the counterfeiting of the money of another nation. Following are some classic examples.

Timeline of Counterfeiting	
Year	**Event**
1768	Imperial Russia strikes counterfeit Dutch gold ducat coins during the Russo-Turkish War. This continues for a hundred years, until a formal Dutch protest in 1868.
1775	King George III of England attempts to disrupt the economy of the rebellious American colonies by ordering the paper money of the colonies to be counterfeited.
1806	Emperor Napoleon I of France orders the counterfeiting of Banco-Zettel bank notes of Austria and of Russian bank notes in an attempt to disrupt the economy of these two nations during the Napoleonic wars.
1918	Austria accuses the United Kingdom of counterfeiting Austria's paper money during World War I.
1919	The Hungarian communist government of Bela Kun forges bank notes of Austro-Hungary.
1930	The United States questions if counterfeit $100 bank notes are being produced in the Soviet Union under the authority of Soviet Premier Josef Stalin.
1941	Nazi Germany launches "Operation Bernhard," government-sanctioned counterfeiting of British bank notes in an effort to disrupt the British economy during World War II.
1992	The United States Central Intelligence Agency is accused of distributing counterfeit Iraqi bank notes following the first Gulf War following the liberation of Iraqi-occupied Kuwait by the United States and its allies.
2005	India accuses Pakistan's government of printing counterfeit bank notes of India.

The names of those responsible for much of the counterfeit U.S. currency now circulating worldwide may never be known, but all indications are that the majority of the better fakes are originating in Lebanon, Iran, and in North Korea. Some of the fakes are likely made under government authority, but at least in the case of Lebanon it is more likely enterprising individuals who are responsible for the bogus money.

Key-Date Altering

Although some coins may be counterfeits, others may be genuine coins on which a date or mint mark has been changed, added, or removed. Such alterations are made to change an otherwise low value coin into a key date for which collectors may be expected to pay a lot of money.

Alterations are usually encountered on collector coins, rather than coins meant to circulate as money. That's because it makes sense to alter a common date coin to a much rarer date coin when collectors are willing to pay a premium for the rare coin. It makes far less sense to alter a coin that is just going to be used in circulation.

What was the racketeer nickel?
When the Liberty Head design was introduced in 1883, the reverse design initially featured a large letter V, but without the word "cents." Enterprising individuals gold-plated the coins and attempted to pass them as the similar $5 gold Half Eagle coins. The government quickly responded by changing the design on the nickel to include the all-important word "cents" below the large V.

Here's a list of some of the U.S. coins more commonly encountered that are counterfeited or altered:

- **1877 Indian cent:** On genuine coins, the weakly detailed central area of the reverse, and the angular but flat base to the hook of both 7s in the date must be present. Be aware other dates are occasionally altered to this date.
- **1909-S Indian cent:** On genuine coins, the mint mark appearing at six o'clock on the reverse below the wreath must be thin, symmetrical, with small serifs and smooth curves. Mint marks are known to be artificially added to altered examples. The blank on which the coin was struck should have pale golden-yellow or wood grain color.

- **1909-S VDB Lincoln cent:** The initials of the designer, Victor David Brenner, appear at six o'clock on the reverse of cents struck early during the year, however later coinage dies discontinued these initials. The mint mark appearing below the date is square and box-like, with a tiny notch and a raised lump in the upper serif. The initials VDB are slightly off-center to the left, with the center bar of the B slanting upward from left to right.
- **1943 Copper Lincoln cent:** Copper-plated fakes are magnetic (1943 cents are normally composed of zinc and steel), while copper composition counterfeits are made by altering the 8 on the 1948 cent.
- **1913 Liberty Head nickel:** Spot fakes by looking at the date under magnification; it will be obvious the date has been altered. It is well documented that there are only five specimens of this coin, and the whereabouts of all five are well known.
- **1937-D Three-Legged Buffalo nickel:** On genuine coins, what appears to be a stream of raised dots should be present between the belly and the ground. You should also see a mottled appearance to the back of the rear leg and the back of the Indian's neck. Watch for the missing leg to have been artificially removed on altered coins.
- **1916-D Mercury dime:** Altered coins with added mint marks are rampant for this date. The mint mark appearing left of the base of the fasces near six o'clock on the reverse is boxy, with the top and the bottom of the curve of the D being angled rather than rounded, with the inside of the D appearing as a triangle, with square rather than pointed serifs. The mint mark must have the same amount of wear as does the balance of the coin.
- **1932-D Washington quarter:** You should see a square, tall, and angular mint mark below the reverse wreath at six o'clock. Under magnification, you'll also see reverse raised die polish marks. Watch out for altered coins with added mint marks.
- **1932-S Washington quarter:** Genuine examples have a square, boxy mint mark with serifs parallel to each other. A raised die line appears above the D in "dollar" on most genuine examples. Coins with added mint marks exist.

- **1921 Walking Liberty half dollar:** A stylized 2 with a flat but slightly curved base must be present. Watch for alterations to other coins to create this date.
- **1804 silver dollar:** Counterfeits of this coin made overseas are common. All genuine examples are accounted for, with their ownership being well documented. Don't expect to find an unknown but genuine example.
- **1889-CC silver dollar:** Be suspicious of all cleaned examples. A raised die line should be present in Liberty's cap between the banner and leaf in the cap on most examples, with a faint die crack appearing from the point of the bust through all four date digits. The mint mark appears at six o'clock on the reverse just below the wreath.
- **1893-S silver dollar:** Watch for a diagnostic die scratch in the top of the T and "rabbit ears" die chip in the left foot of the R in "liberty," with the date slanting upward to the right. The mint mark is in the same place as on the 1889-CC silver dollar.
- **1928 silver dollar:** The 1928-S silver dollar is common, but under magnification you'll see the surface has been disturbed if the mint mark was removed. The mint mark on Peace silver dollar coins such as this appear at about 8 o'clock on the reverse near the rim between "one" and the tail feathers. The mint mark on these coins is small and can be difficult to see.

An 1804 silver dollar.

Counterfeiting Techniques

Any coin or bank note might be counterfeited. In general, the more desirable the coin or note, the greater the chance someone is counterfeiting it. Here are seven types of counterfeiting and similar problems to watch out for—casts, electrotypes, transfer dies, spark erosion copies, contemporary counterfeits, reused bank note paper, and retooled coins.

Casts

Most coins are struck, not cast. Casting is a crude, slow way to make a coin. There are several telltale indications that a coin is cast. First look for a seam along the edge of the coin where the two dies making the cast replica were joined. In more sophisticated counterfeits, watch for marks where this seam was filed down to remove the evidence, especially on ancient coins.

Ancient coins are subject to being copied by casting. Among U. S. coins, colonial period and territorial coins are the most commonly cast copied.

Cast counterfeits may have a soapy feel, because cast rather than struck metal surfaces have a different texture that is soapy to the touch. Under close examination, you'll often see small bubble-like depressions or lack of detail appearing on the coin's surfaces. Cast counterfeit coins are usually underweight compared to their genuine counterparts. This is because counterfeiters make cast coins out of base metals instead of precious metal. Expect cast coins to be comprised of low-value metals such as lead, pewter, tin, or zinc.

Interestingly, many cast coin "counterfeits" were made as souvenirs rather than to deceive collectors.

Electrotypes

Counterfeiters make an electrotype copy of a coin by impressing the image of a genuine coin into a soft substance, leaving a negative image of that side of the coin. This negative impression is then electroplated to once more make a positive impression. The problem with this technique is that you can only make one side of a coin at a time and then the two sides must be fused.

You can spot electrotype copies by the seam created by fusing the two halves together. Also, if you drop an electrotype copy, it will usually thud rather than ring because of the difference in metal consistency. The weight of an electrotype coin is also either too heavy or too light when compared to a genuine example of the same type. (You can find out how heavy a coin is supposed to be in most coin catalogs.)

During the nineteenth century, mint employees sold electrotype coin replicas to collectors. For this reason, you'll find both older examples and recently made electrotypes.

Interestingly, electrotype copies are popular with museums. First, valuable coins don't have to be placed on exhibit, and second, both sides of a coin can be simultaneously displayed.

Transfer Dies

When an image from a genuine coin is transferred to a die from which additional coin replicas are to be made this coinage die is called a transfer die. The genuine host coin must be sacrificed in the process since the impression is made onto a steel composition working die. The counterfeiter is then free to strike as many copies as he wants until the dies wear out.

In the process of making the transfer die, all of the surface features of the host coin are transferred, including every blemish, bag mark, and contact mark. Because no two genuine coins are exactly alike when coins are too perfectly matched, right down to identical bag marks and blemishes, there is good reason to be suspicious of their authenticity.

Counterfeiters also take shortcuts, often matching the undated side of a coin with several different coinage dies of the opposite side on which the date appears. Once again, if the reverse of two coins of the same design and denomination are too perfectly matched—even if the dated sides are different—there is reason for concern.

Spark Erosion Copies

In this counterfeiting technique, a coin and a steel die from which further coins are desired to be made are both immersed into an electrolytic bath, with the coin facing the die. An electric current is then passed through the coin. A spark jumps from the coin to the die, etching the coin's image onto the die in the process. This process must be repeated to get images of both sides of the coin onto obverse and reverse dies. Counterfeit coins are produced from the die.

FACT

The "micro O mint mark" variety 1903 Morgan silver dollar was recently declared to be bogus by a third-party authentication service after years of being accepted as genuine. Careful study of several New Orleans silver dollar reverse images proved the same die had been used to make coins with several different dates, suggesting that the reverse image came from applying the transfer die counterfeiting technique.

Before the counterfeiter can use these dies, they must be polished to remove pitting caused through the etching process. Counterfeiters typically fail to polish into the areas of the finer design details, leaving telltale pitting marks that will appear on the counterfeit coins. This polishing also leaves the dies with a mirrorlike, almost prooflike, surface that is also transferred onto the bogus replicas.

Contemporary Counterfeits

Contemporary counterfeits are fakes made to be used as currency. They're called contemporary because they're produced during the period the coins are actually being used. Since they are "funny" money, there is a collectors' market for these coins. Because contemporary counterfeits are meant to fool the public—not savvy coin collectors—they are not well made. They often simply contain substitute metals, such as lead or copper, instead of the precious metals in many coins prior to 1964.

Reused Bank Note Paper

Recently, however, forgers have found ways to wash the ink off genuine notes, then reuse the blank notes to print their bogus product. In 1997, authorities discovered that Libyan bank notes were being washed out, and the paper was recycled to make counterfeit notes of Brazil and Germany. During 2005, authorities learned that a similar technique was being used to make good quality counterfeit U.S. $1,000 bank notes, legal tender notes that were often purchased by collectors for a premium above $1,000.

Counterfeiters have tried many different techniques to make fake bank notes look like the real thing. One of the major reasons paper money forgeries are usually easy to identify is because counterfeiters can't duplicate the specially made paper on which bank notes are printed.

Retooled Coins

While not technically counterfeiting, retooling—if done with bad intentions—is an unsavory practice, so we'll include it here. Retooling is when you rework the major design elements of a coin to appear less worn than they really are. This may improve the appearance of a coin, but it reduces the desirability of the coin to collectors. To spot a retooled coin, examine it under magnification. Watch for raised stubby short lines or unusual smoothing in the fields.

Three "Most Wanted" Counterfeiters

It is useful to know what to watch for regarding counterfeit coins and bank notes, but there still has to be a person behind the forgeries. Thanks to modern technology and the Secret Service, most amateur counterfeiters are apprehended before a significant number of counterfeit coins or notes are circulated. It wasn't always this way. In the past, some counterfeiters made entire careers of making and spending their own phony cash. Some of these counterfeiters gained such reputations that their coins or notes are collected today.

An Infamous U.S. Counterfeiter

Most of the more notorious U.S. counterfeiters produced bank notes rather than coins. Likely the most important coin forger in U.S. history, however, was a mint employee named Theodore Eckfeldt. While Eckfeldt was employed as a night watchman at the mint, he borrowed coinage dies, then used the mints presses to reproduce examples of older coins sought by collectors. Eckfeldt's "restrikes" include such notable coins as the 1804 Draped Bust silver dollar, 1836 Classic Head half cent, and the 1840 to 1849 Coronet half cents. Eckfeldt was eventually caught and dismissed from the mint. Ironically, today Eckfeldt's replicas are sought as legitimate restrikes, and his coins are listed in virtually all books on coin collecting.

FACT

The Secret Service receives its authority in Title 18, United States Code, Section 3056. Within this authority is the right to detect and arrest anyone committing an offense against the laws of the United States as they relate to coins, currency, and any other obligations and securities of both the United States and any foreign government.

The name of the employee is unknown today, but another great U.S. classic rarity, the 1913 Liberty Head nickel known from five examples, was also produced inside the mint. Once again, these coins are listed in all U.S. coin catalogs. They are valued at more than $1 million each.

Infamous World Coin Counterfeiters

Carl Wilhelm Becker is likely the most famous non-U.S. counterfeiter. Becker began his career in 1806 and continued until his death in 1830. Becker made his own coinage dies, using genuine ancient coins as the host blanks for his ancient coin counterfeits and fantasy issues, and then he sold his work to wealthy collectors. Today Becker's counterfeits are sought by collectors of ancient coins. His counterfeits are nicely illustrated in several books.

Slavei Petrov, better known to coin collectors simply as Slavei, is the dean of modern counterfeiters. Officially Slavei, who lives in Bulgaria, claims to make reproductions, but his ancient coin replicas have been confused with genuine coins, even among collectors. Some, but not all, of Slavei's work carries his name in obscure places within the coin designs.

Modern Replicas

Because of the problems with counterfeiting, there are laws regulating how money can be reproduced, such as in books, and how money can be mutilated, such as to make jewelry. Modern U.S. bank notes, for example, cannot appear in print at actual size. They must be either 1.5 times or under .75 times the actual size of the real note. Photographs and printed illustrations of coins are not as restrictive. In general, U.S. laws now permit coins to be reproduced at actual size, as they often appear in coin catalogs.

Generally it is illegal to deface coins and bank notes. However, as long as the mutilation of a coin, U.S. or foreign, is done without fraudulent intent, it is legal to do so under current laws. For example, you can make coin jewelry, including cutout and engraved coins, under current interpretations of Section 331, Title 18 of the United States Code. Also, you can legally make novelty items, such as two-headed coins and gold plated coins.

chapter 11

Investing in Coins

It's a stereotype that all coin collectors are wealthy. Another myth is that all old coins are valuable. People who believe these have a lot to learn about the values of collectibles, and they need to learn a lot about investing as well. Investing in coins is not a simple task.

Considering Coins as an Investment

Anything can become an investment if you work at it. For example, if you purchase stock, you cannot put it away in a drawer and expect that it will become more valuable later. Without managing your stock portfolio, you are at the mercy of the whims of the market and the fates of the companies in which you invested. If you don't monitor their performance, you won't know when to sell or purchase additional stock.

One big difference between coins as a hobby and coins as an investment is your emotions surrounding them. An investor is willing to sell at the right moment. A collector has an emotional attachment to his collection. If you truly are to invest in rather than to collect coins, you must separate yourself from the emotional appeal of what you have.

Coins and other forms of collectibles are no different when it comes to investing in them. Without managing your coin collection you will be at the whims of the market. You can manage your coin portfolio yourself, or you can hire a trusted dealer to help you.

As you begin investing, understand that it takes money to make money, regardless of if it is in real estate, stocks, bonds, commodities, collectibles, or anything else. If you have a modest position in anything, you can expect a modest return. If you have a serious position, although the downside risks may be greater the opportunity for significant asset appreciation is also there. All investments are the same in many respects; only the item in which you choose to invest differs.

Choosing Coins as an Investment

Why choose coins to invest in rather than stocks and bonds? You can liquidate stocks or bonds with a telephone call to a broker, but coins are not as readily liquidated, nor is the price as well defined.

This lack of a defined price can work for or against you depending on your knowledge of the market in which you are dealing. When you sell stock, a broker looks up the current price and sells for you at that price. When you sell coins, however, you must first determine their condition, if there are any problems with the coins or their packaging, and then negotiate with the potential buyer. It's not as easy, or quick, a process.

If coins are your investment of choice because someone told you that coins are a super investment, reconsider. If coins were truly such a great investment, no one would invest in anything else. Coins are similar to any other investment: If you don't understand what you are investing in, you are shooting in the dark.

People who make money investing in coins fully understand the product and the market. If you don't have confidence in your knowledge of both, either educate yourself further or simply remain a hobbyist.

Investing Wisely

It's the sad truth that most people who invest don't invest wisely. For example, most people who invest in the stock market buy stocks of businesses they like, on recommendations from friends, or advice from professional brokers. Most people invest the same way they would bet on a horserace—by picking the name of a horse they like, and hoping the horse wins. Few investors do their homework and actually study the market and reports on companies before investing.

Many inexperienced investors in coins do the same thing. They pick up unreliable tips from hobby publications, people selling coins on television, or other sources that may have their own agenda. Instead, wise investors understand investing trends, set goals, recognize that coins are a commodity, know their markets, monitor their investments, and hopefully have some fun in the process.

Understand Investing Trends

An understanding of the current trends in coin collecting is important. For example, perhaps silver dollars are popular at the moment. But later, there may be less interest in collecting silver dollars, and some other type of coin will become popular. Tastes in collectibles change. The rare coin market is whimsical. What is popular today may not be as popular tomorrow. You as an investor must be ready to change with these changes in interest.

Unless you are certain tastes in collecting are going to change, do not buy something in anticipation that it will become popular later. On the other hand, if a series of coins being made currently is popular and increasing in value, question if should you get involved with them, and if so should you resell into this bull market. Once the series ceases production, interest in it may wane and prices may drop. This has happened many times in U.S. coin collecting.

FACT

Between 1971 and 1978, the United States issued Eisenhower dollar coins both for circulation and for collectors. The collector versions—struck in proof and housed in brown boxes—gained popularity and increased significantly in price. Unfortunately, interest in these coins decreased after the series ended in 1978. Today the proofs are worth a fraction of what they were worth at the height of their popularity.

Investing in coins is no different than investing in any other commodity or stock item. Strike when the market is hot. For example, during early 2005, it was discovered that there were two seemingly rare varieties of the recently released Wisconsin quarter struck at the Denver Mint. (Each shows an extra leaf on the cornhusk on the reverse of the coin.) The price for these two varieties skyrocketed. But once it was determined just how many of these two varieties actually exist, the market began to adjust downward accordingly. The time to sell for an enormous profit quickly evaporated.

These two varieties will likely continue to command a premium in the future, but it would be foolish to assume these scarcer varieties will at some later date once again rise to the lofty prices they realized immediately following their initial discovery.

Another story in recent history illustrates the importance of understanding trends perfectly. Between the 1960s and 1980s, coin collecting gained a reputation as a great investment that likely would outpace all other investments. Suddenly, there was a dramatic increase in coin collectors. But since there is only a fixed supply of collectible coins, this new influx of demand for the fixed supply caused prices to increase.

At the same time, the prices of gold and silver began to rise dramatically, reaching their zenith during 1980. There were two reasons for this. First, two wealthy Texans, the Hunt brothers, manipulated the silver markets, eventually losing a lot of money in the process. Second, this was also a period of high inflation during the presidency of Jimmy Carter. Since many available coins were comprised of gold or silver, the price of these coins increased accordingly. The prices increased not because coins were a good investment, but because of inflation and market manipulation.

Once inflation was brought under control and laws were changed to prevent manipulation of the gold and silver markets, the value of most gold and silver coins first decreased, then leveled off at more reasonable prices.

Set Goals

Coins can be a good investment, but you have to be pragmatic about coins if you are to treat them as an investment instrument. Separate the hobbyist in you from the investor. You must, as with any other investment, set a goal for yourself. When your coins reach the price you set as your goal, sell the coins. If you can't bring yourself to sell your coins, your coins are a collection, not an investment.

Recognize Coins Are a Commodity

Investment coins are a commodity. Coins are a long-term durable good, and they are nonconsumable objects. They may require storage and security, which can involve additional overhead. You may want these coins authenticated and graded by a third-party certification service to further protect your investment. This, too, involves additional cost.

When you invest in coins, you take delivery of a commodity. This is not a paper transaction. If someone proposes you invest in coins by paying them and receiving a paper certification that they are holding them for you, ensure the coins really exist. There are plenty of scams involving investing in coins. You want to take delivery. If you don't have access to your coin investment, how can you liquidate it when the time is right?

The urban legend that coins are a good investment is fueled by hobby publications that offer coin values on a weekly basis. This gives the false impression coin prices change that rapidly. There will always be a few price fluctuations each week, but in general most of the coin market remains steady for long periods of time.

Beware that commodities do not always increase in value. Sometimes they depreciate, and coins are no exception. You can either gain or lose on your coin investment. Plan an appropriate exit strategy if your coins do not perform as well as you hoped they would.

Know Your Market

If you invest in coins, it's critical that you know your market as well as your product. This cannot be emphasized enough.

Here's how to test your market. Buy something at a modest price that you perceive to be offered at a price low enough that you can sell it elsewhere for a profit. Now, go sell it. If you were wrong, your loss should be minimal and you learned a valuable lesson along the way. Master this learning curve before you begin to invest any serious money in coins.

Monitor Your Coin Investment

One of the differences between investing in collectibles and in traditional paper investments such as stocks, bonds, certificates of deposit and the like is in trying to keep track of their values. You can check the Internet, watch financial programs on television, or read a newspaper to get the price of stocks and other such paper investments. You can also telephone your broker for up-to-the-minute prices.

With coins, though, it's harder to determine—and track—their values. Since no two coins are truly identical, you need first some assurance you are purchasing what you were told you were buying. Especially when you are buying coins as an investment, you may want to buy slabbed coins encapsulated by the more generally accepted third-party certification services. Certainly, some investors purchase unslabbed coins, but hopefully they understand grading and the coin market well enough to be able to still ensure themselves a profit.

Once you have established your coins' date, mint mark, variety (if any), and grade, then you need to identify a reliable source of pricing information. Then use that information to determine if your coins are appreciating, depreciating, or doing nothing.

There is a certain amount of excitement in investing in coins. Many people who make money buying and selling coins, both dealers and pure investors, find the negotiations to be more rewarding then simply watching the stock market and telephoning a broker when they see an opportunity to sell for a profit.

There is no national bid board that determines the absolute value of a specific coin in a specific grade at any moment. But by comparing several pricing sources, you can get a range in which your coins should be valued. Then you should be prepared to negotiate the price at which you will sell your coin, just as you probably negotiated the price when you bought it.

It is this negotiation that makes coins either a good or a bad investment. Your skill at identifying the appropriate person to sell a coin to you, and your skill at negotiating not only the appropriate buyer, but the price at which he will buy that coin from you is where the true coin investor makes his money.

Yes, there is skill involved in investing in coins. You must understand the product and its value fully, and you must be able to negotiate to realize a profit.

The Magic of Turnover

A good investor makes more money through the investment vehicle he has chosen than through some other investment vehicle. For example, if you are good at making a profit buying and selling real estate why would you want to invest in the stock market? Using the same logic, if you believe your negotiation skills are good enough to make significant money in the rare coin market, go for it!

But here's the bad news. There are exceptions to this rule, but in general most coins do not appreciate as quickly as more mainstream investments. So, you may wonder, how does anyone make money in the coin market? The answer is: turnover.

Making money in the coin market is no different for any other investment. "Buy low, sell high" is just as true for coins as it is for stocks. The key to turnover is doing this over, and over, and over again. Purchase a coin, resell it for a higher price, then take the money to do the same thing over and over.

Coin dealers typically make small percentage profits from the sale of each coin. If a dealer is only realizing a 5 percent profit from the turnover of his merchandise, it is the velocity of that turnover that makes the difference. If he turns over his merchandise ten times a year at 5 percent on each turnover, he has just increased his value by 50 percent annually.

Coin investors need to follow this same scenario. The secret is turnover. This is why coin investing is managed investing. Either you or a coin dealer with whom you are working hand-in-hand is continuously purchasing coins at a price low enough that the coins can be resold almost immediately for some profit.

FACT

You might have heard about someone selling a very rare coin for more than $1 million. What most people don't understand is that from the moment that investor bought the coin, he was already searching for the next buyer—at a higher price. The speed of turnover will determine if the investment was worthwhile.

"Managed investments" is a key phrase here. If you choose to do all your own buying and selling, you need to first arm yourself with a full understanding of your coins as the commodity or product, then an understanding of the market, and finally how you will maneuver through this market.

Working with a Dealer

You may find there are coin dealers who will help you invest in coins. Before doing this, however, check to make sure the dealer has a good long-term track record regarding coin investments for other individuals. Also make sure that rather than the dealer simply selling you coins to hold for long periods of time, this dealer is going to use you instead as his bank, contacting you to get the coins back as soon as he has someone who is willing to pay even more than you paid for them.

Working with an Auction House

You may also want to familiarize yourself with several of the major auction houses that specialize in selling coins. You may be able to purchase some coins for prices lower than what you understand to be their current market value, and in reverse, these auction houses may become a good vehicle through which you can maximize selling your investment coins.

No matter if you buy and sell on your own, with a dealer, or with an auction house, where you buy is almost as important as is what you buy. If you can't purchase at a reasonable price, you won't be able to sell for a profit. You can't assume the coins will appreciate in value later. They may not. They may never appreciate; they may even depreciate!

What most people don't understand is that a dealer cannot succeed unless he has a reliable way of continuously restocking. It's surprising that *selling* coins is not that difficult; there are trade and hobby shows, auctions, and other sources through which to sell that are available almost continuously. *Buying* coins is the real challenge.

Investing in Specific Types of Coins

You can invest in coins virtually at any level. If you want to invest a few dollars, you simply need to purchase coins of such a value. If you want to invest heavily, you will have to determine if you want quality or quantity. There is no right or wrong answer here. You can make money from either, but you still have to ensure you purchased them at a price that allows you to resell them for a profit.

Once again this is also where you must understand your product. If you are purchasing a $500 face value bag of U.S. silver quarters, you must understand that it is likely a waste of your time to check the bag for rare date coins. It was likely checked before the bag was ever sealed. This is why it is a commodity. The value of the bag will fluctuate with the price of silver. Buy and sell it accordingly.

If you want to invest in an individual rare date U.S. quarter ensure the coin is genuine; it is in the grade as claimed; that it does not have problems such as nicks, bruises, tooling, or having been cleaned; and that you are purchasing it at a price that you are comfortable with so that you can resell it for a better price later.

Just as many collectors collect certain types of coins, many investors invest in certain types of coins. Here are some specifics on them, including classic collectible coins, bullion-related coins, modern made-for-collector issues, hoards and treasure finds, and paper money.

Classic Collectible Coins

Most coin investors envision investing in well-established, perhaps in famous, rarities. There are many desirable coins that are scarce or rare. These coins stand out above the other available coins either because of their relative scarcity compared to the continuing interest in them, or because these are otherwise relatively common date coins in very uncommonly nice condition.

These are the coins that likely have the best opportunity for price appreciation in a bull market. In a bear market, they likely will depreciate less in value than will the more commonly encountered collector coins. Regardless, the same rules apply as before. Understand the condition in which the coin has survived, identify any potential problems with the individual example, ensure the price is modest enough that you should have room to sell the coin for a higher price, and understand the market sufficiently to know where you will likely resell it. This is a managed rather than a passive investment.

Bullion-Related Coins

Do not pay a collector premium for a coin that will only resell for its bullion content. For example, nineteenth- and early twentieth-century French gold 20-franc coins circulated as money when the gold standard was still applicable in France. Today they trade for their intrinsic value, not for a collector premium.

Recognize bullion coins for what they are. These are coins that either are obsolete or are being currently produced that will trade for their intrinsic value, not for their potential collector value. Buy and sell them accordingly.

During the same period, U.S. gold $20 double eagle coins circulated as money. In 1933, the United States went off the gold standard. There are many common dates and many worn examples that will trade for prices closely associated with their intrinsic value. However, there are better dates and superior high grade coins that sell for collector premiums. For example, a 1924 Saint-Gaudens double eagle in mint state 60 is commonplace; a 1921 double eagle in any grade is not. Understand the difference before buying either as an investment.

Modern Made-for-Collector Issues

Some coins are made specifically for collectors rather than to circulate as money. These specially made issues are typically limited edition collectibles. Before you invest in them, determine if there will be a significant secondary market for these coins.

For example, proof and mint sets are issued annually. During the period in which the mint is shipping them, the value often escalates, but it then settles after the supply is distributed. However, there are years in which fewer sets are made than others. You can take your chances and order in anticipation of getting a scarcer issue, but develop an exit plan if the investment goes sour.

As another example, modern NCLT commemoratives are usually bad investments. Interest in them usually evaporates almost as soon as does the publicity surrounding their initial offering. Ensure that there will be continuing demand for these coins following their initial offering before buying them as an investment.

Hoards and Treasure Finds

We reviewed the pitfalls regarding hoards and treasure earlier. The person who typically profits from these finds is the finder, not the buyers with irrational exuberance for the lore spun around the find.

Quality and scarcity become important when buying a coin from such finds as an investment. If you can't read the date on the coin, who is going to want it later regardless of if it comes from a famous find or not? Buy the coin that is not only of good quality, but appears to remain scarce despite the new supply now entering the market. Otherwise this becomes an impulse rather than a rational investment purchase.

Paper Money

Paper money, especially U.S. paper money, can be a good investment. Once again understand first what you have, the condition it is in, and the collector interest for it.

Everyone hoards Series 1935 and 1957 silver certificates, $2 Federal Reserve notes, and $1 Federal Reserve notes signed by Joseph Barr. Barr served only briefly as treasurer of the United States, however notes bearing his facsimile signature were printed even after he was no longer in office.

Identify existing markets where there is an interest in buying and selling, and in what they are buying and selling. Invest accordingly. Your notes signed by Joseph Barr are common today. They will likely always be common.

Since the bank of issue for a specific bank note may be of importance, don't be afraid to invest some money in specialized books on the subject. The knowledge you gain will pay for itself.

chapter 12

Selling Coins

Anyone can purchase coins or other collectibles. All it takes is money. Selling is the true art. Many a collector has learned the hard way that perhaps you can't realize the money you think something is worth without investing time and perhaps additional money to achieve your expectations.

Preparing to Sell

If you are the collector or if you are disposing of someone else's collection, ask yourself these questions:

- Is there a detailed inventory of the collection?
- Does the inventory include specific information on dates, mint marks, condition, and estimated retail values for a specific time?
- Are you able to identify coins or bank notes of significantly higher value than other coins or notes?

Next, do some research into the collection. If you understand what you are selling, you may do well and realize a fair price. But if you don't, someone with superior knowledge may take advantage of you.

You want to get a fair price for your coins. On one hand you don't want to offer a bargain to someone significantly more knowledgeable than yourself. But on the other hand, you don't want to grossly overstate what you have in terms of condition and value. These are especially pitfalls when someone inherits a collection, but has no personal interest in or knowledge about collecting.

Coin catalogs can help here. They identify the rare from the common coin. Unfortunately, the prices published in many catalogs are optimistic and at best are frozen in time on the date the book went to press. Market prices fluctuate continuously and are often different than what may appear in print.

When you've done your homework, know the value of your coins or notes, and are ready to sell, you have a big decision to make. To whom do you want to sell? You could sell your coins to other collectors, to dealers, to an auction house, on the Internet, or at flea markets.

Selling to Other Collectors

The most logical thing is to sell collector coins or bank notes to someone who collects them. There is no middleman, and you will probably get the best price for what you are selling from a collector.

Unfortunately this may be wishful thinking. You have to first find a collector who is interested specifically in what you have to sell. For example, a collector looking to complete a date set of Roosevelt dimes may not be interested in your silver dollars. Even if he is interested, he may want them only so he can resell them himself. In such a situation, he isn't looking to collect them, but to become the dealer who will resell them. You can expect such a buyer to want a deep discount from what you perceive as a retail price.

Family involvement in your coin collection has many benefits. One of them is that the family understands what you have, what it is worth, and where to sell it if you are no longer able to do so yourself.

Security is another problem you will face when selling to a coin collector. How do you find the buyer/collector? If you publish an ad in the local newspaper, you are announcing to the world that you have a coin collection, possibly opening yourself up to theft. How much can you trust the person examining your coins? Stay close by when he or she is examining your coins, or you might later find you didn't get every coin or bank note back. Or, the person examining the collection may not be that careful handling the coins or notes. Before you meet with the potential buyer, ensure that each coin or note is properly packaged so it will not be damaged when it is examined.

Another challenge when selling your coins to a collector is that unless you already have a network of collector friends, it may cost you time and money to find someone interested in buying all or part of your collection. You need to first establish that what you have is worth going to all this trouble, then learn enough about what you are going to sell that you will be in a good position to bargain when an offer is made.

Yet another challenge is that the buyer you finally find might not have sufficient funds to buy everything. Perhaps he will pick only the best items? Before you meet with the potential buyer, take a moment to think through how you'll handle this situation.

Selling to Coin Dealers

Many people don't like the idea of selling coins or bank notes to coin dealers. We have all heard horror stories regarding some coin dealer who ripped off a customer, selling what the dealer purchased for many times more than what the dealer paid for it.

There are bad apples in any profession. Unfortunately in coin collecting it sometimes appears as if all coin dealers are guilty by association. This simply isn't true. If a dealer truly offers very low purchase prices not only will his competition eventually outdistance him, but his own poor reputation will likely eventually put him out of business. This is a competitive business. Competitive prices, when buying and selling, are important.

Coin dealers, just like any other businesspeople, are entitled to a profit. Just how much of a profit they are entitled to is the ethical question. Most coin dealers are honest, willing to make a modest profit from a quick turnover of a lot of merchandise rather than a huge profit from a single purchase.

Coin dealers do not hold onto coins until at some later date the coins become more valuable. Turnover is important in all businesses. The business of dealing in collectible coins and bank notes is no different. If a coin dealer buys your coins this morning he is looking to resell them this afternoon if possible.

FACT

You do not have to sell outright to a coin dealer. If you arrange a consignment agreement, the dealer does not have to invest in your holdings and can sell them for you for a percentage of what he can get. This may be a superior arrangement to selling to that dealer.

The advantage to selling to a dealer is that it's faster than having to hunt for a collector. However, because in this situation you are a wholesaler selling to a retailer, you're not likely to sell the coins for as much as you would to a collector.

If you determine it is in your best interest to consign a coin collection to a dealer, first ensure everything is packaged so it can be viewed but cannot be switched. Make the agreement in writing, and include a detailed inventory list. Set a date by which either the coins have to be sold or you renegotiate your arrangement. Make certain your coins are insured while in the hands of this third party.

Selling at Auction

Auctions are a glamorous way to sell your coin collection. Once again the amount of time, effort, and additional money you are willing to invest must be considered. Time is a particularly important factor with an auction. Things consigned to an auction sell when the next auction date is scheduled, in some situations many months later.

Auction houses do not hold auctions every day. They happen at intervals that allow time to accumulate and prepare consignments for sale. This may include advertising or other publicity. It may include illustrated auction catalogs if the auction house sells particularly important or valuable consignments.

An auction is the ideal economic climate in which to sell anything. The price realized is based on supply and demand. It is the job of the auctioneer to get as much interest drawn to the auction as possible to increase the demand for the fixed supply of whatever is to be sold.

Understand what you have and be willing to accept its true value to someone other than yourself. Do you believe you can get a better price for your collection at an auction than if you try to sell it yourself or sell it through a dealer? If so then this is the sales method for you.

Not all auctioneers are created equal. Some auctioneers sell household goods to a local audience, other auctioneers sell specialty items into local markets, and still other auctioneers sell specialty items to national or to international audiences. Each of these auctioneers has standards and values that merchandise they are willing to accept must meet. You can't expect a major coin auction house to take an interest in a minor value collection.

The Local Auctioneer

A local auctioneer may be willing to accept almost any coin collection. Low value coins often sell to unsophisticated bidders for more money than they may be worth at many of these sales, however rarer or more expensive coins or notes typically sell for too little. Be careful what you consign. Make certain the auctioneer has some experience selling numismatic objects. Local auctioneers sell virtually anything they perceive as having value, so the auctioneer may or may not have experience selling coins and notes. Ask the auctioneer how potential bidders get to preview coin consignments in a secure environment. Before handing over your objects for consignment, make sure to sign an agreement with the auctioneer that spells out whether the consignment is covered by your insurance or the auctioneer's. The agreement should also clearly state that the auctioneer takes full responsibility for theft or damage to the property while it is in his possession.

An auction sounds like the best way to sell my coins. Can I auction off my entire collection?
Not all coins or bank notes can be sold at auction. Auction houses are only interested in certain items or groups of items that have significant value worthy of their time and trouble.

Small Market Specialized Auctioneers

Some auctioneers specialize in selling coins and notes. They range in size from one-man operations to those with large staffs. Some of these companies specialize in coins of the United States, while others may sell bank notes, foreign, and ancient coins as well. Other auction houses have specialty departments that are fully dedicated to selling coins.

Such auction houses have one thing in common. They want coins, notes, or sets of coins or notes that are at least one level above the average. There is no reason to accept consignments of material someone can get virtually anywhere, even if it is collectible.

You as the consignor have to judge if what you want to sell is worthy of being auctioned rather than sold outright to a coin dealer.

Once again it's important to consider your market. For example, if you have a collection of Pennsylvania transportation tokens, you don't want to consign this collection to an auction house in Chicago. You need a "home" market to realize the best possible prices.

Similarly, if you have coins worth $10,000 or more individually, it isn't a particularly good strategy to consign them to an auctioneer who conducts sales at local coin shows drawing an attendance of perhaps 300 people. The good news is the auctioneer is going to know this and watch out for situations like this. A major auction house with a national or international audience will likely decline to accept consignments that are not of the appropriate value and rarity that is expected by their potential bidders.

Major Market Specialized Auctioneers

Everyone dreams of consigning their coin or bank note collection to a major rare coin auction house with a national or an international reputation. Everyone dreams of having that auction named after themselves, with a biographical sketch of the collector included within the published auction catalog.

For most collectors this is exactly what was just described—a dream. Many times major auction houses that specialize in coins or bank notes, or have departments that specialize in these fields, have feelers out at all times to people or their heirs known to have valuable coin collections. Such auction houses know where many of the major coin collections are located, be they held by private collectors, museums, or universities. This is how they got to be major auction houses. They don't just wait for collectors or their heirs to approach them.

Select your auctioneer based on the reputation and track record of that auction house. Compare several auctioneers. Ask for copies of past prices realized, then make your choice.

If you truly believe you have individual coins, notes, or sets of either that are worthy of such an auction house, don't be intimidated. Approach the company to get their opinion regarding if your material may do well in their auctions or not. Despite their size, these auction houses will still accept anything from a single item to many items that fit what they anticipate their customers will want.

Negotiating with the Auction House

If you decide to sell your coins or notes at an auction, there are some very important things to keep in mind. First, make sure that the auction house has a legal local auction license and is bonded. You also should sign a contract with the house that includes the consignor's fee, any buyer fees, and reserves.

The consignor's fee is the percentage of the price realized that the auction house keeps. Fees vary and are often competitive, especially for particularly desirable consignments. Some coin auction houses have been known to offer negative percentage fees for especially significant consignments, in other words, rather than charge the consigner, they pay the consigner an additional percentage of the price realized.

This brings up the second point to be negotiated—buyer fees. This is the fee a successful bidder is expected to pay above the actual price the successful bidder actually bid. It is typically a percentage of the successful bid. The negative buyer's fee, when offered, is paid to the consigner from this buyer's fee. Otherwise the buyer's fee will help to defray overhead the auction house must absorb.

Reserves are an important aspect of auction negotiation terms. If you have a coin estimated to be worth $1,000, why take the risk of it only realizing $200 if there is no reserve value through which the true worth is protected? If the reserve is not met, you will be expected to pay a fee in order to get that item returned to you. This reserve must be negotiated. If the item does not meet the reserve, you might want to allow the auction house a second opportunity to sell the item rather than pay them a reserve fee to get it returned to you.

Auction houses specializing in selling coins and bank notes to a national or to an international audience typically publish an illustrated catalog of what is to be offered. Some of these auction catalogs are printed in hard copy, with some of these catalogs viewable on the Internet. Do not expect smaller auction houses or individual auctioneers to publish auction catalogs, however if your collection is consigned to a major auction house you will want the right to proofread the description of what you have to sell before it is published. You will not likely have any right to demand a specific grade or description be assigned to your consignment. But if there are any inaccuracies in the description, you should have the right to have them changed prior to publication of the catalog.

Not every lot in an auction catalog is illustrated, however if some lots are to be illustrated find out in advance if your consignment may qualify for this treatment. Also, find out if the auction house charges you something extra to illustrate these items. This too is negotiable.

An individual acting as an auctioneer or a small auction house likely lacks the resources and time to publicize an auction to the same extent as can be expected by a major auction house. The amount of publicity your consignments will receive is not a negotiable point, but it behooves you to learn just how much publicity will be drawn to the auction, and if this publicity should be sufficient for the auctioneer to successfully sell your coins or bank notes for a good price.

Also learn what the written policy of the auction house is regarding when you will be paid. Some auctioneers may pay consignors in a very short period of time following the sale, while others may require sixty or ninety days to first collect from the bidders, then to do the appropriate accounting, and finally to pay you.

This brings up the final important negotiation point. If you consign something to an auction, but the auctioneer advices you it may be a significant period of time until your consignment will be auctioned, you may want to inquire about the possibility of receiving a cash advance on your consignment. An advance, when available, is typically a percentage of what the estimate of the price to be realized will be. Ensure if you accept an advance you will not be expected to pay interest on that advance. Understand if your consignment fails to reach its estimate you may be liable to repay part or all of this cash advance.

Selling Online

It appears almost to be an automatic reaction today that if individual collectors, coin dealers, or auctioneers don't tell collectors what they want to hear, they simply sell the coins or bank notes themselves using the auction services on the Internet.

In theory, it is easy to sell something online. But in fact, it can cost a lot of time and money. You have to first establish a reserve price as well as an estimate of what you expect to be the final price realized. You need to accurately describe each lot, including grading each item. You also need to illustrate each item to maximize its price. Once the item has sold, you have to receive the payment, pay the Internet provider for its services, then package and ship the merchandise to the successful bidder.

If collectors, coin dealers, and auctioneers all tell you your coins or bank notes are not worth what you think they are, remember that you may be legally liable for any misrepresentation you present when selling these items on the Internet.

Do not always believe the prices you see listed on the Internet. Those people listing items for sale sometimes are able to manipulate bids either to entice someone else to bid higher, or to be able to show someone elsewhere what appears to be the price an item realized on the Internet when their intention is to sell that item to this other person.

Selling on the Internet is not for everyone. Ask yourself if the time and effort you will expend are worth your efforts.

Selling at Flea Markets and Garage Sales

Selling your coins or bank notes at a local flea market or garage sale is another option through which you can sell your collection, but again first examine your outlay of time, effort, and additional money before using this method.

Security is important, so ask yourself the following questions:

- Do you own suitable display cases to house your wares?
- Do you have a secure place to keep the money you receive?
- Will you accept checks? How do you know they will clear?

The items and sets you want to sell need to be individually packaged to make them look nice and also to protect them when someone wants to examine them up close, and to make them more conspicuous so someone will not be able to simply put them into their pocket and walk away without paying for them. When a coin or bank note is properly packed, write the grade or condition and the price you expect to receive for each item offered on the packaging.

Pricing at a flea market or garage sale is based on the audience you anticipate. It is not uncommon to find coins or bank notes at a flea market that are relatively common yet are priced optimistically. Depending on the audience, you may do well or you may waste your time. Know your market and price what you want to sell accordingly. Don't be dishonest. Accept a realistic price.

Check with local authorities or with your accountant regarding sale tax on what you are selling and what is required of you regarding sales tax collection and payment to the proper government authorities. Be aware of current IRS regulations regarding reporting the sale above certain weights of precious metals, and of cash transactions above certain levels, these being $10,000 or more at the time this book was written. You may be required to get the social security number of your client and to report that information to the IRS.

Making Donations

An often overlooked way to liquidate coin collections is by contributing them to an appropriate institution. You may want to contribute coins, bank notes, or other related numismatic items to a favorite charity, university, or numismatic institution such as the American Numismatic Association or the American Numismatic Society.

Check with your tax accountant first, but there are often tax benefits that can be derived from making contributions. Ensure you have first established a fair market value in writing from a generally accepted evaluator for what you want to contribute prior to making the contribution. Make certain you receive a receipt for the contribution from the place to which you made your donation. The IRS will likely also require documentation regarding what you initially paid for what you are contributing.

Local, state, and federal (IRS) tax laws change all the time. Check with your accountant before you sell to ensure you understand what taxes you might have to pay. This is why people sometimes wait to sell coin collections until after they have retired and are in a lower tax bracket.

Some contributions are made with stipulations. Perhaps you want your contribution to be a legacy, and the organization will not be permitted to resell it later. You'll have to negotiate such stipulations first with the organization to which you want the coins or other collectibles to be donated.

chapter 13

A Brief History of Ancient Coins

13

Coins and coin collecting date from a very early period of history. Although most collectors think of the coins struck by the early independent city-states of Greece as "ancient," coins were also invented separately in China and India.

Collecting Ancient Greek Coins

Nobody knows for certain who invented coins, but it is generally accepted that coinage as we now know it began in the Greek region of Lydia in Asia Minor.

Greek Coin History

There are several periods of coinage through which the Greeks evolved. For practical purposes, it can be accepted that Croesus of Lydia was using lumps of electrum (a mix of gold and silver) stamped with his symbols as coins following their invention about 650 B.C., although merchants may have been producing their own coins in Lydia prior that. Here are the seven periods of ancient Greek coinage:

- The archaic period of about 650 B.C. to 480 B.C. is the timeframe when crude issues typically depicting human or animal iconography first appear.
- The transitional period of 480 B.C. to 415 B.C. is when significant advances in artistic workmanship can be observed, with reverse designs often replacing what appear to be meaningless incuse designs.
- The finest art period of 415 B.C. to 336 B.C. is the classic period of the masterful celators, or coin die engravers. The workmanship of these celators involves elegantly proportioned figures of man, beast, or mythological characters, and it often shows motion. The city-state of Syracuse on the island of Sicily was center stage at this time. Such celators as Euainetus and Kimon signed their work.
- The later fine art period of 336 B.C. to 280 B.C. depicts the earliest contemporary portraiture, especially that of Alexander III ("the Great") of Macedon and of the many successors, kings, and tyrants who followed him. Seated figures are the dominate reverse subject.
- The period of decline of 280 B.C. to 146 B.C. is also the historic time of the rise of the Hellenistic monarchies in Macedonia, Syria, and Egypt, with the encroachment of Rome gaining momentum. Coin

design workmanship imitates that of earlier times, but it lacks the masterful work of the past.

- The period of continuing decline of 146 B.C. to 27 B.C. is also the time of the expansion of Rome. Locally struck bronze coinage issues are now plentiful, with a marked decline in style and workmanship on all Greek coinage.
- The imperial period of 27 B.C. to A.D. 268 is also the time that Rome dominates the Greek world. Greek imperial and Roman colonial coins that began at the time of the Roman conquests are eventually phased out. Cities in the now Roman East and West receive the right to produce bronze coinage at local mints, but the right to issue most precious metal coinage is retained by the mints at Rome and Lugdunum, both controlled by the imperial government.

Greek Coin Theme Collecting

Some popular ways of collecting ancient Greek coins are by region or individual city-state, by a specific ruler such as Alexander "the Great" of Macedon, by denomination, or by design. Collectors who choose to collect specific designs appearing on coins may collect coins depicting buildings, mythical creatures or gods, animals, athletes, or anything else that interests them. One of the nice things about collecting coins of ancient Greece is that there are no limits to what to collect or how to collect it.

Greek Coin Denominations

Weight standards dictated the denominations used by the various Greek city-states. More than one standard was in use, making it even more challenging to define the denominations briefly.

FACT

Six major weight standards dominated the coinage of the ancient Greek city-states: the Attic, Aeginetic, Babylonian, Persic, Phoenician, and the Rhodian standards.

Here are the coin denominations most often encountered by collectors, based on the obol:

- Decadrachm (10 drachms)
- Tetradrachm (4 drachms)
- Didrachm (2 drachms)
- Drachm (8 obols)
- Tetraobol (4 obols)
- Triobol or Hemidrachm (3 obols or half drachm)
- Diobol (2 obols)
- Trihemiobol (1.5 obols)
- Obol
- Tritemorion (¾ obol)
- Hemiobol (half obol)
- Trehemitartemorion (⅜ obol)
- Tetartemorion (¼ obol)
- Hemitartemorion (⅛ obol)

Two additional common denominations are the litra used at Syracuse on Sicily and the stater used at Corinth in Greece.

Greek Coin Identification

Perhaps the most daunting task the average collector faces when collecting ancient Greek coins is how to identify them. Many coins of ancient Greece have either no legend, a legend in Greek that is abbreviated, or a legend in Greek letters that is beyond their knowledge.

There is a saying in coin collecting that is often ignored: "First the book, then the coin." Uninitiated collectors may be surprised to learn just how many books there are about ancient Greek coins. Some of these books may be scholarly and challenging to understand, others are aimed strictly at collectors. These books address identifying the coins, the denominations, and their values.

Some Greek coins display the badge of the local city of issue, which was later called its heraldry. Something as simple as an owl on a coin may suggest the coin was issued by Athens, while a coin depicting the winged mythological horse Pegasus may suggest the coin was issued by Corinth.

Greek Coin Dating

Greek coins do not carry dates as does our modern coinage. You can't simply read the year 323 B.C. on a coin of Alexander the Great. Nonetheless most ancient Greek coins can be dated to a specific period, if not to a specific year.

The style of some coins identifies the period of their issue. As an example, silver tetradrachm coins depicting Alexander were issued within his lifetime, but also almost until the time of the Roman occupation of Macedon about two centuries later. When a large group of such coins are examined, it becomes obvious just how much the design style declines over a period of time. Because of this, the style from a particular period helps to identify about when an individual coin was issued.

Another way to date Greek coins is by their magistrate marks. These marks appear on many Greek coins. They assist in dating coins since information on the years in which magistrates were in power is in some instances known.

Regnal years is another way in which many ancient Greek coins can be dated, especially those issued by the later empires such as that in Syria. A coin may have, as an example, "Year Eight" on it in Greek figures. This would be the eighth year of the reign of the particular monarch in whose name that coin was struck.

Even the coins of ancient Judaea were struck in the names of first their local rulers and later in the name of the Roman procurators who governed them. Since the years in which these people ruled are known to us, the coins can be dated accordingly. You can find this information in books on ancient coins.

Athenian silver tetradrachm.

Collecting Ancient Roman Coins

The Greek world evolved from one of many independent city-states to a world in which larger empires such as those in Egypt and Syria dominated. These in turn were replaced with the ever-expanding Roman world. The Romans were heavily influenced culturally and economically by the Greeks, but the Romans were not a Greek people. Once Rome came to dominate the known world, its coinage quickly displaced the Greek coinage.

Roman Coin History

Roman coinage evolved separately from that of the Greeks, however it was influenced by Greek coinage. At first barter was the main way to conduct business in Rome. Soldiers were paid in salt, referred to as "salarium," the forerunner for our word "salary."

Eventually Romans cast large bronze blocks on which an animal might be depicted. The value of the block depended on which animal was depicted. For example, if an ox appeared on a coin, the coin was valued at one ox.

In 187 B.C., Rome officially adopted the silver denarius as the center of its coinage and economy. The denarius would remain part of the Roman coinage system throughout the balance of the time of the Roman Republic, and throughout much of the period of the Roman Empire.

During the period of the Roman Republic, the denarius often carried the name of the moneyer authorized to issue the coins. The coins often depicted a scene of historic importance from the moneyer's family history, or perhaps a pun on the moneyer's name. Eventually many of the Roman Republican denarii came to depict the personification of Roma on the obverse, with a chariot on the reverse. Roman Republican coins can be dated by the moneyer named on them.

Silver denarius of Augustus.

About the time of Julius Caesar, the ruler or members of his family began to be depicted, this being the time of the Roman Empire. This tradition would continue until the end of the empire, although the tradition is continued even today on coins of many countries.

As Rome expanded and conquered its neighbors, Roman coinage displaced whatever coinage had been formerly in use in these places. There are two coinages that are generally recognized and collected.

FACT

In A.D. 286, the Emperor Diocletian changed the weight of the gold aureus to sixty to the pound rather than seventy to the pound, then introduced a better purity silver coin to replace the badly debased denarius and double denarius or antoninianus. New minor bronze denominations followed in 295 or 296.

Roman colonial coins are those coins issued under Roman authority by locally based mints in western provinces. These coins are bronze, while Rome retained the right to produce gold and silver coins at its mints at Rome and Lugdunum. These Roman colonial coins usually depict the Roman ruler or a member of his family, although there are often references to mythology or other subjects of interest to the city of issue on the reverse. Roman colonial coins carry Latin legends.

Greek imperial coins are those coins, mostly bronze issues, that were authorized and struck by locally located mints of the empire in formerly Greek city-states. Again the coins typically depict the emperor or a member of his family on the obverse, with perhaps a subject of interest to the local inhabitants on the reverse. These coins have legends in Greek rather than in Latin.

Roman Coin Theme Collecting

Collectors of Roman coins usually try to collect Republican coins by moneyer, or a portrait gallery of the emperors, their families, and the usurpers who lived long enough to strike their own money through their coins. Some people try to complete a representative portrait set of "the 12 Caesars," the emperors between Julius Caesar and Domitian over a period of a little more than 100 years. Others may choose to collect portrait coins of the empresses, perhaps of the Julio-Claudian rulers or others. The reverse types are so varied on Roman coins that the reverse types can also be a popular way to collect these coins.

Roman Coin Denominations

The Roman coinage system was constantly evolving and changing, however two systems dominated the coinage of ancient Rome. The first system, based on the uncia, was as follows:

- As (twelve uncia)
- Semis (six uncia)
- Triens (four uncia)
- Quadrans (three uncia)
- Sextans (two uncia)
- Uncia

The second system, based on the introduction of the denarius in 187 B.C., was as follows:

- Gold aureus (25 silver denarii)
- Gold quinarius (12.5 denarii)
- Silver denarius (16 copper asses)
- Silver quinarius (8 copper asses)
- Orichalcum (brass) sestertius (4 copper asses)
- Orichalcum dupondius (2 copper asses)
- Copper as (4 copper quadrantes)
- Orichalcum semis (2 copper quandrantes)
- Copper quadrans (¼ copper as)

Roman Coin Identification and Dating

The Latin or Greek legends on coins of Rome, Roman Colonial issues, and Greek Imperial coins help identify and date Roman coins. It has already been mentioned that the moneyers named on the denarius coins of the

Roman Republic help date these coins. Coins of the Roman Empire are easily dated by the name of the emperor or member of his family appearing on the coins and also by the government positions that the ruler may have held at the time the particular coin was struck.

Such segments of Latin legends such as COS III tell us that the emperor named on the coin was holding the annual office of consul for the third time. The year of this third consulship is known from historical records and appears in easy-to-read charts published in many books on ancient Roman coinage. Collectors can in many cases date Roman imperial coins to an exact date for this reason.

The following are the most important legends to watch for on these imperial Roman coins:

- **Tribunicia Potestas:** Tribunician power (It appears as TR.P on coins.)
- **Imperator:** Emperor or his victories (It appears as IMP. on coins.)
- **Consul:** Annual office of consul (It appears as COS. on coins.)
- **Pontifex Maximus:** Priests of the gods (It appears as P.M. on coins.)
- **Pater Patriae:** Father of his country (It appears as P.P. on coins.)

Collecting Ancient Indian Coins

Ancient India is a gold mine of coins to be collected, however due to the many languages and scripts, most collectors need to really research them before becoming seriously involved in this section of the hobby.

Indian Coin History

India's coinage may have begun as long ago as 558 B.C. if the collector wants to consider *satamana* ("bent bar") metal ingots of pre-Mauryan India as coinage. The use of these metal ingots as money was in decline by 478 B.C., about 150 years before the conquest of northern India by Alexander the Great. At that time, India was not a united nation as it is today, but a subcontinent comprised of many independent and semi-independent states, many of which issued their own coinage.

Coinage of some of these states are more prominent than are others. For example, Mauryan coinage was at its height about 273 B.C., while cast coinage of the Sungas dynasty didn't appear until this dynasty established itself in central India in 187 B.C.

FACT

During the third to the first century B.C., crude coins on which punch marks appear dominate the collecting landscape of ancient India. By the 330s B.C., the Greeks influenced India's coinage due to conquests and the cultural legacy of Alexander.

Among the important numismatic areas are the Hindu coinage of about 130 B.C. to A.D. 100, the Indo-Scythian and Indo-Parthian coinages of about the same time, the coinage of the Kushans of the first century A.D., the coins of the Gupta Empire of the fourth to sixth centuries A.D., and the coinages of the periods of the barbarian invasions of medieval India from about the time of the fall of Rome to the time of the rise of sultans of Delhi beginning in the twelfth century. Islamic states and their subsequent coins follow between the thirteenth to the sixteenth centuries (Islamic coins of Khudavayaka struck by the Samanids were first issued about A.D. 915), then domination by the Mogul emperors with their own unique coinage, and finally the encroachment of European traders who in turn issued their own coinage.

Indian Coin Theme Collecting

Indian coins are complicated to collect. There is no particular way to form a collection, however some people choose to collect simply by time period, a particular ruler or ruling family, metal composition (such as only gold coins), or perhaps by a certain symbol that may appear on coins.

The coins of the European trading companies that appear in late medieval Indian history are consistent with their European counterparts. Although these coins are crude in appearance, they are easier to understand and collect.

Indian Coin Denominations

Coins of ancient and medieval India are available in gold, silver, and in base metals (particularly copper and bronze). It's interesting to note that gold remained an important part of Indian coinage throughout its history, while in western Europe silver coinage dominated during the Middle Ages.

There is no easy way to describe the denominations of coins used in India since during many periods it depended on what local ruler or empire controlled a particular region.

The inscriptions on Indian coins can be challenging to read. But inexpensive books on Indian coins are available. If you don't want to become a scholar in the process, you can just familiarize yourself with the more common coinage types to become proficient in collecting Indian coinage.

Collectors will find that, with few exceptions, a nice representative collection of coins of ancient or medieval India can be collected for a modest price.

Collecting Ancient Chinese Coins

China doesn't always get the credit it deserves for its long history. This includes a tradition of odd and curious or primitive money dating back centuries before coins as we know them were first invented. As far back as the eighteenth to the eleventh centuries B.C., northern China was an agricultural society ruled by the Shang dynasty.

Chinese Coin History

It has been suggested that the first *pu* coins could date from as far back as 2255 B.C., but the earliest inscribed bronze pieces that could be considered to be coins date from the reign of Ch'eng Wang, which began in 1155 B.C. The first formally produced primitive money mimicked functional items that were equal to the money item in value when bartering. These were called "knife and space money" and they date from about 1122 B.C.

In ancient China, gold was legalized as a medium of exchange in 1091 B.C. Metal trade tokens are known from the Shang dynasty, about 900 B.C., but it wasn't until 540 B.C. that round bronze money with an obverse character that translates to "valuable" first appeared. This is generally accepted to be the first true coinage of China.

The Emperor Wang Mang officially replaced primitive money with coins by A.D. 10. But it was the T'ang dynasty in A.D. 618 that began issuing coins with the square characters so well known to many collectors.

There is about two thousand years of Chinese "cash" coinage to be collected, most of it being incredibly inexpensive when compared to other areas of coin collecting. It appears paper money was introduced as banker drafts about A.D. 804. By 1154, paper mills were in operation in China.

Unlike Europe, China had no true medieval period. The cash coinage continued unabated until in 1757 the Chinese city of Canton was opened as a port for foreign trade. In 1842, Hong Kong began using westernized coinage. In 1861, the round silver dollar or 1-yuan coins, which are now popular with collectors, were issued in Fukien province. In 1889, the Canton Mint became the first modern facility to strike coins in China. During the early twentieth century, modern coinage as we know it began, following the fall of the last imperial dynasty.

Early Chinese coin.

Reading Chinese Coin Characters

Several books can aid you in reading the characters appearing on Chinese coins. Chinese coins issued prior to the final imperial issues are undated, but can be dated to the reign of a particular emperor or a usurper through the Chinese character legends.

The obverse of Chinese cash coins typically have four Chinese characters placed at 12, 3, 6, and 9 o'clock. The characters at 12 and 6 o'clock are the emperor's name and title, while those characters appearing at 3 and 9 o'clock announce the coinage is current. The reverse of most cash coins depict characters at 3 and 9 o'clock. The "boo" character at 9 o'clock identifies the item as a coin, while the character at 3 o'clock identifies the mint of issue.

Chinese Coin Theme Collecting

Collectors typically collect an individual example of each emperor's coinage, although there are specialists who collect in some other manner.

Collectors of post-1912 coinage seek coins struck along the model of European coinage. These are dated issues to be collected by date, mint mark, and other traditional ways of collecting such as by theme.

Chinese Coin Denominations

Most Chinese coins issued prior to 1912 were only issued in the denomination of 1 cash, although higher denominations exist.

Collecting Medieval Coins

Coin collectors usually think of medieval coins as the hand-hammered, paper-thin coins of Europe, although this is a narrow view of what is available to be collected. Both medieval Byzantine and Islamic coins are available as well. The Byzantine Empire began its life as the Eastern Roman Empire and for that reason is typically treated as an area of ancient collecting. Islamic coinage is typically ignored as a separate collecting area. Many issues of India from the same period are also considered medieval coins.

In general, medieval coinage begins with the fall of the Roman Empire in A.D. 476 and continues until each individual coin-issuing entity began to use machines rather than manpower alone to produce its coinage.

Medieval Coin History

Silver rather than gold coins dominate the medieval period of European numismatics. However, Islamic and Byzantine coins are dominated by gold.

Medieval European coin collecting is not a particularly popular area since most of the coins appear to be very similar until studied closely. They are unattractive crudely struck paper-thin coins often merely depicting a cross on one or both sides.

Medieval Coin Theme Collecting

Most collectors of medieval European coins collect deniers of various rulers. The English and French coinage systems were sufficiently organized that collecting a sample coin of each ruler is a possible collecting theme, but many collectors concentrate on the more famous personalities in whose name coins were struck. These include Charlemagne and Frederick Barbarossa.

Collectors typically collect Byzantine coins in a similar manner to how Roman coins are collected—attempting to assemble a set of coins in which each piece represents a different ruler.

Medieval Coin Denominations

Gold coins typically encountered are the solidus, semissis (half solidus), and tremissis (third solidus). Silver coins are the miliarense (1/12 solidus) and its half, the siliqua. Although there are a number of small denomination bronze or copper coins, the most commonly encountered coins will be the follies (180 to the gold solidus) and the nummus (7,200 to the gold solidus). This coinage system was used in the later Roman Empire, then in the Byzantine Empire, with parts of the system being borrowed for use in other medieval European countries as they evolved.

Although there were many coin denominations issued during the medieval period of European coinage, the most commonly encountered are the following.

- **Bracteates:** These paper-thin silver coins have an image on one side that is struck through so as to show the same image in retrograde on the other side.
- **Deniers:** This is a small silver coin known in some countries as the pfennig, penny, and the like. This is the basic coin of the medieval coinage system.

- **Obols:** This is a half denier.
- **Groschen:** These large silver coins appeared late in the medieval period, following the discovery of significant silver deposits.
- **Talers:** Praguer groschen of 12 pfennig value introduced in 1300.

Medieval Coin Identification

The most commonly encountered coin is the silver denier, based on the Roman coin denomination the denarius. These medieval coins typically include Gothic or similar character inscriptions that are often in Latin. Since many of them are abbreviated due to the small diameter of the coins, it's very challenging to read them.

On occasion the iconography/heraldic devices can assist in identifying such coins, but it takes practice coupled with the use of several specialized books on the subject for the average collector.

Medieval Coin Dating

We take it for granted today that our coins carry the year in which they were produced, but this wasn't always so. It is generally accepted that the first modern Christian dated coin in Europe is an obscure issue of Valdemar II of Denmark dated 1234. Dating of coins didn't become commonplace until after 1501, so all Christian dated coins prior to this are collectible. The most commonly encountered coins will likely be those of Saxony. Many early Christian dated coins prior to 1501 are known from only a few examples, however this isn't a popularly collected field, so coin prices are very reasonable.

Many Byzantine coins can be dated by the regnal year (year of the reign of the emperor named on the coin) expressed in Roman or Greek numerals. Mint marks and even the individual mint shop within the mint can often be identified as well.

chapter 14

A Brief History of World Coins

When someone uses the term *world coins,* most people think of coins produced during the past 100 years or so. People are always impressed with any coin dating from the 1800s. Yet coins go back thousands of years. Even modern coins typically encompass issues of the past 500 years. There is a lot out there to be collected.

Medieval Versus Early Modern

Machine-produced coins were introduced into different countries at different times in history. For this reason machine-struck coins of England, for example, appear significantly earlier than do machine-struck coins in Russia. It isn't difficult to identify one method of manufacture from another. Just examine the fabric and appearance of the individual coins.

In most parts of Europe, the economy was predominantly agrarian from approximately the fall of the Roman Empire until the Renaissance. As the Renaissance advanced and the modern European economy went from barter to money, the need for coins also increased dramatically.

Silver mining in such places as Bohemia became increasingly important as did the demand for higher denomination coins in significant numbers. The discovery of gold and silver in the Americas became just as important. So did the need to be able to produce coins from the metals being mined not only in larger numbers, but of sufficiently consistent purity, weight, design, and diameter. Modern machinery could fill this need.

The Early Modern Era

Medieval coins are generally defined as coins produced completely by hand, whereas early modern coins are those coins produced using hand-operated machinery. The method of manufacture determines the period into which the coin fits.

European Coins

England began to use milled coinage in 1662. The country used the pound system, which consisted of a confusion of pence, shillings, florins, pounds, and crowns. This continued until a decimalized currency system was introduced during the 1970s.

The Netherlands began its modern coinage in 1586 when the Earl of Leicester as governor-general of the Netherlands limited the number of mints in operation to one mint for each province. In 1602, the States-General introduced a uniform system of denominations and coin types. The Congress of Vienna established the Kingdom of the Netherlands in 1815. The Netherlands joined the European Union currency union in 2002.

France began using the centime-franc coinage system during the sixteenth century, the system being established by the Valois kings. The mint in Paris began using machines to strike coins by 1640 during the reign of Louis XIV. Magnificent gold and silver coins followed. Decimal coinage was introduced in the 1790s during the French Revolution, and France adopted the euro in 2002.

Italy and Germany are fascinating areas to collect since each was divided into states until late during the nineteenth century, and many of these states issued their own coins. Despite the diversity of issues, the system was not chaotic, since each coin-issuing entity made the denominations, weight, and purity of their coins consistent with those of other states.

FACT

In 2001, the euro currency system replaced the coins and bank notes of twelve European Union countries. This is the largest currency union in history.

Spain became a unified nation in 1492. Its coinage system, based on the gold 8-escudos and 8-real coins, is remembered today because the coins were cut into pie-piece shaped "pieces of eight" to make change. Spain's coinage system was also used by its vast Spanish colonial American system of mints. The system survived through the Napoleonic invasions, but during the late nineteenth century, it was replaced with the more modern decimal peseta-based coinage system. This system was continued through the dictatorship of Francisco Franco during the mid-twentieth century and beyond, but it was finally retired in favor of the euro in 2002.

Russian coinage modernized during the reign of Czar Peter the Great, who ruled between 1689 and 1725. In 1711, machine-struck coins were first produced at the newly constructed Moscow mint. In 1719, the mint and its machinery was moved to St. Petersburg. Czarist Russian coinage continued through 1917, with Soviet coins and notes being issued through the early 1990s, this in turn being followed by the coins and bank notes of the newly independent modern states that include Russia and the many breakaway states that were formerly parts of Soviet Europe and Asia.

Islamic Coins

Islamic coinage, just like any other coinage, is complex. There are common coins and there are rare coins. The many Islamic coin-issuing entities produced minor denomination coins in copper or bronze, with higher denomination dirhems in silver and dinars in gold. During what in Europe would have been the Middle Ages, gold rather than silver was the primary coinage metal driving the economy of the Islamic world. Unlike the mostly fractionalized nations of Europe, the Islamic caliphates of this period were united and flourished. Due to Islamic laws forbidding images, few coins depict anything other than an Islamic slogan.

Many collectors are squeamish about collecting Islamic coins because they are unfamiliar with the Arabic script and calligraphy typically appearing on these coins, and disappointed by the lack of any iconography other than this artistic script appearing on most issues.

You can identify these Arabic legends or slogans with several specialized coin books on the subject. Most of these coins are simple to read with the assistance of such a reference. The price of even the gold dinar and silver dirhem denominated coins, is typically reasonable when compared to U.S. and modern world coin prices.

Chinese Coins

The coinage history of China is similar to that of Islam; there is no true medieval period for their coinage. In 1861, round silver dollar, or yuan, coins were issued in Fukien Province. Two years later, Hong Kong, already under British control, opened its own mint to strike European-style coins. In 1889, imperial China's first modern mint opened in Canton. The yuan or dollar was declared to be the central coin of economy in 1910.

China's modern period begins at this point. Some of the most desirable Chinese coins from this period are the Communist Army issues of the civil war period of the 1930s. Even many of the low denomination coins are rare. Coinage of the Peoples' Republic of China begins in 1955. Although today China issues precious metal "Panda" coins, it wasn't until 2004 that it became legal for Chinese citizens to own gold.

Coinage in the Americas

The indigenous people of North America used barter rather than coins until the time European traders and settlers introduced money as we know it. The greatest impact came from the early settlers who established New Spain, New France, New Netherlands, New Sweden, and New England. Each of these colonies and its governing authority in Europe vied for supremacy over this new world, with Great Britain eventually coming to dominate North America. The coinage of the British colonies is described in Chapter 15: A Brief History of U.S. Coins.

New Spain

New Spain actually included part of North America (Mexico) as well as Central and South America with the exception of Portuguese Brazil. At least one very rare token is known that can be linked to Florida, but most of the Spanish colonial American coin issues were struck at mints scattered about their possessions in Mexico and points south.

The primary mission of the Spanish colonial American mints was to strike as many gold and silver coins as was physically possible, shipping most of them back to Spain where the treasure ships in which they were loaded were typically impounded by local bankers owed money by the Spanish crown to finance the monarchy's costly wars in Europe.

Initially the coins were made by rolling the gold or silver into a cylinder of precious metal from which the coinage blanks were cut just as a disk could be cut from a corncob. For this reason these barbarically made coins were called cobs. Machine struck coinage followed, using a collar to make the coins round. Machine techniques ensured better quality coins, with more consistent weight as well.

Spanish colonial American coins can be collected by denomination and date, however the mint mark and the initials of the mint master also appear in the legends on the reverse. These mint marks and initials are important, since some are rarer than others.

You can use a good foreign coin book to identify the many mint marks appearing on Spanish colonial American coins. In general, the most common coins carry the Mexico City mint mark (a small O resting on a larger M).

The Spanish colonial period ended during the early nineteenth century, varying from country to country depending on when the local revolutions succeeded. The awkward Spanish system based on the gold 8-escudos and silver 8-real coins was soon replaced with decimal coinage systems that are still in place today.

Most of the coinage struck for New Spain was produced in Central and South America due to the abundant gold and silver mines throughout that region. Many of these coins circulated in North America during the colonial period simply because there were few coins being imported into the North American colonies from elsewhere. It wasn't until 1857 that it became illegal for foreign precious metal (gold and silver) or specie coins to circulate as currency in the United States. A majority of these foreign coins were struck at mints somewhere in New Spain.

You can collect Spanish colonial American coins by denomination, date, and mint mark in a similar manner to collecting coins of the United States. Some are rare, while others are not. In general the most common Spanish colonial American coins are those struck at Mexico City. The mint mark for this mint is a large M on which rests a small O.

Spanish colonial American silver coins were struck in 8-, 4-, 2-, 1-, and half real denominations, with gold coins struck in 8-, 4-, 2-, 1-, and half escudo denominations. The smaller denominations are "pieces of eight."

New France

The Company of the Hundred Associates was organized to colonize New France in 1627. Montreal was founded in 1642 followed by the founding of Louisiana in 1699. The Gloriam Regni coinage produced for all French overseas colonies in 1670 was shipped to Acadia and Canada the same year. A chronic shortage of coins for Canada and other French territories led to the countermarking of Spanish coins with a fleur de lis for local circulation. In 1685 playing cards were specially marked as currency to pay French military troops stationed in Canada, but these proved to be unpopular.

France continued to make coins for its colonies. Louis XV ordered 6- and 12-denier copper coins for the colonies in 1716, while a copper 9 deniers was sent to New France under his authorization in 1721. Four years later, the ship *Le Chameau* sank off Cape Breton Island on its way to Quebec and Louisbourg, loaded with gold and silver coins.

France ceded Canada to England in 1763. In the ensuing years, privately issued and banker tokens were produced and circulated throughout Canada. In 1858, the first federal issues were minted.

FACT

Canada's colonial coinage period ends in 1857. Its large cents were introduced in 1858 just as the United States ceased issuing theirs. Canada introduced its silver dollar in 1935, the year the U.S. ceased producing its silver dollar.

Today Canada has a decimal system of coins and bank notes similar to those used in the United States. Collectors tend to either collect Canadian coins by denomination, date, and mint mark, or they collect colonial issues. Collectors in Canada refer to their modern coinage as "decimals."

Modern World Coins

There are almost a countless number of modern world coins to be collected. Collectors can choose between coins meant to circulate as money, precious metal coins meant to trade as bullion, and the many commemorative coins struck by mints for the benefit of governments' coffers.

Some people collect coins of a specific country, others collect by a specific theme appearing on coins regardless of their origin, and still others choose the daunting task of collecting a single coin from every coin-issuing entity in the world. Ways to collect are limited only by your imagination and creativity.

Evolution of the Use of Coins

One of the more important events in modern world coin history occurred in 1484. That's when the Archduke Sigismund of Austria (at Tyrol) declared 60 kreuzer value in silver coins to be known as the gulden groschen, in turn this gulden groschen being valued at one gold gulden. In 1520, Count Stephen Schlik and his brother struck large diameter silver coins at Joachimstal in Bohemia. The coins were soon known as the Joachimstaler, then as the thaler, taler, dalder, dollar, and other similar names. Large denomination coins were taking center stage.

Modern technology slowly replaced the old fashioned way of making coins by hand. Steam presses eventually replaced human and horse power. As European monarchs began to gain better control of their countries, these monarchs centralized their power. During the Middle Ages it had been common for local mints to be in operation throughout the realm for convenience of coinage distribution.

This centralization of power also led to centralized coinage production as well. The number of mints in most countries began to decrease as they developed centralized minting facilities.

As the modern economic world dawned, coinage was in regular use primarily throughout Europe, Asia, and the Americas. Australia and Africa followed once these two became viable modern economic regions. Coinage in India, just as in Italy and Germany, was eventually centralized as was the government.

Modern Innovations

The first truly modern innovation in coinage was modern machinery and modern energy methods to run those machines. This was followed by a reduction machine, which made identical working coinage dies of the appropriate size from a master coin design model.

Dates and mint marks became commonplace on coins. Most countries began using Christian calendar dates, but even today there are countries that do not.

As technology improved, so did the metals that could be used to make coins. Nickel, aluminum, and many different alloys were employed. Some of these metals proved to be more durable than their precious metal predecessors. In 1933, the gold standard for coins was abandoned, and during the 1960s the silver standard was abandoned worldwide.

Today circulating coinage no longer is based on the intrinsic value in each coin. Faith in the government and the local economy is why we accept modern coins as money.

Modern technology also allowed circulating coins to vary in shape. Scallops, six-, and even eight-sided coins were produced. The edge of coins is sometimes reeded, other times appears with a lettered legend, while other times may appear as an interrupted combined reeded and plain edge.

Braille appears on some modern coins. Holographs have been developed for security purposes. Ringed bimetal coinage was made popular after its introduction in 1981 by the Italian state mint.

The Commemorative Revolution

Commemorative coins have existed almost since the first coin was struck. It didn't take long for monarchs to realize that the thing depicted on coins could double as propaganda tools. As a result there are such ironies in history as a Roman coin honoring the emperor for defeating the Parthians when in fact the Parthians captured the emperor!

From the sixteenth to the nineteenth centuries, magnificent German talers and multiple talers (double talers and other higher denominations) were struck to honor coronations, births, deaths, weddings, and baptisms. Other commemorative coins were issued by various coin-issuing entities, but the number of commemorative coins being issued remained conservative.

All this changed when in 1952 Helsinki, Finland, hosted the Olympic Games. A single coin with either of two dates on it was issued. It was a conservative start, but by the 1970s it had become apparent to governments that striking Olympic coins could help finance the Games. The Games held in Germany during the 1970s was a high water mark in which a significant number of different Olympic coins were issued.

Canada's Royal Canadian Mint Master James Corkery, with the assistance of his marketing director, Robert Huot, perfected the idea with coins specially produced and marketed to help finance the Montreal Olympic Games. From this point forward, modern commemorative coins were issued more and more frequently.

A Canadian commemorative.

Another important name regarding innovative modern commemorative coins is that of Derek Pobjoy, whose family owns the Pobjoy Mint in Great Britain. Pobjoy, realizing the value of producing coins for nations that do not have their own mints, began competing with the British Royal Mint, Royal Canadian Mint, and other government-owned mints for contracts to produce business strike coins for circulation, and also to strike commemoratives.

A modern U.S. commemorative.

Pobjoy, and now other mint owners, obtained the rights to strike commemorative subjects of their choice, then to market the coins as well. All that the nation whose name appears on the coin has to do is collect a fee. Pobjoy selected designs that were marketable either to coin collectors or to the general public, regardless of if the subject appearing on the coin has anything to do with the country of issue or not.

Profits derived from the sale of commemorative U.S. coins today are approved by Congress to support private organizations or projects, many of whom have nothing to do with the subject appearing on the commemorative coin.

The Bullion Revolution

Modern circulating coins no longer contain precious metal, however there is still a need to trade precious metal due to its intrinsic value. If precious metals such as platinum, gold, and silver are to be bought and sold in ingot form the authenticity and quality of the metal content must first be assured through an assay. An assay, which involves destructive testing, takes time and money. For this reason, it is more logical to trade such metals in the form of coins. Coins can be more easily authenticated and make an assay unnecessary.

Austrian Maria Theresia silver taler.

An interesting example of a bullion coin is the Austrian Maria Theresia silver taler coin. Dated 1780, the silver taler wasn't introduced as a bullion coin, but the coin became so popular it evolved into an international trade coin. Through its history it has been struck by at least eleven different mints—each time with the date 1780. And it is still struck today.

FACT

Occasionally mints continue to strike bullion coins using a date from the past. Mexico restruck gold 20-peso coins dated 1959, while Austria still strikes gold ducat coins dated 1915 and Maria Theresia talers dated 1780.

The first modern bullion coin struck for the sake of the precious metal it contains rather than to be redeemed for its face value was the South African Krugerrand. The Krugerrand was introduced in 1967, and it contains an ounce of gold. South Africa is on a currency standard using the rand, however the "Kruger" rand is not technically a denomination.

Later competing programs originating in other countries—including the platinum, gold, and silver American Eagle coins issued annually by the United States—have legal tender values at which they are to be honored even if the value of their metal content goes below this face value. The face value of these coins is set so low that it would take a catastrophic drop in the value of precious metals for this to happen, but this arrangement has a psychological value to precious metal investors.

The Paper Money Revolution

The hobby of collecting paper money is becoming more and more popular. It is a logical branch of coin collecting considering we usually desire to hold more paper money than coins for the purpose of buying goods and services. The wide use of paper money is actually a recent phenomenon brought about by the end to both the gold and the silver standards during the twentieth century. Prior to that time paper money was not widely accepted, often with good reason.

Evolution of the Use of Paper Money

China was using "flying money" bankers drafts by A.D. 804, drafts that could be cashed in cities beyond the city where the draft was initiated. Metal currency was abolished in favor of paper money in 1277 by Kublai Khan, although coins were later reinstated. By 1280, the Mongol Yuan dynasty was using paper money widely in China.

The use of paper money in Europe grew slowly over the course of several centuries. Scholars generally credit Marco Polo with introducing it when he returned from a trip to the court of Kublai Khan.

During the nineteenth century, privately owned banks in the United States issued their own paper money, currency that in theory was supposed to be fully backed by the same value in specie (precious metal coins) on deposit at the bank. In fact these banks often printed more paper money than could be redeemed. If there was a run on the bank to redeem its paper money for specie, the bank simply closed. These are called "wildcat" banks, and their paper money is called "broken" bank notes by collectors since the bank would go broke.

The issuance of paper money was eventually centralized, with the government assuring banks deposited sufficient reserves with appropriate federal government agencies before their bank notes could be issued. These "National Bank" notes carry the name of the local bank, but they were in fact issued federally. A generation of bank notes later all paper money was being issued exclusively by the federal government. Today all paper money is issued by the Federal Reserve Bank.

Bank notes that are printed on crispy, yellowed paper are replicas. The paper has been dipped in vinegar to give it this appearance. Genuine older paper notes look similar to a well-worn note you may have in your wallet.

These many broken bank, National Bank, and modern note issues are all of interest to collectors. This is a growing part of the coin collecting hobby. Collectors of U.S. bank notes should be aware that although condition is important, the many signature and other varieties can make a big difference in values. So can the serial numbers on a note. Some people seek very low serial numbers, while others may want serial numbers that repeat or have some other pattern to them.

Another popular collecting area is U.S. bank notes with a star at the end of the serial numbers. These "star replacement notes" are notes that replace a note destroyed due to some printing problem at the time it was first printed, reusing the same serial number.

Inflation and Bank Notes

The wildcat banks of the nineteenth century are not the only reason paper money has sometimes been given a bad name. Germany, Hungary, and Yugoslavia each experienced hyperinflationary periods in their modern history in which notes valued as high as in the billions of their currency denominations would be issued, yet purchased very little. At one time following World War I, Germany issued bank notes in denominations exceeding one billion marks, yet they barely purchased a loaf of bread! Want to impress your friends? Collect high denomination inflation notes. Noncollectors have no idea the notes are almost worthless!

Commemorative Bank Notes

Commemorative bank notes have been around since the 1890s, but it has only been since the 1990s that they have become popular. A significant number of such notes are now being issued, once more opening the door for another collecting opportunity. Unlike modern commemorative coins, many of which are noncirculating legal tender issues with questionable redemption potential, these bank notes are made to circulate.

chapter 15

A Brief History of U.S. Coins

It isn't necessary to fully understand the coins and currency of the United States in order to collect them, but knowing their history will make them real, rather than soulless dates and mint marks to be assembled into a collection. You can gain an understanding and appreciation by learning the economics and history behind these coins. One coin may be worth more than another, but why? This is what separates the numismatist from the coin collector.

The British Colonies

British colonists founded Jamestown Colony in 1607, and the Plymouth Company was granted a charter in 1606. The Pilgrims arrived at Cape Cod fourteen years later. The Dominion of New England was formed in 1686 as the English established thirteen colonies up and down the east coast of what is now the United States.

Currency of New England

The first mint actually located in North America was in Massachusetts, and it began minting coins in 1652. The coinage of colonial Massachusetts is different from other colonial period coins in that the coins were actually struck in Massachusetts rather than imported from abroad. The date 1652 was retained on this coinage because the British crown ordered production to be stopped, although the colony continued production through 1682 in defiance of the British decree.

FACT

It is generally accepted that colonial coin collecting begins with the four denominations (two pence through shilling) issued about 1616 for use on the Sommer Islands, later known as Bermuda. Since a hog is depicted on these coins, they are generally known as Hogge Money.

The Massachusetts silver composition willow tree coinage was followed by similar coins depicting an oak tree, then coins depicting a pine tree. The pine tree shilling coin was struck with the date 1652 regardless of when the coins were minted to circumvent decrees by the British monarchy forbidding the colony from making more coins.

Maryland and Other Colonies

In 1658, Cecil Calvert had coins made in England for his colony in Maryland. Other coins originating in England but circulating in British North America were elephant tokens, which depicted an elephant on the obverse.

A pine tree shilling.

The list grew quickly, much to the glee of today's colonial coin collectors. In 1688, King James II authorized American plantation tokens for the British colonies. In 1690, Massachusetts got back into the action at the end of King William's War by issuing Colonial bills of credit to soldiers. Only a few years later, in 1703, South Carolina issued paper money to pay for its military incursion into Florida, which at the time was populated by hostile Indians and owned by Spain.

The Confederated Period

During the colonial period, coins and tokens were issued for or imported and used in the colonies of Maryland, Massachusetts, New Jersey, New York, Rhode Island, and for merchants' use throughout the colonies. During the period of Confederation the states of Connecticut, Massachusetts, New Hampshire, New Jersey, New York, and Vermont issued their own coins, while others were issued privately and circulated as well. Kentucky can be considered part of this list, however the tokens attributed to that state were issued in England, with some doubt regarding their circulation in Kentucky.

In general most collectors consider a coin to be colonial rather than a foreign coin if the coin in question appears in the colonial coin section of *A Guide Book of United States Coins* by Richard Yeoman.

Some colonial period coins, such as those issued for Maryland, were made specifically for use in that colony, while other colonial period coins were simply foreign imports initially produced for use in Ireland or other such places. Prior to 1795, coins were issued by several of the states, however once the Constitution replaced the Articles of Confederation a centrally controlled coinage system became necessary.

Eighteenth-Century Coinage

In 1722, Rosa Americana and Hibernia coins were issued by William Wood under a patent granted by King George I. Then in 1764 the Currency Act prohibited new American Colonial paper money issues. Continental paper money, local tokens, and coins followed during the American Revolution. The dollar-decimal system we know today was adopted July 6, 1785. In 1792, the first federal coinage rolled off the presses, with our coinage as we now know it commencing the following year.

A significant number of privately issued tokens on which George Washington is depicted appeared between 1783 and 1795. Since these tokens are listed in the Yeoman book, most collectors consider these to be part of the U.S. colonial group to be collected.

The Decimal Plan

The first true United States coinage was the 1776 Continental dollar and the 1787 Fugio cent. The concept for our decimal coinage first appeared in

1783. Pattern Nova Constellatio coins were issued dated 1783, all of which are expensive rarities today. The patterns of 1783, sponsored by Robert Morris, were rejected the following year by Thomas Jefferson, who at that time was a member of the House of Representatives. Jefferson championed the dollar and its decimal smaller denominations as the basic unit for our future currency system.

The First U.S. Coinage

U.S. coinage began when the Mint Act passed Congress during 1792. Cents and half disme coins (later renamed half dime) were struck under the authority of the United States during that year, but for practical purposes these can be considered patterns rather than circulating coins.

True United States coinage began during 1793. Copper half cents and copper cents, neither of which were considered to be legal tender at the time, were produced during that year. The silver half dime first appeared during 1794, the silver dime in 1796, the silver quarter in 1796, silver half dollar in 1794, and the silver dollar in 1794. Gold coins were not issued until 1795 because of legal problems regarding bonding for the mint officials responsible for producing these coins. Among gold coins the $2.50 quarter eagle was first issued in 1796, the $5 half eagle in 1795, and the $10 eagle in 1795.

Ironically, while minor denomination silver and copper coins were divided by decimal divisions of the dollar (with the exception of the quarter) the gold denominations were divided by halves and quarters, mimicking the Spanish gold 8-escudo coin and its fractional "pieces of eight" denominations.

1793 U.S. cent.

More denominations would be added to this mix during the nineteenth century. All U.S. coins at this time were specie. Their face value was intended to equal their intrinsic value. Unfortunately due to world metal price fluctuations, this would quickly become a problem.

Nineteenth-Century Coinage

Many changes took place in our coinage during the nineteenth century, but at the same time the Seated Liberty design dominated most of the silver coinage, while the Coronet portrait of Liberty dominated most gold coins. Due to a lack of the technology that exists today, coinage dies were not always consistent, resulting in the many desirable varieties of coins of the same date among collectors today. For this reason, specialized books on just about every nineteenth-century U.S. coinage series identify rare and unusual coin varieties.

Undervalued Gold and Silver to 1806

The rising price of gold and silver on the world market quickly resulted in the mass export of U.S. precious metal coins. Silver dollar and $10 eagle coin production ceased in 1804 for this reason. Other silver and gold denominations continued to be minted, but they are scarce today because so many of them were melted. 1821 was a particularly bad year in which many gold coins where exported since their gold content exceeded their face value.

Collectors should be aware the silver dollars minted in 1804 are dated 1803. The famed 1804-dated silver dollar coins worth more than $1 million each were actually struck many years later as presentation pieces given to foreign dignitaries.

Seated Liberty half dollar.

Minor Denomination Coins to 1836

Low denomination silver coins were produced in small numbers between 1794 and 1836. The large cent coins were produced annually with the exception of 1815, a year in which there wasn't sufficient copper available from which to strike them.

The half cent was never a popular denomination. Production was interrupted after 1811 and didn't commence again until 1825 when the Baltimore firm of Jonathan Elliott & Company ordered coins of this denomination directly from the mint. Beyond that there was so little demand for the half cent that in 1830 and 1831 excess inventory was melted.

You should be aware the coin design changes that appear throughout the nineteenth century often indicate a change in the weight of precious metal in these coins.

The coinage shortage reached crisis proportions. The only currency that was circulating was lightweight foreign coins. Statistics indicate there was less than one coin for every person living in the United States in 1830. Paper money printed by private banks that was often insufficiently backed by precious metal coinage was being issued by "wildcat" banks.

On June 28, 1834 a new law was passed reducing the weight of standard gold, at the same time putting the United States on a gold standard. This was followed by another law implemented on January 18, 1837, that revised the coinage laws. Not only did new coinage appear of a lighter weight by 1836 than was the earlier coinage, but these revisions also encouraged gold mining in Georgia and North Carolina. In 1835, government branch mints opened in Dahlonega in Georgia and at Charlotte in North Carolina to mint coins from this gold. A branch mint also opened in New Orleans the same year, but silver coins were struck there.

Another result of the law changes was the revival of the silver dollar in 1836 and of the gold $10 eagle in 1838. Only a few years earlier, in 1832, Andrew Jackson blocked the rechartering of the Bank of the United States, a move that encouraged state banks to flourish.

The California Gold Rush

The amount of gold mined in the Appalachian Mountains was never significant. Many of these mines were abandoned once gold was discovered in California. The California Gold Rush is particularly important to coin collectors. The gold dollar and $20 double eagle denominations were introduced in 1849 and 1850 respectively due to the gold rush, with the branch mint at San Francisco opening in 1854 to fill the need for coinage in the west.

Prior to the establishment of the San Francisco Mint, local assayers often produced their own gold coins, which collectors call pioneer gold. Fractional denominations of 25 and 50 cents and 1 dollar were also issued.

California gold coin denominations of 25 and 50 cents on which a small bear appears at six o'clock on the reverse are gold-plated fantasy issues made at a much later date than the dates appearing on the coins. These were made for the jewelry industry.

The nineteenth century was marked by experimentation with coin denominations. In 1851, a silver composition 3-cent coin was introduced just as the price of silver was rising above that of the face value of other silver coins. Two years later the weight of all silver coins excepting the silver dollar was reduced for this reason. The 3-cent coin proved to be unpopular due to its diameter. The seldom-used coin was appropriately nicknamed "fish scales." Today it is challenging to find these tiny, paper-thin coins in better grades, with the value of these better examples reflecting their scarcity.

Despite the lack of public interest in the 3-cent coin, the complementary $3 gold coin was introduced during 1854. This denomination also proved to be unpopular with the public. Today virtually any $3 gold coin is rare and can be expected to command a significant price.

Part of the nation's coinage was overhauled during 1857. The half cent ceased production, the diameter and weight of the cent was reduced, and all foreign coins were demonetized, that is, they were no longer legal tender. The cent would go through further reductions in weight during the 1860s, evolving to the standard the denomination uses today.

The Civil War and Beyond

The Civil War rocked the nation, its social order, and its currency system. As fear of the war gripped the nation, the public hoarded all metal coins. During 1861, the government suspended payment in specie, while the Confederacy seized the branch mints situated in the southern states. However, the Confederacy was unable to keep the mints open due to a lack of metal from which coins could be struck. Although the Philadelphia Mint continued to operate, it was the mint in more remote San Francisco that produced most of the silver coins throughout the war.

FACT

Half dollar and 1-cent coins were struck for the Confederacy during 1861, but they are rare today. Beware of the many replicas, souvenir copies, and fantasy pieces that are readily available.

Paper money was not trusted due to the wildcat bankers, however the government began issuing paper money in denominations between 5 and 50 cents to supplement the chronic coinage shortage beginning in 1863. The government placed a 10 percent tax on all private bank note issues. Merchants began issuing their own 1-cent weight and diameter tokens during 1862 due to the situation. Because these tokens depicted either patriotic themes or advertised the company issuing them, they are known as either patriotic or merchant Civil War tokens. This is a popular collecting area today.

During 1864 the ill-advised 2-cent coin was introduced, followed by the 3-cent coin composed of nickel even though the silver coin of the same value continued to be struck as well. Joseph Wharton, a mining baron who held a monopoly on all nickel mines in North America, used pork barrel congressional legislation to ensure the 3-cent nickel and the nickel composition 5-cent coin of 1866 were introduced. His nickel, of course, was used to produce these coins.

Following the war, an overabundance of Indian Head cents caused the mint to reduce the number struck each year through 1877. Most of the rarest dates in the series are for that reason those dated between 1866 and 1877. In

1869 the Carson City, Nevada branch mint opened due to the discovery of silver within that region.

The Law of 1873

The Law of 1873 is important to coin collectors. This law placed the country on a gold standard, demonetized silver, legislated yet another change in the weight of silver coins, while abolishing the 2-, 3-cent, and half dime coin denominations. At the same time the Trade dollar was introduced in hopes of competing with the Mexican silver peso in international trade, especially in the Orient. The Trade dollar failed and in 1887, became the only U.S. coin ever to be demonetized. Also during 1873 the superintendent of the Carson City mint was fired for intentionally debasing gold coinage.

Three unpopular coin denominations may have been abolished during 1873, but Congress then introduced the silver 20-cent coin only two years later. This coin was so similar in diameter, weight, and design to the quarter that it was immediately rejected by the public and was only minted through 1878.

People who fail to learn history are doomed to repeat it. In 1979 the Susan B. Anthony dollar coin was introduced, a coin so similar to the circulating quarter that it was almost immediately rejected by the public.

Only a year later, during 1879 through 1880 the gold $4 Stella was issued, however this was meant to be a pattern for a possible metric coinage. Few if any ever circulated. Today these are some of the outstanding rarities in the United States coinage series.

The Bland-Allison Act

Joseph Wharton knew how to get pork barrel coinage legislation through Congress, and others were quick to learn from his example. During February 1878, the Bland-Allison Act was passed following heavy lobbying by the silver mining companies. Through this act, the government was mandated to purchase $2 to $4 million in silver bullion value on a monthly basis, the bullion to be coined into silver dollars. The silver dollar had not been minted since 1873 and was not popular in circulation. The new Morgan design silver dollar proved to be just as unpopular as its predecessors.

Huge quantities of unwanted Morgan silver dollars sat forgotten in bank vaults until after the 1950s when coin collectors and silver speculators demanded their release. With the exception of several low-mintage issues, most Morgan silver dollars are common, although they are one of the most popular areas of coin collecting today.

During 1890, the Bland-Allison Act was repealed and the Sherman Act passed. Under the Sherman Act, silver could be paid for with Treasury notes that in turn were redeemable in gold or silver dollars coined from purchased bullion. Once it was realized the notes were being regularly redeemed in gold that was promptly exported, the Sherman Act was quickly repealed.

In 1893, the Carson City Mint was shut down, and a panic ensued due to nervousness about the government's commitment to the gold standard. In 1900, the Gold Standard Act put the country on a single standard.

Twentieth-Century Coinage

Most U.S. coins encountered by collectors will likely be from the twentieth century. This is a century of transition, a century in which the public would see first the demise of gold coins as currency, then the demise of silver coins, finally ending the century using nonprecious metal or fiat coinage (and bank notes) as money. Specie coins are those coins whose intrinsic and face value were meant to be equal, while fiat money is coinage and bank notes that do not contain and are not backed by precious metals.

The Nation to 1933

In 1906, the Denver Mint opened, followed by minor denomination coins being struck at branch mints for the first time only two years later. A minting facility would strike cents at West Point, but no mint mark would be applied, making them impossible to differentiate from the Philadelphia issue cents.

Do not confuse the D mint mark on coins! The Dahlonega mint only struck gold coins, and it closed in 1861. The D mint mark appearing on coins beginning in 1906 stands for Denver.

President Theodore Roosevelt impacted the future of our coinage directly. Roosevelt allegedly carried an ancient Athenian silver tetradrachm because he liked its artistic beauty. Roosevelt encouraged the redesign of our coinage that resulted in such classic designs as the Buffalo nickel, Mercury dime, Standing Liberty quarter, Walking Liberty half dollar, Indian Head Quarter Eagle, Half Eagle, and Eagle gold coins, and the St. Gaudens Double Eagle gold coin. Beginning in 1909 with the Lincoln cent, prominent Americans appeared on our circulating coinage.

Silver dollar production ceased after 1904 due to a lack of demand for the coins. The Pittman Act, passed in 1918, authorized needed silver to resume their production, which began in 1921 and continued through 1928 when supplies once again were exhausted. The silver dollar was revived one last time in 1934 to once again subsidize silver mine owners, but it ceased production permanently the following year.

Off the Gold Standard

Things changed rapidly following the Roaring Twenties, especially regarding the crash of 1929, the ensuing Great Depression, with subsequent events leading up to World War II. In 1929, the dimensions of paper money were reduced for economic reasons, with the country going off the gold standard by presidential decree in 1933. Gold coins were no longer legal as

Walking Liberty half-dollar.

currency, and many of them were melted. It wasn't until 1974 that private ownership of gold was legal again in the United States.

The importance of paper money in the U.S. economy increased as gold coins no longer circulated. In 1934, the Federal Reserve banking system was implemented.

During World War II, certain metals were needed for the war effort, so alternate materials were used in the cent and nickel. Between 1942 and 1945, a copper-silver-manganese mix replaced the usual copper-nickel composition in the nickel, while during 1943, the normally 95 percent copper cent was produced of steel coated with zinc. Between 1944 and 1946 salvaged cartridge casings were used to make cents.

War nickels can be differentiated from other nickels by the large mint mark P, D, or S that appears above Monticello on the reverse.

Commemorative coinage was first introduced during 1892. By the 1930s so many commemoratives were being issued each year that the collecting public lost interest in the series, and the final commemoratives of this series were issued in 1954. The commemoratives issued through 1954 are considered to be the classic series, whereas the series beginning in 1982 is the modern series.

Proof sets were first offered during 1936, but ceased production after 1942 due to the war. During 1947, uncirculated mint sets were introduced, followed by the modern proof set in 1950. Both are issued annually and can be purchased directly from the U.S. Mint in the year of issue or from coin dealers at a later date.

Coinage Act of 1965

The next major event in twentieth-century U.S. coinage was due to the Coinage Act of 1965. This law took the United States off the silver standard. In 1965, the silver composition dime and quarter were replaced with copper-nickel coinage, and between 1965 and 1970, the 90 percent silver half dollar was replaced with a debased silver-clad half dollar. Beginning in 1971, the half dollar also became a copper-nickel coin. Silver certificate bank notes were still redeemable in silver through 1968, but after that date they were relegated to the status of legal tender at their face value.

The Dollar: Paper or Metal?

During 1971 the circulating dollar coin was revived, however as a copper-nickel coin. After 1987, the traditional 38.1 millimeter diameter dollar size was replaced with the Susan B. Anthony dollar. This coin was so similar to the quarter in diameter, color, and weight that it was never popular; however when German bankers discounted its value at coin exchanges during 1980 the future of the coin was doomed. The Susan B. Anthony dollar was struck between 1979 and 1981, with additional coins struck in 1999 to fill inventory while the new golden color Sacagewea dollar coin was being prepared for issuance the following year.

The dollar denomination coin didn't circulate well when it was composed of silver. It hasn't fared well as a nonprecious metal coin either.

While other countries have forced a coin of a similar denomination into circulation by withdrawing its paper equivalent, the United States has steadfastly continued to issue dollar bills simultaneously for political reasons. This is likely why the dollar coin fails to circulate.

The Sacagawea dollar.

The Sacagewea dollar coin met with resistance from the public. During 2000 and 2001, a significant number were produced, but most found their way to Ecuador once that nation dropped its own currency system in favor of the U.S. dollar. Sacagawea dollar coins struck beginning in 2002 were primarily made for collectors.

Modern Commemorative Coins

Beginning in 1982 the United States resumed commemorative coin issues. Collectors generally consider the commemoratives of 1892 to 1954 to be a separate series from this so-called "modern" commemorative series.

The commemoratives first issued in 1982 are noncirculating legal tender issues. Beginning in 1999, the United States joined a growing number of countries issuing circulating commemoratives as well. The statehood quarter coinage program is a ten-year program available in proof and mint sets, but also available from circulation. Its introduction created a renewed interest in coin collecting within the general public.

Starting Your Collection of U.S. Coins

No one can predict the future of coin collecting, but the statehood quarter program and the commemorative nickel program that followed beginning in 2004 have caught the attention of the general public. If U.S. coinage continues to offer something of interest to the general public, it can be expected the coin collecting hobby will expand.

The Pennies in Your Pocket

Regardless of the area of your collecting interests, be it older coins or those now being made, you are likely to begin your introduction to the hobby by checking the coins in your pockets. Among the first coins you are likely to encounter will be the U.S. 1-cent coin, or the "penny." Although you will usually see the Lincoln cent with the Lincoln Memorial on the reverse, this design was only introduced in 1959. A date set of these coins is a modest undertaking, but often becomes a great place from which to begin a collection. You may choose to stick with this denomination, progressing to the Lincoln cent of 1909 to 1958 on which two wheat ears appear on the reverse.

If you would like to broaden your collection within the same denomination, you can also collect the Indian head cent of 1858 to 1909 and the short-lived flying eagle cent of 1857 and 1858. To illustrate to what extent even a low denomination coin collection might involve, there are the large cents of 1793 to 1857 that precede the small cents that begin with the Flying Eagle design.

Other U.S. Coin Denominations

The 5-cent coin, or nickel, began during 1866. The 10-cent coin, or "dime," was introduced in 1796. The quarter, or more correctly the "quarter dollar," was first issued in 1796. Both the half dollar and dollar coins made their debut in 1794. Any period within any of these denominations might be sufficient to satisfy the ambitions of a collector, however there are also a number of additional U.S. coin denominations that are no longer in use. Any of these might also become a coin collecting theme.

Copper Half Cents

The half cent denomination began in 1793 and ended in 1857, when the value of its copper content exceeded its face value. There are several major designs to be considered either for a representative type set or to collect by date. These are the 1793 Liberty Head Left, 1794 to 1797 Liberty Cap Right, 1800 to 1808 Draped Bust, 1809 to 1836 Classic Head, and the 1840 to 1857 Coronet designs.

Silver Composition 3-Cent Coin

The diminutive 14-millimeter diameter 3-cent coin composed of silver was never popular and was dubbed "fish scales" by the public. It was issued between 1851 and 1873, part of its circulation coinciding with the nickel composition coin of the same denomination. There is one major design on this issue, with three sub-varieties, one being the coins of 1851 to 1853, with modest modifications made on the issues of 1854 to 1858 and again on those beginning in 1859.

FACT

One of the United States' more dubious failures was the copper 2-cent coin, introduced during the Civil War when coins were typically being hoarded. It was the first U.S. coin to carry the legend "In God We Trust." The 2-cent coin was produced with a single design of a union shield on the obverse between 1864 and 1873. The denomination was never popular with the public and was quickly phased out for this reason.

Nickel Composition 3-Cent Coin

Nickel composition coins first appeared in 1865 due to pork barrel legislation in Congress instigated by Joseph Wharton, who had a monopoly on the nickel mines in North America. At 17.9 millimeters diameter, this coin was larger and more popular than the silver composition coin of the same denomination, but neither ever circulated very well. The coins were initially thought to be a convenience in post offices because at the time it cost three cents to mail a letter. This coin, only issued with a single design throughout the series, was last struck in 1889.

Silver Half Dime

Before the United States had nickels or 5-cent coins we had silver half dimes. Although the denomination was struck between 1794 and 1873 it fell victim to Wharton's lobbying for the nickel as we know it today when the nickel composition coin was introduced during 1866. Between 1794 and 1795 the Flowing Hair design was issued, with the Draped Bust with Small Eagle reverse issued between 1796 and 1797, Draped Bust with Large Eagle reverse between 1800 and 1805, Capped Bust between 1829 and 1837, and Seated Liberty between 1837 and 1873.

Silver 20-Cent Coin

The 20-cent coin was issued between 1875 and 1878, making it one of the two shortest lived denominations of U.S. coins. The coin was easily confused with the quarter and quickly rejected by the public.

Gold Dollar

The silver dollar already circulated when during 1849 the gold composition dollar was introduced due to the gold rush in California. The small, 13-millimeter diameter coin was never popular. Between 1849 and 1854 a Liberty Head design was issued, modified to a thinner 15-millimeter diameter coin with Small Indian Head between 1854 and 1856, then modified again to depict a Large Indian Head between 1856 and the demise of the denomination in 1889.

Gold $2.50 Quarter Eagle

It may appear to be illogical to issue such a denomination, but the $10 Eagle was issued alongside its half, quarter, and eventually its double denominations. U.S. minor denomination coins based on the dollar include our quarter dollar, still in use today despite it being illogical to our decimal coinage system. Quarter Eagle types are Capped Bust Right (1796 to 1807), Capped Bust Left (1808), Capped Head Left (1821 to 1834), Classic Head (1834 to 1839), Coronet or Liberty Head (1840 to 1907), and Indian Head (1908 to 1929).

The same logic that was behind the 3-cent denomination was used to introduce the never popular $3 gold coin issued with "Indian Princess" obverse design between 1854 and 1889. In general these coins should all be regarded as rare regardless of the date or grade in which they are encountered.

Gold $5 Half Eagle

Considering that modern commemorative gold coins of this denomination are struck today the half eagle is the only U.S. coin denomination that has been produced at all eight U.S. mint facilities. The circulating half eagle was struck with Capped Bust Right with Small Eagle design between 1795 and 1798, Capped Bust Right with Heraldic Eagle between 1795 and 1807, Capped Bust Left in 1807 to 1812, Capped Head Left in 1813 to 1829, Capped Head Left in 1829 to 1834, Classic Head in 1834 to 1838, Coronet or Liberty Head without reverse motto (In God We Trust) between 1839 and 1866, Coronet or Liberty Head with reverse motto in 1866 to 1908, and Indian Head from 1908 through 1929.

Gold $10 Eagle

The eagle was an enormous denomination that typically represented more than what the average worker earned in a week. Designs to collect are the Capped Bust Right with Small Eagle (1795 to 1797), Capped Bust Right with Heraldic Eagle (1797 to 1804), Coronet or Liberty Head without reverse motto (1838 to 1866), Coronet or Liberty Head with reverse motto (1866 to 1907), and Indian Head (1907 to 1933).

Gold $20 Double Eagle

The Double Eagle was introduced due to the gold rush in California, however the denomination was so much greater than the weekly wages of the average working person that the coins often functioned in transactions involving transfers between banks.

$10 Eagle.

The short-lived gold $4 Stella of 1879 to 1880 comprises very rare coins (only 460 were minted) with either Flowing Hair or Coiled Hair design. The denomination was actually a pattern meant to conform to the metric dollar being used by international monetary unions.

The designs to collect are Coronet or Liberty Head without reverse motto of 1849 to 1866, Coronet or Liberty Head with reverse motto (value expressed as "Twenty D.") of 1866 to 1876, Coronet or Liberty Head with reverse motto (value expressed as "Twenty Dollars") of 1877 to 1907, Saint-Gaudens without reverse motto of 1907 to 1908, and Saint-Gaudens with reverse motto of 1908 to 1933. Surviving Double Eagle coins dated 1933 were not officially released and are subject to confiscation by the Secret Service.

chapter 16

A Brief History of Bank Notes

Although bank notes have existed for more than a thousand years, they have not been around as long as coins. The hobby of bank note collecting is in many respects still in its infancy, although its popularity has been gaining rapidly in recent years. There are many similarities between coin and bank note collecting, and many hobbyists collect both. There are some subtle differences between coin and bank note collecting as well that will be addressed in this chapter.

Foreign Bank Notes

The history of paper money is longer than most people realize. There is evidence the Kao-tsung dynasty in China used paper money about A.D. 650 to 683, although no examples survive. Paper receipts called Jiao Zi issued for metal coins on deposit were introduced in 1024 in China. Kublai Khan went as far as to abolish metal coins in 1277. Marco Polo is generally credited with bringing the concept of paper money to Europe, however the priest William of Rubruck reported paper money being used in Mongolia to the court of Louis IX of France as early as 1255. It appears King James I of Catalonia and Aragon may have beat both of them, issuing paper money as early as 1250.

FACT

Movable type was invented by Pi Sheng in China in 1041. By 1403 a type foundry existed in Korea. All this happened before Johannes Gutenberg independently invented moveable type in 1452 in Europe.

Ever since moveable type became popular, governments have continuously attempted to improve on paper money printing techniques in order to stay one step ahead of counterfeiters.

The first true bank note was issued by the Stockholm Banco in Sweden in 1661. The activities of the bank were a precursor to what was to later come. The bank issued notes of greater value than were the precious metal reserves to back the notes, forcing the bank to eventually close.

Paper money was first issued in North America in 1685 when the paymaster for the French army in Canada issued promissory notes when the ship carrying the pay in specie (precious metal coins) was late arriving. The notes were to be redeemed when the hard cash arrived, however due to counterfeiting, inflation, and note discounting the issue was not a success.

The First U.S. Bank Notes

Massachusetts issued "old Charter" bills in four denominations to meet provincial payrolls during King William's War in 1689. The notes were only valid

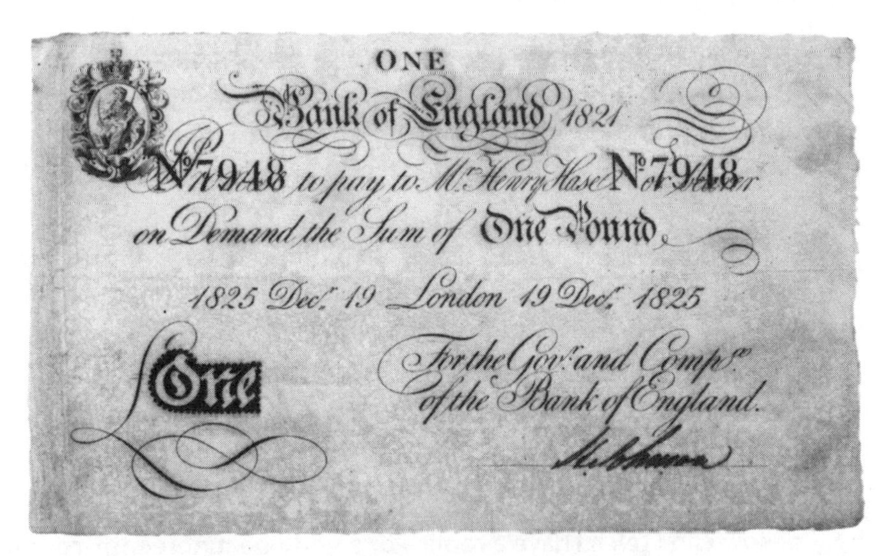

A British nineteenth-century bank note.

for paying taxes, giving the Massachusetts colony a way to issue un-backed paper currency and even to recall it at the pleasure of the colony.

Bank notes first appeared in 1732, issued by the New London Society United for Trade and Commerce, a bank that had unsuccessfully applied for a charter. Additional private bank issues would follow until these banks would finally be legislated out of existence during the nineteenth century.

The New London Society United for Trade and Commerce intended to back its paper money issues with real estate holdings rather than with specie. By the time of the American Revolution, both the rebelling British

A U.S. bank note.

colonies and the Continental Congress were issuing paper currency "not worth a Continental." After the war ended Alexander Hamilton rescued the fledgling United States by proposing that the federal government assume all war debt the individual states had incurred. He raised tariffs to pay for the debt.

The Bank of the United States that followed served as the central bank for the United States, but in fact it was a federally chartered private bank. President Andrew Jackson refused to recharter it in 1832, leading to the later financial crisis known as the Panic of 1837. Replica $1,000 Bank of the United States notes are common.

How can I tell if I have a replica or a genuine nineteenth-century U.S. bank note?

Most nineteenth-century bank notes were printed in a single step, however the authorization signatures and the serial numbers were typically added by hand. The hand written signatures and serial numbers fade at a different rate than does the ink from the note vignette.

With the absence of a central bank state, chartered banks followed, with many banks issuing their own paper money. The sole reason for the existence of many of these banks was to issue paper money rather than to act as reputable banks. In theory this paper money was supposed to be backed by specie, that is, gold and silver coins of the same value. The idea was that anyone could redeem the notes at the bank of issue for metal coins. In fact the banks commonly issued paper money in values far beyond the amount of hard currency they had on hand. When someone came to redeem a note, bankers would make an effort to give the client paper notes from another bank where possible.

Runs on banks occurred due to a lack of confidence in the economy or the bank, and many people attempted to redeem their notes for specie on short notice. Often the bank simply closed. Since the bank went broke, these notes are called broken bank notes. The banks themselves were referred to as wildcat banks.

Paper Money During the Civil War

During the Civil War, individual banks, states, and the Confederate States itself issued paper money that later became worthless. The most common of these notes were issued in Richmond, Virginia. National Currency was introduced by the federal government to help finance the Civil War. The National Currency Act of February 25, 1863, and the National Bank Act of June 3, 1864, paved the way for a seventy-year issue of National Currency notes issued in the name of federally chartered local banks. Banks were required to purchase government bonds that were deposited with the Treasurer of the United States as collateral for the notes to be issued, thus eliminating the wildcat or broken bank notes of the earlier period. Individual banks could issue National Bank notes up to 90 percent of the total value of the collateral held for them at the Treasury. If the bank of issue closed, the notes would still be honored.

Small size bank notes lacking the legend "In God We Trust" on the back are not error bank notes. No U.S. bank note included this legend on it until October 1957, during the Eisenhower administration. Prior to that time only coins bore this legend.

Large size National Currency notes were issued in three charter periods, those of 1875, 1882, and of 1902. Small size notes, the same size as the Federal Reserve notes now in circulation, were issued until March 1933 and through May 1935 respectively, in two varieties.

The Twentieth Century to the Present

By the twentieth century, banking laws were changing and U.S. paper money was becoming increasingly centralized. Fewer independent banks could issue their own paper money, and those that did were being monitored closely by the Federal government to ensure their paper would be honored even if the bank of issue failed.

Once President Franklin D. Roosevelt took the United States off the gold standard during 1933 the public no longer had a choice between gold coins or paper money of the same face value from which to choose. Although the unpopular silver dollar was still being produced through 1935, the public had little choice but to either carry huge amounts of silver composition minor denomination coins or to use bank notes. Those notes with clauses on them stating they could be redeemed in gold were no longer honored in return for specie after 1933; however silver certificates could be redeemed for their face value in silver on demand until 1968.

Today none of our circulating bank notes can be redeemed for precious metals, however. Our paper currency continues to circulate due to the public's trust in both our government and in our economy. Currently all U.S. bank notes are printed by the Bureau of Engraving and Printing at facilities in Washington, D.C. and at Fort Worth, Texas.

The Hobby of Bank Note Collecting

Bank note collecting has been growing in recent years, with prices for more desirable older notes escalating due to the increased demand posed against a fixed supply. This is a similar scenario to that when coin collecting expanded significantly during the 1950s and 1960s.

One of the exciting things about bank note collecting is that collectors may still find desirable notes folded into old books, in dresser drawers, or in old wallets. In general the large size notes last issued for series 1923 (silver certificates) have more value than do their more modern smaller size constituents, but the popularity of the smaller size notes has also increased.

How to Collect Notes

There are many ways to form a collection of U.S. bank notes. Some people seek a representative sample of a series, one of each series, denominations, or even a note from each Federal Reserve district for a particular series.

You can collect notes by the signatures on them, by the type of note issued (reviewed below), or even by special serial numbers. Some people seek particularly low serial numbers while other collectors relish "radar"

A 1923 silver certificate.

notes in which the numbers repeat in some fashion, such as 12121212 or 123454321.

The series date appearing on the front of all U.S. notes is not the year in which the note was printed, but the year in which the design type was first introduced. When the signature facsimile of the treasurer of the United States or of the secretary of the Treasury changes, a letter is simply added behind this series date. Major design elements of the note must change in order to change the year of the series.

Notes found in circulation today are Federal Reserve notes, with a green seal identifying them as such. There have been many other federal note issuing authorities in the past. Collectors may want to assemble a representative collection of these notes.

Demand Notes

Issued in 1861 these were payable "on demand" by the assistant treasurer of the United States at Boston, Cincinnati, New York, Philadelphia, and St. Louis.

Legal Tender or U.S. Notes

There were five issues of U.S. notes between 1862 and 1923 by the U.S. Treasury department. Only the series of 1869 is designated as a Treasury note. Unsecured legal tender notes of the Civil War period are known as "greenbacks."

Compound Interest Treasury Notes

These notes were issued under congressional authority given in 1863 and 1864, the notes paying 6 percent semi-annually compounded interest and being payable three years after their issue. These notes were meant to help finance the Civil War.

Interest Bearing Notes

These notes were the successors to the Treasury notes. They were issued to help finance the Civil War. Since each of these notes has an expiration date most were redeemed, making them rare today.

Currency Certificates of Deposit

Authorized in 1872 and repealed in 1900, currency certificates of deposit were printed in $5,000 and $10,000 denominations only. The $5,000 notes were payable at the place of deposit or in settlement of clearinghouse payments, while the $10,000 notes were receivable on deposit from national banking houses.

Silver Certificates

First authorized in 1878, silver certificates were backed by specie. They were redeemable for their face value in silver. Silver certificates are still legal tender today, but they have not been able to be redeemed for silver since 1968.

Gold Certificates

First authorized in 1863, gold certificates circulated until the United States went off the gold standard by presidential proclamation in 1933. Until that time these certificates were redeemable for their face value in gold.

Refunding Certificates

These $10 notes, rare today, were issued in 1879 to discourage specie payment from the government by offering 4 percent annual interest on this issue. The interest compounding was stopped by an act of Congress in 1907.

Treasury or Coin Notes

These notes were authorized in 1890 as a vehicle through which the Treasury could purchase silver bullion. The Treasury could determine if and when to pay out gold and silver for their redemption. Mass redemption of these notes caused a financial panic and almost bankrupted the Treasury during 1893.

National Bank Notes

This is a very popular area of bank note collecting. Collectors often seek notes issued by a bank in a favorite town, by the state, or seek a representative sample of a note issued by a bank in each state where such notes were issued.

National bank notes were authorized from 1863 through 1928, and they were backed by government bonds. Individual banks were chartered, then were authorized to issue notes of uniform appearance to those of other authorized banks but identifying the bank of issue. Banks so chartered could only issue up to 90 percent of the total U.S. government bonds they deposited with the Treasurer of the United States.

Federal Reserve Notes

These are notes issued by the U.S. central bank, the Federal Reserve Bank. Until 1968 they were partially backed by gold certificates or gold certificate credits, however today they circulate on faith in our system and in our economy. Federal Reserve notes are now the only notes being issued for circulation within the United States.

Technical Components of U.S. Bank Notes

Although many collectors collect notes either by series, denominations, or some other method, there are specialists who are interested in the more complex technical components of bank notes. Among these are the plate position numbers, the small capital letter and number that appear in the upper left corner below the denomination numeral. These numbers identify where on the sheet that particular bill was printed. Modern notes are printed in thirty-two-note sheets divided into four quadrants, with two vertical rows of four notes each.

Plate numbers are another important component. This is the number in the lower right corner identifying the face plate from which the note was printed. This plate serial number is different from the serial number of the individual note.

Federal Reserve symbols appear on all pre-1996 bank notes identifying one of twelve Federal Reserve banks for which the note was issued. So if you choose this collecting theme, you have twelve different notes to collect for any series to this point. Here are Federal Bank reserve symbols:

Federal Reserve Symbols

Number	Letter	City
1	A	Boston
2	B	New York
3	C	Philadelphia
4	D	Cleveland
5	E	Richmond
6	F	Atlanta
7	G	Chicago
8	H	St. Louis
9	I	Minneapolis
10	J	Kansas City
11	K	Dallas
12	L	San Francisco

How to House Your Notes

Collectors often use innovative ways to protect their paper money collections, however commercially produced plastic sleeves are available in which to place them. Polyvinyl chloride or PVC, as was discussed in the chapter addressing housing coins, is a problem regarding paper money as well.

Do not fold notes as the paper will eventually wear out and tear. It is also not advisable to store currency in leather or plastic wallets, as contact with either of these materials will negatively affect the notes. Notes that are framed should be matted in the same manner as a photograph, otherwise the note may later stick to the glass. Direct light is another thing to avoid when storing or displaying notes since direct light can fade the inks and age the paper.

One seemingly easy way to store paper money is in a scrapbook or in a photograph album in which the notes will be placed behind a sheet of clear plastic. If notes are mounted in a scrapbook this may involve glue, which will damage the notes upon their removal. If a photo album is used the chemically treated paper on which the notes are placed may impact the notes adversely.

Bank Note Production and Mistakes

It may be mere trivia to learn how bank notes are made, but it's helpful to understand if you want to collect error bank notes, which is a popular field within bank note collecting. On occasion error notes may even appear in daily commerce.

Production

Intaglio, or "line engraved," printing techniques in which the intricate details of the designs or vignettes are hand-tooled to varying depths into the steel plates are used to print all U.S. bank notes. This makes counterfeit detection easier since forgers can seldom come close to duplicating this process. The paper on which our currency is printed is also difficult to duplicate. It's a special mix of 75 percent cotton and 25 percent linen with red and blue imbedded fibers.

Our bank notes are printed at the Bureau of Engraving and Printing (BEP) located in Washington, D.C., and Fort Worth, Texas. Notes are printed using fast drying ink in thirty-two-note sheets that are later cut into individual notes. The sheets are first fed into a printing press to print the back design, then a second time to print the face. The sheets are trimmed, cut into two sixteen-note sheets, then sent to the Currency Overprinting, Processing and Packaging Equipment (COPE) Pak machines in which they are overprinted, examined, counted, and packed into 10,000-sheet stacks.

FACT

Modern security features have been added to our recent bank notes in an effort to foil counterfeiters. These high tech features include a security thread imbedded in the paper, micro-printing, watermarks, and an optical device that changes when the note is viewed from different angles.

Printing cylinders then print the black overprint Federal Reserve Bank seals and letters, and the green Treasury seals and serial numbers on the face of each note. Sheets are then collated into stacks of 100, cut into individual notes and banded into "bricks" of 100 notes that are strapped together into 1,000-note packages. Following further inspection, sorting, and packaging the notes are shipped to the twenty-six branches of the twelve Federal Reserve banks. The notes are disseminated to banks as needed from these banking centers.

Mistakes

Paper money production is not foolproof. Error bank notes do slip past the inspectors and are popular with collectors. There are many minor errors that may be encountered, however unless these error notes have significant eye appeal they may not be of any particular premium value to collectors.

First and Second Printing Errors

First and second printings are the first two steps in the printing process. The first printing adds the black print to the paper, and the second printing adds the green print that includes the treasury seal and serial numbers.

- **Board breaks:** These are a blank area of a note caused by a piece of the printing cylinder having broken prior to the sheet having been fed into it.

- **Double denominations:** These are the most desirable of all error notes. They occur when during the second phase of printing the sheet of notes was fed into the wrong press, resulting in a different denomination appearing on each side of the note. These are rare.
- **Incomplete printing:** These errors, or even completely blank backs of notes, occur when inking is incomplete on a printing cylinder. These errors have good eye appeal.
- **Ink smears:** These are relatively commonplace but still of interest to collectors when the smear is particularly noticeable.
- **Inverted printing:** This occurs when a sheet of notes is fed backward in the second printing step. This is a sought-after error by collectors.
- **Multiple printing:** This happens when the sheet of notes is fed through a press one too many times. These are desirable errors.
- **Off-register printing:** This occurs when the alignment of the sheet is off when it is fed through the press.
- **Offset errors or blanket impressions:** This type of error may occur when the paper flow between the two printing cylinders is interrupted, transferring the impression from one cylinder to the other and in turn overprinting one side of a note with a reverse impression of the other side. These are common error notes, but they are popular with collectors.

Overprint Errors

An overprint error occurs either when a note goes through a printing process more than once (leaving an additional image on one side), or when ink remains on the printing drum and causes an overprinted second image. Double overprints, ink smears, inverted overprints, missing and incomplete overprints, overprints on the back, and misaligned overprints are similar to the same errors in the first and second printing stage, however these errors occur with the sixteen-note sheets. Other popular overprint errors include:

- Mismatched serial numbers or letters are popular among collectors and may occur at this stage of printing.
- Partially turned digits occur when a digit sticks during the serial number printing process. Unless this is particularly graphic it is not an error that commands a significant premium.

- Wrong stock notes occur when a sheet of notes of one denomination is inadvertently mixed with sheets of another denomination, then overprinted.

Fold and Cutting Errors

There are several folding and cutting errors that may result in an extra piece of paper on a note, a missing piece, or perhaps a gutter interrupting the design—the more graphic the error, the greater the selling price.

"Star" Replacement Notes

A star appearing following the serial number on a bank note is referred to as a "star" replacement note. This happens when an error is detected by the BEP on a note. The notes are destroyed, but the serial numbers are reused, with a star following them. Star notes themselves are seldom error notes since this would mean the replacement note would have some error on it, but star replacement notes are popular with collectors. Some series have more star replacement notes than do others. Collect these in crisp uncirculated condition or better where possible.

chapter 17

Exonumia

17

The term *exonumia* doesn't likely appear in too many dictionaries. It is a broad term first introduced by numismatic researcher Russ Rulau during the late twentieth century to cover all nonlegal tender collectibles usually associated with the coin collecting hobby. The most common exonumia items are tokens, medals, and scrip, however in a broader sense it can also include patterns, essays, pieforts, political buttons, and even error coins.

Tokens

Tokens are misunderstood even by many coin collectors. They are a nonpermanent substitute for money. For a piece of metal (or plastic) to be impressed with a design and to be designated as a token rather than as a coin or a medal, the item at one time was exchanged for goods or services as a substitute for coins or currency.

Condor Tokens

The very unusual name for this type of token is taken from the name of author James Condor, who cataloged this type of token in his book *An Arrangement of Provincial Coins, Tokens, and Medalets, Issued in Great Britain, Ireland, and the Colonies*. More correctly these emergency issues should be called provincial or merchant tokens.

During the late eighteenth century, the Royal Mint in England chose to produce silver and gold coins, while generally ignoring production of base metal small change coins. These low denomination copper coins—including the farthing, halfpenny, and penny—were desperately needed to keep commerce going, but the mint appeared to be insensitive to the needs of the masses.

Exonumia is a more structured and sophisticated area of the hobby than might be expected by those who do not participate in it. There are catalogs listing many of the collectibles and their values, organizations for such specialized collectors, and shows at which exonumia has its own special area and shows catering exclusively to exonumia specialists.

Local merchants began issuing their own tokens in the proper weights, metal content, and diameter for these denominations, however the merchants needed to be careful to ensure the designs appearing on these issues were not similar to those appearing on the king's coinage or risk being accused of counterfeiting. Thousands of different merchant tokens were issued throughout the British Isles during this period.

U.S. token.

Hard Times Tokens

Following the American Revolution, the economy of the fledgling United States had its good times and its hard times. During good times, citizens prospered, and coins flowed freely in circulation ranging from copper half cents to gold $10 eagles. During economic slumps, it was natural for the average citizen to hoard all the metal coins that could be acquired.

Private merchants, just as in England before them, occasionally issued merchant tokens during this period. Merchant tokens were of the same weight, diameter, and metal content as were the coins for which they were a substitute, but just as in England the merchants changed the designs to avoid being accused of counterfeiting. Merchant tokens were free advertising for the merchant who authorized them since information about that business appeared on them.

Politically motivated hard–times tokens were also issued, although they were meant to circulate as well as to spread propaganda. This is the time of the political intrigues pitting President Andrew Jackson against those in politics who opposed him regarding the Bank of the United States. The Bank of the United States was actually a privately owned bank in which the government deposited its money, under an arrangement through which the bank got to keep the interest earned on the deposits. Jackson opposed renewing the bank's charter. The political and economic intrigues that followed resulted in one of the more notorious stock market crashes and ensuing recessions in American history.

Civil War Tokens

During the American Civil War, once again there was fear of economic collapse. Citizens began to hoard all specie, grinding the economy to a halt.

The government came up with several innovative substitutes for currency, including fractional denominated paper bank notes between the values of 10 and 50 cents, and encased postage stamps.

Merchants once more took matters into their own hands, producing thousands of varieties of Civil War tokens of the diameter, weight, and metal content of the recently introduced small cent. (In 1857, due to the increased cost of copper, the weight and diameter of the Large Cent was decreased from 10.89 grams and about 28 millimeters to 4.67 grams and 19 millimeters.)

FACT

Any token on which the issuing vendor is either identified merely by initials or not at all is called a maverick. Collectors find it challenging to identify maverick tokens.

You can collect two major categories of Civil War tokens. These are merchant tokens and patriotic Civil War tokens. The merchant tokens are simply those 1-cent size tokens on which advertising for the merchant issuing them appears. Patriotic tokens are those in which a patriotic theme such as "Army and Navy" or "Union Forever" appears instead of the person issuing the token.

It has been estimated that more than 10,000 different Civil War tokens were issued. On April 22, 1864, a law was passed prohibiting the private issuance of any 1- or 2-cent coins, tokens, or other devices to be used as money, followed by an additional law on June 8, 1864, prohibiting the use of any privately issued coinage of any form.

Transportation Tokens

Transportation tokens are still in use today. Each token can be vended to receive a ride on a transportation service. Since the cost of a ride often changes, so do the tokens that can be accepted within a vending machine allowing entry to the transportation service.

Because each local transportation service typically issued its own tokens, thousands of different transportation tokens can be collected. Many of these tokens name the transportation company or the city in which the service is offered. Some of these tokens may even depict a trolley, bus, or other mode of transportation. All are collectible.

The easiest way to collect transportation tokens is by theme. Perhaps you will collect only transportation tokens from a specific city or state. Perhaps you will collect only transportation tokens depicting trolleys. The theme can be anything you want it to be, but it is much less frustrating to specialize than to attempt to collect virtually every transportation token available.

Ration Tokens

Shortages occur during wartime. During the Civil War, the shortages included copper coins due to the rise in the value of copper and the insecurities of the public. During World War II shortages included the metal for striking certain coins (copper 1-cent coins from 1943 to 1945 and nickels from 1941 to 1945), food, and other consumable commodities as well. People could only buy products such as gasoline and dairy products with cash and the appropriate ration stamps or ration tokens.

The most commonly encountered ration tokens are red or blue cardboard-like fabric disks that could be redeemed along with the appropriate amount of money for either meat or dairy products. Several varieties of these tokens exist.

Vending Machine Tokens

The most commonly encountered tokens are those that vend goods or entertainment services such as pinball games or amusement rides. Since these are a substitute for coins, they are considered tokens rather than medals.

The best way to collect tokens is once again by a theme. This theme could be tokens issued by a specific company, for use in a specific geographic place, or perhaps that depict some particular person, place, or thing. It can be frustrating to attempt to collect virtually every token since there are so many different tokens issued.

Even the gambling industry issues its own casino chips or tokens. Some of these tokens have a plug of silver in the center, while others are composed of base metal. Most name the casino at which they are to be used, and many of them are attractively designed in hopes people will take them home as souvenirs rather than redeem them. This benefits the casino because it costs the casino less than the token's face value to make each token.

You can purchase attractively packaged sets of casino tokens, however ensure that the individual tokens in each set can be vended or redeemed within the casino, otherwise you are simply purchasing a made-for-collectors set that likely is overpriced and perhaps nonredeemable.

Vending machine tokens also involve the darker side of the hobby since peep show tokens also fall into this category. Although some of these tokens simply name the establishment at which the tokens can be used, some of these tokens can be very graphic.

Military Tokens

Military canteen tokens were issued throughout the later twentieth century. Most of them identify a military unit or a post exchange at which the tokens can be redeemed. These tokens are a substitute for coins, especially in areas where a threat is possible. At any give moment the local military authorities can withdraw these tokens, ensuring that if they fall into enemy or black market hands they cannot be used by someone other than the persons to whom they were issued.

Trade Tokens and the Company Store

Trade tokens were issued privately to be used in trade. Many of these carry a legend that begins "Good for ________" with a monetary value such as "five cents" following. Most trade tokens do not have dates on them. Some are simply good for one cigar, a beer, or some other commodity, rather than having a monetary redemption value at a store. Not all trade tokens are easy to identify. Some tokens only bear the initials of the issuing entity. Since these are not easily identified, they are known as mavericks until someone identifies what the initials stand for. Some collectors specialize in researching such tokens.

Trade tokens were issued to encourage people to do business with a particular business. Many of them identify the business and often the city in which the business existed. For this reason collectors often gravitate toward collecting trade tokens from a favorite city, such as where they were born or now live.

Trade tokens are sometimes referred to as store cards, since such tokens were issued to be used in a specific store rather than in a community at large. Company stores can be considered part of this, but company store issues are different. At one time it was legal to pay employees in scrip rather than in U.S. currency. This scrip, or company store money, was redeemable only at the company owned general store. The company dictated the price of goods at this store, often at inflated prices. Employees who changed employers would have no money until the new employer paid them, considering they were not paid in a universally accepted federal currency. For this reason today, employees must be paid in U.S. currency.

Company store tokens are particularly popular in the communities from which they originated. In general company store money has a "home base" where it is more avidly collected and for that reason has more value there. However, some scrip of better known companies is collected nationally

Love Tokens

Love tokens are coins on which one side has been planed smooth, then engraved (typically by a professional jeweler) with a short message of love or the first name or initials of a loved one. Love tokens were initially popular in Great Britain, and they gained similar popularity in the United States from the 1880s through the early twentieth century.

The most commonly found love token will be on a U.S. dime, however love tokens are known using coins ranging from a cent to a gold coin as the host. Love tokens are typically valued by the quality and amount of the professionally engraved art work appearing on them. Each love token should be unique.

Wooden Money

The old saying, "Don't take any wooden nickels," was likely a reference to wooden composition tokens. The origins of such substitutes for coins as money are not clear, however likely began with the siege coinage of the Middle Ages in Europe. During this time it was fashionable for an army to surround a walled city and starve it into submission rather than storming it. Since this might take years to make a city surrender commerce continued within the city during the siege. However as coins became scarce due to the blockade, coinage composed of cardboard, leather, or whatever was still available would be issued, called siege coinage.

FACT

Mexican and American plantation owners occasionally paid their laborers with hacienda tokens—wooden tokens branded with some indication of who issued them and their worth in the company store.

During the early twentieth century, someone got the idea that they could issue a wooden token with a value of five cents that was redeemable with local merchants for a specific period of time, thus inventing the wooden nickel. Today wooden nickels (and other denominations) are made regularly either to draw people to merchants at an event, or as nonredeemable "nickels" meant to advertise something or somebody. Modern wooden nickels have even been issued to commemorate weddings and births. These are not technically tokens since they were never a replacement for currency.

There are so many wooden nickels available that once again it is advisable to choose a theme and collect within that theme. It is unlikely anyone will ever succeed to completing a set of all such issued tokens. Not only that, but it is unlikely a catalog exists in which all such issues have been cataloged.

Medals

Medals are usually made from the same materials as are coins, and may look like coins. Some less scrupulous individuals have been known to issue medals with fictitious denominations on them, then sell the medals to unsophisticated buyers as coins. Study suspicious advertisements for such items carefully to see if the word "coin" is avoided in the ad.

Medals seldom have the same secondary market value appreciation that can be anticipated by collectible coins. They should be collected as art, not as coins.

Medals are different from tokens. A medal may look similar to a coin or to a token, however a medal is a similar object that has never been used as a substitute for money. It is simply an art object that likely commemorates a person, place, thing, or event.

U.S. Mint

The United States Mint has produced medals in addition to coins almost since its inception. The mint has also produced military decorations, which should not be confused with medals or coins, although collecting military decorations is generally accepted as being within the confines of the coin collecting hobby.

Most of the medals produced by the U.S. Mint are high relief art medals meant to be sold to the public as souvenirs. Medals have been struck with the approval of Congress to honor great Americans. An example of this is the single gold medal presented to the late actor John Wayne, with subsequent bronze composition examples being made available to the public for a price.

High relief medals are generally considered to be art medals, while lower relief medals are not. Low relief medals stack easily, as do coins, whereas higher relief art medals do not.

The U.S. Mint also produces an ongoing series of inaugural medals to honor the president and the vice president at the time each takes office every four years. Collectors should be careful not to confuse privately issued inaugural medals for those issued by the mint.

The U.S. Mint has also produced a series of very attractive high relief medals honoring the current secretary of State, secretary of the Treasury, and other important government dignitaries.

Whatever medals are currently being made are available either by visiting the Mint, by mail, or through their Internet Web site.

Commemorative Medals

Medals are issued periodically to commemorate events. Some of these are issued privately, while others are issued under Congressional authority by the United States Mint. All of them are collectible.

Bullion Medals

Bullion medals are those medals containing precious metal that were meant to trade for the intrinsic value of that precious metal rather than because of the art iconography on the medal.

During the 1980s, the United States issues the American Arts medallion series, each of these being either a .900 fine troy ounce or half troy ounce of gold. Once it was realized by Congress that people wishing to hold gold in coinage form preferred legal tender coins to medallions, the American Eagle platinum, gold, and silver coinage series replaced these medallions.

George W. Bush inaugural medal.

Caution is the watchword when purchasing bullion medallions. Some privately produced medallions have nonexistent "denominations" on them. Assure these denominations are legal tender in the country of issue before purchasing such things as coins.

Do not assume because a medal appears to be gold or silver in color that it is solid gold or silver. It may be plated, or it may contain no precious metal at all. Look for something on the medal that gives the metal content, purity, and weight. If this is not present, it is doubtful you have a precious metal medal.

Relic Medals

Relic medals are a memorial of sorts. These medals are struck from metal salvaged from whatever they memorialize, such as a battleship, airplane, or rocket ship. Often these are issued to raise funds for an organization associated with what they memorialize, or the surviving families of those who may have perished in a disaster surrounding what is being memorialized.

Relic medal collecting is a specific area of collecting within the medal collecting field. It may not always be acknowledged on the medal itself that the medal is made from surviving metal from the memorialized object, but with some research this information can usually be found.

Funerary Medals

Emotions always run high when someone has died. Everyone wants to have something left behind as an eternal memorial to the loved one. Prominent people are sometimes memorialized through funerary medals.

During the early twentieth century, high ranking dignitaries attending at least one prominent Chinese warlord/general's funeral received gold funerary medals, while others received medals in silver or in bronze depending on their social position.

One of the more popular American funerary medal types to be collected are those contemporary issues remembering George Washington. Masonic funerary medals are often engraved and for that reason may be unique. These appear periodically at coin shows and in numismatic auctions.

Art Medals

Former American Numismatic Society curator Dr. Alan Stahl once referred to medallic art as "art you can hold in the palm of your hand." True medallic art or medallic sculpture is not necessarily made to commemorate anything, but simply to display art for the sake of art. Such medals are typically produced in extremely limited quantities and many times are only available directly through the artist. Many of the artists are professional sculptor-engravers who also design coins.

Medallic sculpture can appear in many forms. The most popular appears to be cast rather than struck medals, often composed of bronze and made in very high relief. Medallic sculpture is not necessarily round and in some instances may even be free standing. This free standing feature has raised the argument regarding where medallic sculpture ends and true sculpture begins.

Calendar Medals

Some private mints produce medals annually on which a calendar for that year is displayed on one side. The other side typically is medallic art. These medals make great gifts or display items. Although the United States Mint has never issued a calendar medal, Monnaie de Paris (French Mint) has been issuing these medals annually for years. Collecting calendar medals is challenging since most are used as display items, and they seldom appear for sale in collector markets.

Elongated Coins

Although it is technically illegal to deface or destroy our coins or bank notes, the elongated coin, especially the cent, has been with us since sometime during the late nineteenth century. Such souvenir items, produced by placing a coin into a machine that bends it while impressing a new design onto the host piece, are known from at least as far back as the 1892 Columbus Exposition. Elongated cents of this and the 1933 Chicago Century of Progress fair are popular with collectors.

It is virtually impossible to catalog all of the elongated coin designs that have been or are still being made. The best suggestion is to collect by a theme that interests you. It is unlikely anyone can assemble a complete collection.

Coin Replicas

Coin replicas are different from counterfeit coins. Counterfeits were made to deceive; replicas were made to make an otherwise unavailable coin available. An example is the 1862-dated Confederate States of America 1-cent coin made during the 1980s (and possibly later) by the privately owned Georgia Mint. Genuine CSA cents are dated 1861. The mint dated these incorrectly on purpose so as not to confuse the rare genuine issue with their replicas. The Hobby Protection Act now requires that all coin replicas be marked with the word "copy." Those replicas made prior to enactment of this law are not so marked.

Scrip

Most collectors think of scrip as paper money, but scrip also includes tokens that were used for the same purpose. Both fall under the category of exonumia and are avidly collected.

Company Store Scrip

In general you can take it for granted today that when your employer pays you it will be in currency of the United States, but this wasn't always so. At one time it was legal to pay employees with company scrip in the form of paper or metal tokens. These were only redeemable at the company store, at prices dictated by the company. Company store scrip is typically the most popular near where it was issued.

Although in the United States we expect company store scrip to date from no later than the early twentieth century, companies inside Russia and neighboring countries issued paper company store scrip during the 1990s during the tumultuous period following the collapse of the Soviet Union. These are also very collectible.

Paper Scrip

Paper scrip, just as with wooden nickel tokens, has been used on occasion to promote local merchants or local events. Such paper scrip typically has a value assigned to it that the scrip can be used against when making purchases at participating stores for a specific period of time. Sometimes such scrip is good for a service, rather than equating to a dollar amount.

There are also genuine bank notes on which someone has placed a decal over the central front vignette, replacing (as an example) George Washington with Elvis or President George W. Bush on the dollar bill.

Propaganda leaflets resembling paper currency also fall within this category. Propaganda leaflets resembling the currency of an enemy nation on one side but with a message such as suggesting troops surrender to American soldiers appearing on the other side have been dropped from airplanes during several conflicts including World War II, the Korean War, Vietnam War, and the Gulf War.

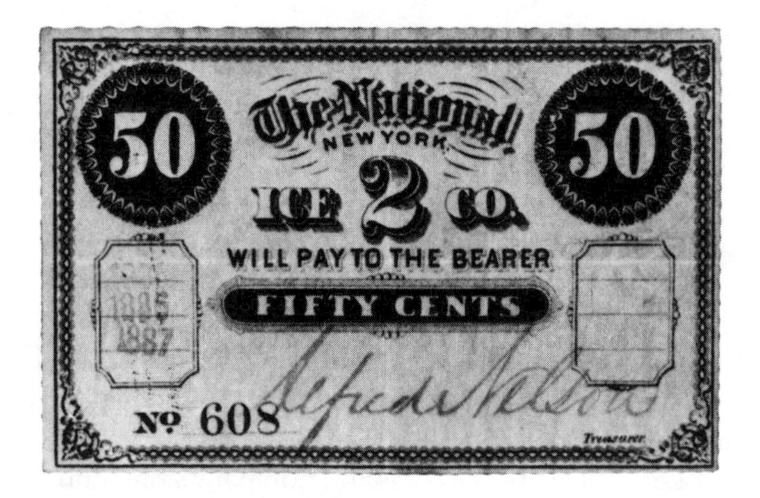

U.S. scrip.

Commercial Paper Scrip

Seignorage is discussed elsewhere in this book. In recent history commercial ventures have learned that seignorage can be of value to themselves, as well as to the government. Companies such as those that own Disney World now issue souvenir paper scrip in dollar denominations that can be obtained on their premises for face value and can then be spent at this full face value at any of their facilities. Where these companies benefit the most is when someone decides to keep the scrip as a souvenir rather than spend it. If it cost such a business five cents to print the note and it has a face value of a dollar then if it is taken home the company gains ninety-five cents profit.

Other Exonumia Items

Exonumia can be considered to be a catch-all term for anything remotely related to coin collecting that a hobbyist wants to include in his collection.

Some of the other unusual things that can fall into this category are coinage patterns, essays, and pieforts, all being specially struck pseudo-coins either produced to test machinery, get an opinion about a proposed pattern for a possible future coin, to demonstrate the abilities of the minting facility, or for collectors.

FACT

Error coin collecting is sometimes considered to be a separate specialized area of coin collecting, but this too can be considered an exonumia field.

Political buttons are often considered to be an exonumia item, this being another popular collectible often associated with coin collecting. Coins that have been countermarked by private individuals or businesses as well as coins chopmarked in the Orient by merchants trying to ensure a silver coin has good silver content are within this realm.

chapter 18

Modern Technology

18

As technology has improved, so has the quality and the consistency of coinage. Like coins weigh the same within minuscule amounts of a gram, their diameter is sufficiently exacting to be usable in vending machines, and the metal composition is precise enough for us to trust in the value of our money. The invention of the collar ensured coins would be perfectly round and allowed reeding, smooth, or lettered edges, all of which discourage counterfeiting. Technological innovation has come a long way, and it hasn't stopped yet.

Substitutes for Coins and Currency

Periodically people prophesy that coinage will at some future date become antiquated and fade into history. The possibility is real, but doubtful. Regardless of the substitute for coinage (and for bank notes as well) that is introduced there is an important psychological need to hold hard cash—something you can hold in your hand and call money. If this weren't true, gold would also diminish as a valuable metal, considering its few uses in industry other than as an adornment. The desire to hold hard currency rather than one of its substitutes is particularly pronounced during periods of economic stress.

Coins are here to stay. There are substitutes for coins (and bank notes), and there will likely be more in the future, but there is still no substitute that is so convincing and reliable that it can displace coinage completely and permanently.

Bank Notes

The bank note is likely the closest thing we have to a true substitute for coins. Although paper money has been around for more than a thousand years, mistrust in it has often caused chaos. For this reason, early Chinese notes carry a warning regarding the penalty for counterfeiting.

Following World War I, Germany experienced one of the worst inflationary periods in history. Paper money was being printed without the full backing of hard assets, and so the purchasing power of these notes diminished virtually by the hour. Finally a new system of bank notes backed by real estate was introduced, and inflation was stopped.

Similar mistrust of bank notes has occurred in the United States. The nineteenth-century "wildcat" banks often printed more money than for which the issuing entity had gold and silver coins on deposit to give real value to that paper currency. When people demanded redemption of more hard currency for these notes than the banks had in gold and silver coin deposits, the banks simply closed their doors and failed.

The bottom line is that even bank notes, as commonplace as they appear in commerce worldwide today, are still only as good as the trust the public puts in them, based on the strength of the local economy and the government behind that economy. No matter how you look at it a bank note is still a receipt for something else of value, be it precious metal, real estate, or the intangible trust in the reliability of the government of issue.

FACT

Due to inflation, coinage was no longer issued in Zaire after 1988. In 1993 Belgium seized forty tons of inflationary 10-million Raire bank notes meant for President Mobuto's private use, notes that were unauthorized by the central bank!

Checks

Bank notes actually originated as promissory notes—in other words, as a check. A check is simply a receipt someone writes to someone else for money that is supposed to be on deposit and is available when the check is redeemed. When someone overdraws their personal checking account, the check will not clear. In many ways this is not that different from a bank note that is not sufficiently backed by real assets or well supported by the trust citizens have in the local economy and government.

QUESTION?

Do people actually collect checks?
Checks are collectible, but only as an esoteric area of the numismatic hobby. Some people collect checks based on who signed them, based on the bank on which they are drawn, or by how fancy the vignettes appearing on some of them may be.

Cancelled nineteenth- and twentieth-century checks are readily available and can be assembled into an interesting and eye-catching collection at modest cost. For example, you could collect checks signed by former U.S. presidents. However this might cost more than other themed collections because of the prominence of the people signing the checks.

Smart Cards

Charge cards began as open credit accounts usable within specific department stores that granted their client credit lines. Eventually, the charge card evolved into the universal payment card used so commonly as a substitute for checks or cash today. Collectors may be interested in finding some of the early twentieth-century credit cards that appear to be nothing more than merely a metal token on which an account number representing the individuals credit account with a specific store is inscribed.

As technology improved, credit card technology evolved as well. The initial credit card token with the account number appearing on it was eventually replaced with a cardboard card, which in turn was replaced with a more durable plastic card. In more recent history a magnetic strip has been added to the plastic card, the magnetic strip being able to be read by specialized equipment, with the charge then electronically transferred appropriately.

FACT

Cities in Denmark have experimented extensively with a "cashless" society in which smart cards would become the only currency vehicle, however even there coins still dominate as circulating money.

During the 1990s it appeared the "smart" card, on which a computer chip was imbedded, might become the next step in currency. This computer chip is capable of storing value electronically. Special readers allow the value on the card to be vended instantly for goods and services, including through vending machines.

Despite the initial popularity of the smart cards the cards failed to become widely accepted. Today they are in sporadic use, but once again the coin as hard currency has come out on top as the perpetual king of currency.

Bank Transfers

Coin collectors might notice that there are a surprising number of $20 double eagle gold coins available on the market in very high grades. This is because at one time the major function of this denomination was to transfer value between banks. The average citizen wouldn't carry a $20 coin. Such a coin represented several weeks wages and had far too great a purchasing power to make it practical. In 1860, eleven years after the introduction of the $20 double eagle, the average wage for a six-day work week for a skilled laborer was $9.72, according to *Historical Statistics of the United States*, published by the U.S. Department of Commerce.

Collectors will also observe that $500 and $1,000 bank notes occasionally appear through collector markets and once in a while over the counter at banks. These are still legal tender, but the highest bank note denomination currently issued by the United States is $100. Once again, these higher denomination notes served a purpose, primarily being used for bank transfers. The value of one of these notes simply represents more money than the average person earned in a week at the time they were printed.

All this has changed in the electronic age. Today banks transfer money electronically, aided by computers. It is no longer necessary to make the physical transactions that were made in the past with either gold coins or with high denomination bank notes.

FACT

During 2000, the Bank of Canada ceased using $1,000 bank notes to deter money laundering by criminals. Interpol has encouraged the European Union to follow this example since 500- and 1,000-euro notes are issued.

Electronic transfers are so commonplace today that any cash transaction involving $10,000 or more in coins or bank notes now requires being reported on a special form to the IRS.

Recent Coinage Innovations

Some collectors think innovations on coins ended with the invention of the collar. Others think the invention of the automatic coining machine brought coinage technology as far as can be expected. This simply isn't true. Early every year government and privately owned mints from all over the world convene during the Basel International Coin Fair in Switzerland. At this fair new technologies are unveiled, some of which will later be used on coinage, while others may be dismissed as novelties or impractical.

Braille

People involved in coin manufacture have always been aware of the need for the sight impaired to be able to distinguish between different coins. The diameter, shape, and edges of a coin are easy to distinguish by feel rather than needing to be physically seen.

Yet it is even more helpful to add Braille to both bank notes and coins to make them easier to identify by the sight impaired. Israel added Braille to its bank notes during the 1970s, and Italy added Braille to its coins during the 1980s.

FACT

The 2003 Alabama quarter is the first United States circulating coin on which Braille appears.

Braille is still not universally used on circulating coinage, but the concept has slowly gained favor in other countries. The shape, size, and varying edges of certain coinage are still the primary ways in which the sight impaired can differentiate between coin denominations.

A 500-lire coin with Braille.

Ringed Bimetal Coins

One of the more sensational and eye appealing innovations in modern coinage is the ringed bimetal coin, an ancient concept revived once more by the Italian State Mint. During 1982, these coins were introduced for circulation in Italy, Monaco, San Marino, and Vatican City.

Ringed bimetal coins have one metal as the center or plug with a ring about this center comprised of a metal of a distinctively different color. Not only are these coins easy to identify by sight and feel, but they are challenging to counterfeit as well. For these reasons ringed bimetal coinage has become popular for high denomination coins issued in circulation in many countries.

For example, in Canada the minor denomination coins between 5 and 50 cents are comprised of nickel, while the dollar coin is a distinctively golden yellow aureate, and the circulating $2 coin is a ringed bimetal coin with a golden color aluminum-bronze center and a white metal color nickel composition outer ring.

A Canadian $2 coin.

The center plug in the first modern ringed bimetal coins is easily removed. France introduced a 10-franc coin where the two metals lock when the image is struck onto the blank, solving the problem.

The concept introduced in 1988 by Monnaie de Paris, the French mint, was to utilize a center plug in which there are several small holes about the edge. When fitted with the ring and simultaneously struck to impress the coinage images, the pressure from the striking causes some metal from the outer ring to flow into the cavities provided in the edge of the center plug, thus locking the two together.

Further innovations have followed. Several countries have now produced ringed trimetal coins using a center plug and two surrounding rings of different color metals.

Ringed bimetal coins are so popular that a Worldwide Bi-metallic Collectors Club was established, devoted to collecting these coins exclusively. The club is so active that it sends a weekly e-newsletter to its members.

The only ringed bimetal coin the United States issued is the commemorative 2000-P Library of Congress $10. This coin has a silver center with a gold ring.

Color-Enchantments

The next logical progression from ringed bimetal coins is to artificially colorize them. But color enhancing the surface can become a labor intensive process. Although this may make a coin attractive enough to market to collectors, it is not practical for mass production for a circulation coin.

The United States Mint has never issued color-enhanced Silver American Eagle coins. Color-enhanced examples of these coins have been painted outside the mint and should not command a premium value due to this colorization—some dealers pay less than the intrinsic value for painted SAE coins since the coins are defaced.

Color-enhanced coins developed accordingly. At first there were coins that were made in very limited numbers and painted by hand meant exclusively for collector consumption. Several mints later developed methods through which significant numbers of coins could be color enhanced using machines, paving the way for possible circulation coins in full color at some later date. Another process that is being studied is enameling.

Holograms

Holographic devices are more challenging to apply to a metal than to a paper surface. The most logical way for this to be done is by placing a decal with the device on the blank surface. Should such a coin circulate the device would quickly wear. For this reason holograms appeared on paper money as an anti-counterfeiting device before the same technology was able to be made practical to be applied to coins. Nonetheless both the Fabrica de Moneda y Timbre (Spanish mint) and the privately owned Pobjoy Mint in England developed the concept for coins separately from each other during the 1990s.

This technology was initially applied only to noncirculating legal tender commemorative coins as a novelty. In 1994, Spain used this technology on some of its higher denomination 500-peseta coins to discourage counterfeiting. The technology has since been used on other lower denomination circulating Spanish coins as well.

Nontraditional Metals

Examine nineteenth- and early twentieth-century coins. The metal composition of these coins will typically be bronze, copper, nickel, silver, or gold. One of the more exciting technologies now being applied to modern coinage is the introduction of other metals.

Using these metals is important because it offers diversity and also because some are harder than others, for that reason not wearing out as fast in circulation, while others such as aluminum are simply inexpensive and work well when issuing very low denomination coins.

Alloys have developed a long way as well. These innovative alloys are important because of their hardness or their inexpensive cost and also because some are distinctively different in color from the more traditional golden yellow, silver white, and copper brown colors of coinage of the past.

The question has to be raised: Will durable plastic coins ever circulate?

FACT

During World War II, inexpensive coins were made for the Nazi-occupied Lodz ghetto in Poland comprised of aluminum-manganese. Manganese is flammable and alleged reports indicate that people burned the coins to warm themselves or to heat meals.

Bank Note Innovations

Paper products have evolved from papyrus through our acid-free archival quality materials of today. Bank notes have improved with time as well, not only regarding the materials on which the notes are printed, but the techniques in which the notes are printed. All this is in a continuing effort to remain one step ahead of counterfeiters.

Counterfeiting has been with us just about as long as we have had money to spend. Coins were the primary target of counterfeiters until such a time as when it became more profitable to counterfeit bank notes. Forgers took full advantage of the fact the average citizen couldn't recognize the many notes issued by the wildcat banks of the nineteenth century, sometimes altering the denomination on a genuine note, while other times making fantasy issues on banks that might not even exist. Since today high denomination circulating money is almost always in bank note rather than in coinage form counterfeiters are more likely to counterfeit bank notes than coins, although such modern coins as Canada's loon dollar and Great Britain's pound coin are known to be counterfeited.

Watermarks

By 1772, Saxony was issuing paper money on which watermarks appear as a security device. Although watermarks are still used on paper money today fibers imbedded in the paper were recognized as a better counterfeit deterrent as early as the 1880s. All U.S. paper money has these specially imbedded fibers.

Simply put a watermark is a design or a pattern imbedded into paper at the time of the paper's manufacture. The watermark is added to the paper by making thicker or thinner layers of pulp at some area of the paper when the pulp is still wet. This is the reason why such images are called "water" marks.

Images of animals, geometric designs, heraldic devices, and the names of either the government of issue or the paper manufacturer have appeared on watermarked paper money. Considering that watermarks have appeared on paper money at least from the eighteenth century, it may appear to be strange, but watermarks as a counterfeit deterrent on circulating U.S. Federal Reserve notes is only a recently added innovation.

Printing Techniques

Embossing, indirect letterpress, and intaglio are some of the many printing techniques employed when bank notes are printed. Serial numbers can be considered a printing technique as well.

Embossing is a process utilizing a metal die to create a raised impression on a piece of paper. Indirect letterpress involves special plate prints on the blanket of an offset press, the blanket then offsetting the image onto the paper.

According to the Bureau of Engraving and Printing, intaglio involves "printing plates [that] are covered with ink and then the surface of each plate is wiped clean which allows the ink to remain in the design and letter grooves of the plates. Each [bank note] sheet is then forced, under extremely heavy pressure (estimated at twenty tons), into the finely recessed lines of the printing plate to pick up the ink. The printing impression is three dimensional in effect and requires the combined handiwork of highly skilled artists, steel engravers, and plate printers. The surface of the note feels slightly raised, while the reverse side feels slightly indented."

Inks that appear as different images depending on how the note is held are quickly becoming part of the basic printing techniques used on modern bank notes.

Complex geometric designs are an important part of bank note printing since it is so difficult for these designs to be duplicated by forgers. Although vignettes and geometric designs have been employed for several centuries it was C. A. Broling who in 1829 first introduced the designs so well known today, using them on Swedish bank notes. The Bank of England Printing Works employed CAD (computer-aided design) technology to produce such complex anti-counterfeiting artwork beginning in 1985.

FACT

Serial numbers were added to nineteenth-century bank notes by hand, however in 1899 Giesecke & Devrient introduced printed serial numbers as they are applied today.

Security Threads

A single thread typically added horizontally to a bank note known as a security thread has become a popular anti-counterfeiting device used on many current bank notes worldwide. This is a distinct thread, often silver in color, that with some care can be pealed off the note, although since without such a thread the note will likely be considered to be counterfeit this isn't a wise idea.

The thread often has micro-printing on it. It may have a hologram as well. Some of these security threads are "windowed," where the thread is weaved in and out of the note through one side to the other as if sewn into it rather than appearing as a single uninterrupted metallic strip.

Front-to-Back Registration

Front-to-back printing registration is one of the marvels of modern printing technology. It involves a design divided into two parts that are printed in perfect registration on the front and back of the note. When the note is held to direct light, these two parts merge to be seen together as a single design or symbol.

Some modern bank notes comprised of polymer go one step further. These notes have a clear or windowed area able to be viewed on either side of the note. The front-to-back registration is then printed on this windowed area.

Micro-Printing

Another modern marvel of printing technology is micro-printing. At one time such technology was something expected to be used by spies—using micro-dots to hide something being smuggled from one country to another. Today micro-printing is widely used as one of the complexities that make vignettes and other standard designs so difficult to duplicate.

Alternatives to Paper

The terms bank note and paper money have long been used simultaneously to mean the same thing. This is quickly changing. In 1983, the Isle of Man used plastic composition bank notes for the first time. Only a year later, Canada began issuing bank notes using Canadian flax rather than U.S. cotton in its folding money. In 1988, Note Printing Australia introduced the world to its first circulating polymer (plastic) substrate bank notes, a note also using a windowed front-to-back registration device and a hologram. Bank notes had gone high tech.

Australian polymer note.

Since that time, NPA has exported its technology to other countries, while Switzerland rushed to develop plastic/polymer materials on which bank notes could be printed. Today Australian and Swiss bank notes can be considered to be the best, technologically speaking, in the world, due to modern printing techniques and the paper substitutes each introduced.

Practicality: Coins or Notes?

There is cost involved regardless of if a coin or a bank note is used as money. As they circulate each wears out and must eventually be replaced. This involves yet more cost, including the cost of destroying the coin or note to be replaced.

Do the Math

Government sponsored studies indicate a low denomination paper bank note will wear out within twelve to eighteen months in circulation, while a coin of the same value will wear out in twenty to forty years. This is a big incentive that in recent years has motivated a significant number of nations to replace their lowest denomination bank notes with coins. Polymer composition bank notes, of course, once again challenge a coin regarding durability, although production costs for such a note may be higher.

There are some disadvantages to high denomination coins replacing bank notes. One disadvantage is weight. Another is the counting machinery necessary when exchanging coins or bank notes for equal value in a foreign currency. This is why banks and foreign exchanges seldom redeem foreign coins, but they will often convert foreign bank notes.

Machiavellian Politics

Canada ceased issuing the dollar bill when the loon dollar coin was introduced in 1987. In 1984, Great Britain began circulating its £1 coin, withdrawing the bank note of the same denomination simultaneously. Despite griping by the general public that they would prefer the old paper bank notes to coins, the governments persisted and today these coins circulate regularly while the government enjoys lower costs.

In the United States, the reintroduction of the dollar coin has failed three times. The United States has steadfastly refused to withdraw the dollar bank note at the same time the dollar coin is being introduced. Congressional opponents of the idea of a circulating dollar coin find ways to justify their math that there is no cost-saving realized by replacing the dollar bill with a coin. Companies that sell the specially made paper used to print U.S. bank notes lobby Congress to discourage legislation that would follow the examples of what has happened in Canada, Great Britain, and in many other countries around the world. Will the United States have a circulating dollar coin that will succeed in its future? Only time will tell.

Precious Metal Coins Today

Today we use fiat rather than specie coins as circulating money, coins of little intrinsic value rather than gold and silver composition coins that are "worth their weight." Collectors may be interested in knowing there is still a place for precious metal coins other than in commemoratives today, but it is in the third realm—that of bullion coinage—that precious metal finds its true modern function.

Maria Teresa Taler

In 1780 Austria struck the Maria Teresa taler, a good silver content dollar or crown size coin that was accepted throughout international trading circles almost everywhere. Some Arab countries countermarked the coins to ensure they were of good quality silver, or to identify that a merchant had checked the coins for authenticity.

The Maria Teresa taler became so successful that the date 1780 remains on subsequent issues still being made at the mint in Vienna today. Since 1780 mints in at least eleven different countries have struck this coin. This is a true international trade coin.

Official Restrikes

Encouraged by the success of the 1780 Austrian silver taler coin, Austria has in modern history continued to strike at least two denominations of gold coins, still using the date 1915 on each. Mexico has restruck gold coins dated 1959. Others exist. There is some assurance to the person who wants to hold gold in coinage form when there is such consistency to the coins this person wants to own.

The Krugerrand

In 1967 South Africa entered the world gold bullion coin market by introducing the Krugerrand. This is a one ounce composition coin that can be traded without the need for a costly and time consuming assay that is necessary when an ingot of gold is sold. Due to good marketing the Krugerrand quickly came to dominate world gold coin markets, only to decline in popularity by 1985 due to the racial separatist South African government policy called apartheid.

The Post-Apartheid World

Other gold bullion coins, including the Canadian Maple Leaf, existed by the time of the apartheid problems, however it wasn't until South Africa's Krugerrand lost its commanding share of the world gold bullion coin market that these competing coins were able to take and successfully hold a significant section of this lucrative market.

Today the Canadian Maple Leaf, Austrian Philharmonic, British Britannia, China Panda, and the United States' American Eagle bullion coin programs among others are household names within the bullion coin markets.

What started as a gold bullion coin market has expanded as well. Today silver and platinum bullion coins are also available to anyone who wants to hold these metals for investment or security. It is possible other valuable metals may at some later date also become popular as bullion coins.

chapter 19

Numismatics as a Profession

At one point or another, most coin collectors daydream about turning our favorite pastime into a full-time profession. There are people whose hobby is also their livelihood, but most people work because they need their day jobs to make a living, rather than because they love what they are doing.

The Coin Dealer

One of the nice things about being a coin dealer is that the profession can be entered on several levels. You can be a part-time dealer, a vest pocket dealer, or a full-time dealer. Some coin stores hire employees, but you must first have a level of expertise before most will take an interest in you. Before you consider coins as a business, take the following into consideration.

Focusing on Pleasure or Profit

There is a difference between participating in a hobby and turning it into a profession. You are in the hobby for recreation, but you enter the same activity as a profession with the goal of making money. But of course, keep in mind there is no get-rich-quick scheme in coin collecting, not unless you are planning to go to jail later!

The business of coins is different from the hobby of coins. Profit is the primary objective in the business. Turnover is the key. You have merchandise to sell, so you can't afford to fall in love with it. You can't add the inventory to your own private collection. If you can't separate the hobby from the business, don't go into numismatics as a profession.

You can derive enjoyment from being in coins as a business, but the excitement is in making deals and handling many desirable coins, but not in keeping them permanently. Let the collector have his own private museum. A coin dealer whose inventory becomes a museum is going to go broke!

Buying Is the Key

The very first thing new coin dealers must understand is that selling inventory is not that challenging. There are many venues through which coins (and bank notes) can be sold at a reasonable pace, but this isn't shoe sales.

When a coin is sold, you can't telephone a manufacturer to order another truck load. Buying is the key to success in this business. But of course, that's buying for the right price so you can realize a reasonable profit later.

You have to establish price levels at which you are willing to buy, and you must stick to these prices. If you start buying at too high a level, your profit margins will suffer. But at the same time if you start buying too low, your prices won't be competitive to what other dealers will pay.

There are many different ways to purchase inventory. Some dealers advertise locally or in hobby publications that they buy coins. Other dealers offer appraisals, hoping to have the opportunity to buy what they have appraised.

Another way to purchase inventory is to visit coin shows, buying at wholesale prices from other dealers or from the public if you rent table space on the bourse. This is a very competitive but challenging way to do business. Everyone at the show is competing, doing the same thing with similar merchandise. If your prices are not competitive, people will go elsewhere with what they want to sell. You will also need a good line of credit or deep pockets to do sufficient business to make it worth your effort.

FACT

Many new coin dealers begin their business using their own collections as their initial inventory. Without a plan to purchase additional inventory, these businesses quickly fold once the initial merchandise is sold.

This is why the entry-level coin dealer must first decide the level of his participation in the business of coins. If you do not have the time or money to support this business full time, you may want to consider either buying and selling by visiting dealers with rented table space at conventions, becoming a part-time or weekend dealer, or working for someone else.

There is always some new, more imaginative way to find and purchase collectible coins, but without some way to continuously restock your inventory you will not have a business. You quickly learn the true meaning of the word "rare" when you sell a rare coin and try to replace it with another.

Understanding Turnover

Museums and collectors keep their coins. Dealers do not. Like any other retail business, the velocity of turnover of the coin dealer's merchandise is the key to success. Profit margins are typically very narrow in the coin business, making the turnover even more important.

There is a common misconception that coin dealers buy for ridiculously low prices, then sell for tremendous profits. There is always a good deal out there somewhere where more profit is possible, but any honest coin dealer will let the sellers know they have valuable coins and will pay them fair wholesale prices. Dealers who are not honest with their clients risk losing their reputations and opportunities to do business once word spreads about their dealings.

A profit margin of 5 to 15 percent may not sound like much, but if you can turn over your merchandise—in any business—several times a year you will likely make a very good living. The coin business is no different.

Coin dealers understand how to turn over merchandise quickly and where to sell it quickly if need be. Once coins are purchased the dealer must decide which coins are worth the time and effort to resell to collectors, and which coins should be sold for their scrap or intrinsic metal value. It takes time and effort to prepare something for the retail market, so sometimes it's better to sell coins wholesale, or to a precious metals dealer.

As an example, there are no rare dates in the silver content Roosevelt dime series of 1946 to 1964. If someone sells a coin dealer a complete date and mint mark set, the labor to assemble the set has already been committed. The set can be purchased and sold intact. However, if someone sells a coin dealer a bag of miscellaneous silver Roosevelt dimes, the coins will likely be relegated to the melting pot at a precious metal establishment or they will be added to a silver dime bag that will be traded as a commodity. It simply isn't worth the labor and time to sort through the dimes to assemble more sets for retail purposes. The cost of labor is simply too high.

Increasing Your Knowledge

The University of Tubingen in Germany has a numismatic program, but there is no such educational system in the United States. Dealers learn about the coin trade by reading, collecting, and gathering experience. You can attend educational seminars at many major coin conventions, the annual summer seminars at the American Numismatic Association in Colorado Springs, Colorado, or forums held periodically at the American Numismatic Society in New York.

There is an old saying, "first the book, then the coin." A surprising number of serious collectors have never invested in the books they should have in their libraries about what they are collecting. This is amazing considering that without this knowledge they are at the mercy of the person from whom they are buying and to whom they may later want to resell.

The best way to learn about collector coins is to purchase some, then resell them to judge your skill and knowledge. Always begin with inexpensive coins, graduating to the more expensive coins once you become proficient.

Do not assume you will deal only in very rare coins unless you are prepared to spend a lot of money on inventory. Common material sells as well. You will need knowledge of both, but above all you will need to learn to grade accurately.

You need to learn how to authenticate and grade coins before you become a coin dealer. Although there are third-party authentication and grading services, the vast majority of the coins (and bank notes) you will encounter will not be encapsulated by these services. You may have to authenticate and determine the grade on coins on short notice. You will also need to know which coins are more valuable than others and learn what a fair market value for each item or set of coins may be. This may sound daunting, but while it's true that there will always be something new in the coin business, a surprising number of transactions may be repetitive.

Getting into the Show Circuit

One of the major reasons coin dealers can turn over their inventory at a reasonable velocity is the coin show. There are local and regional coin shows virtually every weekend of the year, with larger conventions periodically as well. One thing coin dealers learn to do is travel, both to buy and to sell.

Collectors attend coin shows, but not usually in the great numbers that are desirable in order to do a meaningful retail business. Many collectors attending shows have only modest amounts to spend, but it can consume a lot of a dealer's time in the process. What the average collector doesn't appreciate is that dealers attend shows to maximize what they can sell. They are willing to spend time with a collector of some consequence, but they can't afford to spend inordinate amounts of time with collectors who are there more for entertainment than to spend money.

Dealers make most of their money at coin shows by selling inventory at discounted prices to other dealers. These other dealers may want this inventory because they know they have customers at home for the merchandise, or dealers may feel they can add value to their inventories by buying large amounts of merchandise at reasonable prices.

It takes time to get ready for a coin show. Merchandise to be taken to a show must be identified, graded, priced, and packaged. It must then be secured, and at the show it must be displayed.

FACT

A dealer attends a coin show to make money, not to entertain the public. Collectors not prepared to spend money on the bourse should expect dealers to concentrate on paying customers.

Many shows have a period at the beginning of the event that is for dealers only. This is the best time for dealers to engage each other over stock prior to the general public entering the show. Once the public enters the show, some dealers concentrate on the collectors, while other dealers continue to trade primarily with other dealers or combine the two depending on the foot traffic or lack of it.

Coin dealer table at a bourse.

Shows are competitive. Everybody has similar merchandise to sell, and collectors have limited funds with which to buy. It takes skill, showmanship, and an attractively display of merchandise to attract buying customers, while sorting them out from the tire kickers who are wasting their time.

Dealers typically guarantee the authenticity and condition of what they sell, though they often require coins or notes to be returned unsealed in the packaging in which it had been shipped. By insisting on this provision, the dealer protects himself from clients who mishandle or switch merchandise.

Considering Mail Order

One major reason some dealers attend the show bourse is to stock up on coins for their mail order list. A traditional way of doing business is offering a fixed price list to customers by mail. Potential new coin dealers should be prepared to build a mailing list of their own. This will take time and money. You can purchase lists, but the reliability of purchased lists is often questionable.

Once a dealer has established a mailing list (or similarly a Web site), the dealer must find sufficient merchandise to offer on a regularly scheduled listing. Then all of the merchandise must be fully described, fairly priced, and (ideally) illustrated. Mail order business can be very profitable, but it involves significant overhead. You must consider the cost of mailing, printing, imaging inventory, and cataloging.

Boosting Over-the-Counter Sales

The traditional way to buy and sell coins is over the counter in a store. This was a typical scenario for many years, but in more recent history it is becoming a thing of the past due to ever-increasing overhead. Today most coin stores are no longer there to sell coins, but to buy them. The major function of the storefront is to encourage people to bring in their coins and bank notes to dispose of them. The dealer will then sell most of them at coin shows, through a mail order list, at auctions, or via the Internet.

FACT

There are some imaginative ways to attract business. Some dealers hold discovery days on which they offer free appraisals (in hopes of buying what they appraise), others invite a coin club to meet at their facility, and still others hold small auctions at their establishments. This is marketing. What draws people to your shop is only limited to your imagination.

Dealers make some over-the-counter sales at local coin shops, but the same problem exists as when selling directly to the public at a coin show. How much time can a dealer afford to invest in a client if that client is not going to spend very much money? A collector who enters a store to casually browse will likely purchase very little but will require much supervision, while another collector who comes in with a specific list of what he wants will consume less time and will likely spend more money.

The Auctioneer

Another way to get into the business of coins is to become a coin auctioneer. Rare coin auctions are an established way through which many coins and bank notes are sold. However, this is not an easy or inexpensive process. Before you hold an auction, you usually need a published catalog. This catalog in turn costs money since each lot must be described, graded, provided with an estimate of value, and (ideally) illustrated.

Auctioneers likely specialize in either a certain range of values for what they offer, or the type of numismatic merchandise. For this reason there are local auctioneers who likely don't offer anything of more than modest value, while there are national and international auction houses that may specialize is selling expensive rarities. Some auctioneers specialize in coins or bank notes of the United States while others may offer foreign or ancient coins. All this depends on the expertise and the financial backing of the auctioneer.

Auctioneering Laws

Laws governing auctioneering vary between cities and states. There are no federal regulations. Always check with local authorities prior to planning an auction to ensure you are not in violation of the local laws.

It is in the best interest of the would-be auctioneer to take classes in how to conduct an auction regardless of if this is required prior to obtaining a local auction license or not. Running an auction is not as simple as just standing on a podium in front of a crowd accepting their bids.

In some places, a temporary auction license can be purchased for a specific amount of time by virtually anyone wanting to conduct such a sale. There are other places where state licensing may be required, including rigid testing. Some states have reciprocal agreements with other states; in other words if you're licensed in one state you may be able to hold auctions in other states.

Public Auctions

Holding an auction requires a lot of behind-the-scenes work. It's best for the auctioneer and seller to sign a contract. Any reserve price (a minimum price below which it is agreed in advance the item will not be sold) must be established, as must the time period following the sale in which either merchandise must be returned or paid for. All other marketing related services, security for the merchandise, and the auctioneer's fee must be spelled out in this contract. An oral contract is not in anyone's best interest.

Before the auction, the auctioneer usually allows the pubic to view the merchandise. This means the auctioneer has to set up a secure environment for the viewing. This happens regardless of if coins are being sold at a local general merchandise auction or a sophisticated rare coin auction. Usually, the auctioneer puts together illustrated catalogs as well. The auctioneer also must make arrangements to register potential bidders in advance to bid and establish rules of the auction such as if bidders are expected to pay immediately following the end of the auction unless other arrangements have been made in advance.

"Auction fever" is when someone bids far beyond the established value of an object due to the excitement of the bidding competition. Auctioneers and consignors welcome such irrational exuberance.

Anyone consigning to or conducting a public auction must understand there will likely be coin dealers in the audience. These dealers may be representing a client for a fee, or they may be looking to buy at wholesale prices for their own inventory. When this second scenario is true these dealers will bid conservatively.

There are three types of public auctions. English auctions are the traditional type in which bidding begins low and ends with the highest bid being accepted. Coin auctions almost exclusively use this method. Dutch auctions begin with the auctioneer suggesting what he expects to be the highest bid, with ensuing descending bids. There is also the silent auction, typically seen in Japan and other places, where sign language representing a bid is simultaneously flashed by all potential bidders, with the auctioneer picking the high bid from the crowd.

Mail Bid Sales

Instead of holding a public auction, you might consider mail bid sales. Mail bid sales do not require the licensing that is required to conduct a public auction. Once again some form of cataloging of the items to be offered must be prepared, ideally with illustrations. A time and date when the mail bid sale closes must be announced, with the auction house being prepared to accept a significant number of last minute telephone bids.

FACT

"Bid or buy" sales are those mail bid sales in which the client either accepts the published suggested bid price or makes an offer below this figure. If no one bids the suggested bid price, the customer with the highest offer wins.

Mail bid sales, just as with mail order catalogs, require advertising and a reliable mailing list to succeed. There is significant overhead and obtaining merchandise for the next sale will always be a continuing challenge, but this can be a very profitable way to do business if you get a good following of interested clients. Just as with the mail order catalog, the mail bid coin dealer must establish a merchandise return policy. You may require customers to return questionable merchandise (authenticity or grade) within a certain period of time, and still sealed in the packing in which it was shipped to them. It is important to honor all claims regarding authenticity. There are laws against knowingly selling counterfeit coins.

Internet Auctions

You might consider selling coins or notes online. The Internet is the superhighway for selling merchandise. It can involve all the positive aspects of a public auction and of a mail bid sale, but with a higher velocity regarding the transactions. Full disclosure is the key to the Internet. Unfortunately there is a lot of fraud out there and many Web sites fail to properly police their clients.

There are several ways to sell coin-related merchandise on the Internet—using an established auction site such as eBay, creating your own Web site, or creating your own auction Web site.

The first and most obvious way is to use an existing auction-oriented Web site that accepts consignments from others, such as eBay. Many collectors as well as professional dealers use these services to sell coins.

Selling coins or bank notes on the Internet can require a lot of your time and energy. It involves describing, grading, pricing, and imaging each item. You must also collect remittances, clear the checks, package, and ship the merchandise.

You can also establish your own Web site, however this will involve publicity. People won't visit your Web site simply because it is there. You must advertise and link key words to major search engines to draw people to the site. Once a following has been established, it is easier to do business, as long as you can maintain the standards acceptable to your clients.

The third option is to establish your own auction Web site, but this can be costly. Determine what you want to sell, the time and money you are willing to expend, and then identify if you want to piggyback your merchandise on someone else's Web site, establish a site of your own, or build an auction-oriented Web site.

The Archaeologist

Yet another way to make coins your profession is in archaeology. However, this requires formal education. Some professional archaeologists are experts in coins, but this is a narrow field of expertise in which few people are involved on a full-time basis.

Coins as Index Fossils

Coins can help identify an archaeological dig site. Trade routes, information regarding local economics, contemporary culture, technical advancement, and other such information can be derived by coins found at such sites. Coins have helped identify the age of a site and the political boundaries of an area, and in a few cases may depict the only known images of a bygone sovereign.

It is never recommended that coins be cleaned, however considering the poor condition in which most coins are recovered from the ground or water the resident numismatist at a dig site needs to know how to clean up the found coins sufficiently to allow them to be identified.

This is not a glamorous or well-paying profession. More times than not a museum curator familiar with coins may be invited to join a dig or underwater salvage team to help identify coins once they are recovered. Most of these coins can be expected to be in poor shape due to having been in the ground or submerged.

Education

Although there are many amateur archaeologists, those who do this for a living tend to be museum curators or educators who practice archaeology as a sideline as time permits. Professional archaeologists earn doctorates in this field from major universities.

Since there are no universities in the United States with a program relating directly to numismatics as a scientific discipline, it helps to be involved with coins either as a collector or as a museum curator if you are to become involved with coins found at archaeological dig sites.

The Museum Curator

Another profession that can involve numismatics is to be a museum curator. Many museums have coins among their holdings. Some museums have formal collections, however many simply have some coins mixed among other related artifacts. Only a few full-time museum curators specialize in numismatic collections. Most of these curators have graduate degrees in the humanities.

Function of Coins in Museums

Most museums only display a fraction of their holdings at any time. Part of this is due to time, space, and money, however museums also function as repositories. Many of the artifacts housed in museums are there so they will be available for further study at some later date.

Coins can be displayed by themselves, but they are often part of more encompassing exhibits. Some coins are acquired as gifts, others are purchased, while still others may have been part of the find at an archaeological dig site.

Many museums were established with major collections of something initially assembled by a collector or art connoisseur. There is an ongoing controversy regarding if private collectors should be allowed to own coins

Museum display case.

and other artifacts or if this takes away from a museum's ability to acquire these objects. Stifling antiquities laws in some countries have driven the trade in coins and antiquities underground, further depriving museums of the ability to acquire such objects.

Prominent Museums with Coin Collections

As was just mentioned, coins are often part of a larger exhibit rather than being the focus of the entire display as a collection. The following museums that are dedicated entirely or in part to coin collections may be of particular interest to collectors or to professionals seeking to become curators:

- The American Numismatic Association located in Colorado Springs, Colorado, is the largest coin collecting organization in the world. The ANA has a museum specializing in coins, tokens, medals, and bank notes, with a full-time curator.
- The American Numismatic Society in New York City is a scholarly organization specializing in numismatics. Its focus for years was ancient coins, but in more recent history it has made great strides embracing United States coins as well. The ANS has a highly educated full-time curatorial staff that conducts scholarly symposiums.
- The Smithsonian Institution in Washington, D.C., has a numismatic collection and a full-time curatorial staff that supervises it. Budgeting is always a problem since it is a government-owned entity.
- Other museums of importance exist for coins both in the United States and abroad. The British Museum in London, England, is likely the most prominent of these. Once again this museum has a highly educated full-time staff of curators that work with and study this ever-expanding collection.

The Treasure Hunter

Treasure hunting appears to be a glamorous way to work in the coin business full time, but it has its risks and can be costly. People have died attempting to salvage underwater treasure. There is significant cost involved, but the rewards can be spectacular as well.

A Financial Gamble

Think about it. If you are involved in underwater salvage you need a ship, sonar, personnel skilled in diving, diving equipment, insurance, and some very strong financial backers who may not be reimbursed for years, if ever.

You as the treasure hunter should not expect to be paid anything until first you find some treasure, recover it, prepare it for market, and sell it. This can take years. How long can you survive without some other source of income or significant savings? This is not something for the person making monthly payments on a house or with a family to support!

Research and Guesswork

Finding a treasure worth excavating takes research alongside some good old-fashioned guesswork. Depending on where you intend to search, you may require foreign language capabilities to research a lost ship, caravan, or whatever. The reliability of the documents you research is in question as well. This can take time and money.

Treasure Hunters Versus Governments

Governments, including that of the United States, have at times attempted to lay claim to a treasure after a professional treasure hunter has gone to the time and trouble to locate and salvage it. There have been costly court battles regarding ownership of such finds not only between the finder and the government, but with people who claim the treasure due to its previous ownership by an ancestor. Under the circumstances it is amazing treasure hunters succeed as well as they often do.

British treasure trove laws, as an example, allow the finder to keep the find under certain circumstances, while under other circumstances reward the finder with a fee from the price realized once the find has been sold. Not all governments are this generous, which is why sometimes such finds are kept secret and sold discretely.

Treasure hunting can be extremely profitable, but it can be a long, hard task getting to the payday.

appendix a

Glossary

Adjustment marks
Marks made on a coinage blank to ensure consistency when used to become a coin.

Alteration
The act of adding or changing a date or mint mark outside of a mint, usually to create the appearance a coin is a rarity.

Annealing
Heating of coin blanks to soften them prior to being struck with coinage dies.

Artificial toning
Tarnish appearing on a coin caused by purposeful improper storage to create the surface colors now appearing on that coin.

Assay
A destructive test through which the purity of metal can be determined.

Bag marks
Detrimental marks on the surface of a coin caused by banging against other coins when stored in bags.

Bank note
A promissory note issued by a banking agency through which assets are pledged valued at the same amount as the note issued against those assets.

Beaded border
A border of dots around the edge of a coin.

Billon
An alloy of copper and silver also known as potin, but containing more than half copper.

Bit
A pie-shaped piece cut from a Spanish 8-real coin to make change.

Blank
The round metal disk, or planchet, specially cut in preparation for the coin images to be added to make a coin.

Bourse
The area of a coin show where dealers buy and sell coins.

Branch mint
A remote mint facility that aids coinage production centralized at the main mint.

Brockage
An error coin on which one side is struck correctly, however the other side is the incuse mirror image of this other side.

Bullion
Platinum, palladium, gold, or silver coins struck to a specific weight and purity and meant to be traded for their intrinsic value rather than for their legal tender face value. These coins do not command a premium above this precious metal value. They are a convenience, circumventing the need for assaying the metal when it is sold.

Burnishing
A minting process through which coinage surfaces are brightened.

Business strike
A coin made by mass production and intended to circulate as money. The majority of coins encountered in coin collections will be business strikes.

Cabinet friction
The rub a coin receives from movement while in storage in a coin collection.

Cameo
A coinage finish in which the main devices appear to be frosted or otherwise set apart from the background.

Carbon spots
Detrimental oxidation specks appearing on the surfaces of a coin.

Cartwheel luster
The surface brilliance of an uncirculated coin originating from when the coin was first produced. This brilliance disappears when a coin circulates or is cleaned.

Cast
Most coins are produced by being struck rather than cast. A cast coin can be identified either by its soapy surface appearance or by tiny casting bubbles visible under magnification.

Certificate of authenticity
Specially printed certificates may guarantee the coin or coin set being sold is genuine, but be aware there is no guarantee the certificate remains with the coin for which it was originally issued. Such certificates often include metal purity, weight, and other statistics, as well as a serial number specific to that set for which the certificate is being issued.

Chop marks
Small Chinese character marks made on silver coins by Chinese merchants to ensure the purity of the precious metal content of the coins.

Clad coinage
Coins containing copper-nickel rather than silver alloys. U.S. clad coinage began in 1965. U.S. half dollar coins of 1965 to 1970 contain a low grade of silver and are called silver-clad coins.

Clash marks
A ghost-like impression of the image of the opposite side of a coin may appear on the other side. This image is due to the coinage dies having clashed without a coinage blank being in place between them during production immediately prior to the striking of the coin depicting clash marks. These are popular with collectors.

Cleaning
A serious taboo in coin collecting, cleaning a coin usually ruins any collector value it may have.

Clipped
A coin with some metal shaved from the edge, yet still used in commerce as if it is still of the correct weight for the denomination.

Coin
A coined metal composition object identified as having been struck by a coin-issuing government authority, with a specific legal tender face value. Do not confuse coins with medals and tokens.

Coin board
A board, folder, or book with holes of a specific diameter drilled into each page for the coins. Coin boards are typically referred to as penny boards.

Coin cabinet
A wooden or plastic chest of drawers made with slots to display or collect coins.

Coin dealer
A person who works either full or part time buying and selling coins for a profit without first acquiring the coins for collecting purposes.

Collar
The device that holds the coinage blank, also ensuring the blank remains round once the coin images have been struck onto that blank.

Commemorative
A coin struck for a limited amount of time to mark a person, place, or event. Some commemorative coins circulate, while others were made especially for collectors.

Commercial grade
An optimistic grade assigned to a coin that likely is truly a grade lower by most accepted grading standards.

Contact marks
Detrimental marks appearing on a coin from contact with other coins.

Contemporary counterfeit
A fake coin or note produced during the period when the coins were being struck or the notes were being printed to deceive the public, rather than at a later date strictly to deceive collectors.

Copper-nickel
Also called cupro-nickel, this is a coin composition mix used widely on modern circulation coins.

Corrosion
Any form of rust or oxidation appearing on the surface of a coin.

Counterfeit
A replica of a coin made without proper authority and meant either to deceptively circulate or to be sold to collectors.

Countermark
A mark or several marks added to a coin after its initial issue either by a government or by a private individual.

Cud
Occurs when a break in the coinage die interrupts the appearance of the image.

Currency
Although this term technically encompasses all circulating money, it is usually used as a reference to bank notes.

Date
The date appearing on modern coins identifies the year in which the coin was produced. Most coins prior to 1500 lack dates. Some of these earlier coins can be dated through their design elements or by the regnal year of the reigning monarch expressed on these coins.

Debasement
Any time the precious metal purity of coins is decreased the coin is said to be debased.

Deep mirror prooflike (DMPL)
A coin with prooflike surfaces sufficient that a reflection of the person viewing the coin can be seen.

Denomination

The legal tender face value imprinted on a coin or bank note. Ideally coins chosen for a collection will be worth more than this face value.

Denticles

The small notches about the outer edge of the obverse or reverse of many coins at the rim. Also called dentils.

Device

The main design element or achievement on a specific side of a coin.

Die

The tool from which an image of a coin is impressed onto a blank or planchet. Many dies are usually involved in producing coins since dies wear out from use.

Die alignment

The relationship of the alignment between the obverse and reverse dies. Coin alignment is opposites while medal alignment is when both sides correspond exactly to the other.

Die break

When a coinage die begins to break during use, cracks appear on the die and are transferred to coins being struck.

Die crack

The cracks from the die break being transferred from the disintegrating die. These die cracks will appear on coins as raised rather than as incused lines.

Die rust

An incorrectly stored coinage die will eventually rust. When such rust is polished away to use the die, it leaves deep recesses in the die that will be transferred to coins struck from that die.

Die state

The amount of wear on a working coinage die will determine the quality of the detail appearing on coins struck from that die. A late die state struck coin will not have the sharp detail an early die state struck coin will exhibit.

Die variety

A variation from the normally anticipated design of a coin caused by something that altered the individual die from which the coin was struck. Varieties are very popular among coin collectors.

Ding

A small mark appearing on a coin due to the coin having bumped against something.

Dipped

A coin that has been cleaned, likely by dipping the coin into a liquid solution. Collectors do not consider dipped coins to be desirable.

DMPL (Deep mirror prooflike)

A coin with prooflike surfaces sufficient that a reflection of the person viewing the coin can be seen.

Doubled die

A coin struck from a coinage die on which some or all of the images are doubled. This is a more desirable doubling than is strike doubling, in which the coinage blank was struck more than once to achieve the doubling appearance.

Double struck

A coin that was struck more than once by a working coinage die will exhibit doubling, but this should not be confused with a doubled die error coin. Double struck coins are the result of a production problem.

Edge

The side of a coin, not to be confused with the rim, which is the outer edge of the obverse or reverse.

Electrotype

A duplicate of a coin created using electrolytic methods. Metal is deposited into a mold made from the host coin.

Engraver

The person who designs the coinage dies; known as a celator in ancient times.

Error coins

Coins displaying problems due to mistakes made during production.

Essay

Also called an essai, the term represents experimental pieces, pattern coins, transitional, and trial pieces.

Exergue

The small area at about six o'clock on a coin, usually separated from the balance of the coin design by a line, where the date, value, or country of origin may appear.

Eye appeal

The perception of a coin or bank note from the item's outward appearance. This can include toning, strike quality, centering, and other such factors, other than condition.

Face value

The denomination value appearing on a coin or a bank note.

Fantasy issue

A coin that was never officially struck, such as an 1868 U.S. large cent or a coin issued by the nonexistent nation of Sealand.

Field

The open surface of a coin on which there is no design.

Fineness

The purity of the precious metal of a coin, typically expressed in decimal form such as .916 fine rather than as 22 karat. A .916 fine coin has 91.6 percent of that metal in it.

Flip

A 2-by-2 inch clear plastic holder into which a collectible coin is often placed.

Flow lines

Lines that are not always visible that are caused by the metal flow from the center of the coinage blank caused at the moment the blank was struck by the working coinage dies.

Forgery

A counterfeit, an unauthorized coin or bank note meant to deceive.

Friction
Wear appearing only on the highest points of coinage detail on a high grade coin.

Frosting
When coin design elements are set apart from a mirrorlike surface by a sandblast-like or crystallized-metal appearance, this is referred to as frosting or frosted devices.

Galvano
The model for a coin design that serves as a lathe before the design is transferred to a coin-size hub.

Gold certificate
A U.S. paper bank note issued with a gold color seal and a statement that the note is redeemable for the same value in gold or in gold coins. These notes are legal tender; however they have not been redeemable in gold since 1933. The words "gold certificate" must appear somewhere on the note.

Grade
The condition assigned to a coin based on the amount of wear the coin has received from circulation.

Grade rarity
When a common date coin is available in an uncommonly nice condition that commands a premium when sold to coin collectors because of the grade rather than because of the date it is said to be a grade rarity.

Hairlines
Light lines that appear on the surface of a coin due to the coin having been cleaned.

Hammered coins
Coins struck by hand rather than struck by machine.

High relief
The design elements on a coin or a medal are sufficiently high that the item is unable to be stacked. These are artistic pieces usually desired by collectors.

Hub
The steel device made from a galvano with the image of the coin design in positive that will be transferred to the working coinage dies as a negative image.

Impaired proof
A proof coin that has been mishandled and is for that reason less than perfect.

Incomplete strike
A coin lacking part of the design due to a problem during production.

Incuse
When coin design elements are impressed rather than raised above the surface of the coinage blank.

Ingot
A bar, typically composed of precious metal.

Janvier reducing machine
The machine used to produce hubs from galvanos.

Jeton
A counter used on gaming boards or during antiquated accounting practices but also as a substitute for coins.

Jugate

Two busts overlapping on one side of a coin are said to be appearing jugate.

Karat

A way in which the purity of gold can be expressed, based on 24 karat gold being pure gold. As an example, 22 karat gold is actually the fraction 22/24 or .916 fine gold.

Key date

This is an important, rare date and mint mark coin without which a coin series is not complete.

Lamination

A thin piece of metal that separates partially or entirely from the surface of a coin, impacting the design elements in the process.

Legends

The inscriptions appearing on a coin. Blundered legends are legends in which a mistake can be seen.

Lettered edge

A legend appearing on the edge of a coin rather than about the rim.

Liner

A coin on the border between two grades. Liners between the grades about uncirculated and uncirculated are called "sliders."

Lint marks

Miniscule light marks appearing on proofs due to hairlines created from lint originating from the fabric used when the dies were polished.

Love token

A coin on which one side has been planed off and replaced with engraved initials or a name.

Luster

The original glossy radiance of the surface of a coin originating from when it is first struck. Luster must be present for a coin to be considered to be uncirculated or mint state.

Marks

Detrimental blemishes appearing on coins due to contact with other coins or foreign objects.

Master die

The die made from a hub that will be used to make working coinage dies.

Master hub

The original hub made by the portrait lathe. The master hub will be used to make master dies.

Matte finish

A sandblast-like appearance on a proof or uncirculated coin.

Medal

A round metal object struck to honor or commemorate a person, place, or thing, or to display artwork. Medals are not legal tender and do not circulate as money or as a substitute for money.

Medieval coin

Any coin made between A.D. 476 (the date of the fall of the Roman Empire) and about 1500, that was produced by hand rather than machine.

Milling machine

Also known as an upsetting machine, this is the device through which coinage blanks are fed to upset the rims.

Milling marks

Marks left on the surface of a coin when that coin has made contact with the reeded edge of other coins.

Mint

A factory in which coins are made. Bank notes are not made in a mint unless the mint also has a security printing facility.

Mint error

Problems appearing on a coin originating from its manufacture, such as off-center strikes and coins lacking detail.

Mint luster

Also sometimes described as mint bloom, this is the original brilliance that appears on the surface of a coin when it is first struck. As a coin circulates and the surfaces wear, this luster dissipates and eventually is lost. Cleaning a coin will also remove any existing mint luster. There is no way to restore it.

Mint mark

Although mint marks do not appear on all coins, mint marks are initials or other identifying marks purposely placed on coins to identify the mint where coins were produced.

Mint set

A year set of uncirculated coins specially packaged and sold by a mint to collectors. These sets typically have a superior example of the same coins that are being released into circulation during that year.

Mintage

The number of coins produced of a specific date, mint mark, and denomination. Mintage records can suggest the availability of a coin, however they do not indicate the number surviving or the condition in which they survive, but simply the number manufactured.

Mishandled proof

A proof coin that is less than perfect due to handling, cleaning, or some other detriment following its production. Any coin grading less than proof 60 is a mishandled proof. Any proof coin graded less than proof 65 should be suspect.

Modern coin

Any machine-struck coins, typically dating from about 1500 or later depending on when the country of the coin's origin began to machine-strike coins.

Moneyer

The individual responsible for a mint. Moneyer's initials or symbols sometimes appear on their coins.

Mottlod toning

Uneven toning that may present less than desirable eye appeal.

Motto

Legends on coins appearing as inscriptions, such as "In God We Trust."

Nickel

A nickname for the 5-cent coin denomination based on the metal of the same name of which it is partially composed.

Noncirculating Legal Tender (NCLT)

A term applied to a specially struck coin, typically a commemorative, that although the coin has a legal tender value appearing on it, the coin is being issued for sale to collectors rather than to circulate as money.

Numismatist

A person who studies the economics, artistic quality, distribution, and other qualities of coins individually and as groups.

Obverse

The "heads" or face side of a coin.

Off-center strike

An error coin on which only part of the coin design appears due to the blank being out of position when the coin dies struck that blank.

Orange-peel surfaces

Surfaces on a gold coin that glow with an orange or sunset color due to remaining original toning.

Original toning

The glow from the surface of a coin when it was first struck. This original color effect disappears when a coin is circulated or cleaned.

Overdate

A date digit or several date digits impressed over another date digit on a coin.

Paper money

Another term for a bank note, however in recent history bank notes are no longer always made of paper.

Patina

The natural finish on the surfaces of a coin due to exposure to the environment.

Pattern

A coinlike product that is produced by a mint to test or demonstrate a potential new design, diameter, or metal composition for coinage.

Pedigree

The lineage of the ownership of a coin. Some coins can be traced to prestigious collections from the past.

Planchet

Blanks from which coins are produced.

Proof

A mirrorlike surface quality coin struck from higher polished dies and from specially prepared blanks or planchets, to be sold to collectors rather than circulated. Proof coins can typically be identified from their business strike quality counterparts by a squared rather than a round edge rim.

Prooflike

An uncirculated coin with mirrorlike surfaces similar to those of a proof coin.

Pure silver

Silver to the purity of .999 fine or .9999 fine (99.9 percent).

PVC (polyvinyl chloride)

A chemical used in plastic coin holders to make the holders flexible. PVC will react with the surface of coins, causing a green slime to appear on the surface nicknamed "green slime disease" or "PVC poisoning."

Rarity

The desirability of a coin based on the difference between the number of coins available and the demand for these coins among collectors and investors.

Reeding

The notches or grooves that appear about the edges of many coins. The origin of reeding was to discourage clipping or shaving metal from precious metal coins.

Replica

A copy of a coin or bank note made for souvenir purposes rather than to deceive the public or coin collectors. Under the Hobby Protection Act, modern replica coins must be prominently stamped with the word "copy."

Restrike

Coins struck at a later date than the initial issue, but using the same coinage dies. Not all restrikes are officially authorized.

Reverse

The "tails," or back side of a coin.

Rim

The raised area at the edge of the obverse and reverse of a coin. Don't confuse rim with the edge of the coin itself.

Silver certificate

A U.S. paper bank note issued with a blue color seal and statement that the note is redeemable for the same value in silver. These notes are legal tender, however they have not been redeemable in silver since 1968.

Slider

A coin bordering on being graded either about uncirculated or uncirculated, often sold for the more optimistic grade by coin dealers.

Specie

The precious metal of a circulating coin, typically gold or silver content.

Sterling silver

Silver to the purity of .925 fine or .925 percent purity; often misunderstood to be pure silver.

Token

A round metal object issued privately rather than by a government issuing authority, able to be vended or used at a specific place as a substitute for government issued money, sometimes within a certain time period.

Toning

The color changes on the surfaces of a coin due to the coin's contact with contaminants and chemical reactions with the atmosphere. Some collectors seek pleasing toning, while other insist on untoned coins.

Two-by-two holder

A cardboard holder with a see-through center typically of 2-by-2-inch size into which collectible coins are placed.

Type coins
Coins that are an example of their design type, typically collected in order to have an example of this design rather than due to the specific date and mint mark on the coin.

Variety
A minor change or alteration made in the design (also called "type"), date, or mint mark of a coin from what is otherwise the norm.

Vest pocket dealer
A part-time coin dealer who buys and sells at coin shows from an inventory he carries on his person rather than from bourse table space he has rented.

Vignette
The artistic designs appearing on bank notes.

Weak strike
A poorly struck coin on which some of the detail is missing for this reason. Commonly confused with wear.

Wear
The grade or condition of a coin is due to wear.

appendix b

References for Coin Collectors

Books for Your Library

The following is a list of recommended books on specialized and general areas of coin collecting. These books may be available through bookstores, public libraries, or coin club libraries.

Akers, David W. *Gold Dollars.* (Englewood, OH: Paramount Publications, 1975 to 1982 [volumes published for each gold denomination]).

American Numismatic Association. *Official ANA Grading Standards for United States Coins.* (Colorado Springs, CO: American Numismatic Association, 1991).

Bolender, M.H. *The United States Early Silver Dollars from 1794 to 1803.* (Iola, WI: Krause Publications, 1982, reprinted in 1987).

Breen, Walter. *Breen's Encyclopedia of United States Half Cents 1793–1857.* (South Gate, CA: American Institute of Numismatic Research, 1983).

Breen, Walter. *Walter Breen's Complete Encyclopedia of US and Colonial Coins.* (New York: Doubleday, 1988).

Bressett, Kenneth. *Guide Book of United States Currency.* (Atlanta, GA: Whitman Publishing, 1999).

Briggs, Larry. *The Comprehensive Encyclopedia of United States Liberty Seated Quarters.* (Lima, OH: John A. Feigenbaum & Co. 1991).

Browning, A.W. and Walter Breen. *The Early Quarter Dollars of the United States 1796–1838.* (New York: Bowers & Merena Galleries, 1925, reprinted in 1992).

Bruce, Colin II. *Unusual World Coins.* (Iola, WI: Krause Publications, 1992).

Carlotto, Tony. *The Copper Coins of Vermont.* (Chelsea, MI: Pub C-4, 1998).

Charlton, James. *The Charlton Standard Catalogue of Canadian Coins.* (Toronto, Canada: Charlton Press, 2005).

Cline, J.H. *Standing Liberty Quarters.* (Irvine, CA: Zyrus Press, 2006).

Cohen, Roger Jr. *American Half Cents—The Little Half Sisters.* (Arlington, VA: Wigglesworth & Ghatt, Co., 1982).

Crosby, S.ylvester S. *The Early Coins of America.* (Lawrence, MA: Quartermain Publications, Reissues 1974, 1983).

Davis, David; Logan, Russell; Lovejoy, Allen; McCloskey, John; and Subjack, William. *Early United States Dimes 1796–1837.* (Ypsilanti, MI: 1984).

Fletcher, Edward L. Jr. *The Shield Five Cent Series.* (Ormond Beach, FL: Dead End Publishing, 1994).

Fox, Bruce. *The Complete Guide to Walking Liberty Half Dollars.* (Virginia Beach, VA: DLRC Press, 1993).

Fuld, George, and Fuld, Melvin. *U.S. Civil War Store Cards.* (Lawrence, MA: Quarterman Publications, 1975).

Giedroyc, Richard. *Superstition, Urban Legends and Our Money.* (Baltimore, MD: PublishAmerica, 2004).

Guth, Ron, and Garret, Jeff. *United States Coinage: A Study by Type.* (Atlanta, GA: Whitman Publishing, 2005).

Judd, J. Hewitt. *United States Pattern Coins.* (Atlanta, GA: Whitman Publishing, 2005).

Kagin, Donald H. *Private Gold Coins and Patterns of the United States.* (New York: ARCO, 1981).

Kessler, Alan. *The Fugio Coppers.* (Newtonville, MA: Colony Coin Company, 1976).

Krause, Chester L. *Standard Catalog of United States Paper Money.* (Iola, WI: Krause Publications, 2005).

Krause, Chester L., and Mishler, Clifford. *Standard Catalog of World Coins.* (Iola, WI: Krause Publications, 2005).

Lange, David W. *History of the United States Mint and Its Coinage.* (Atlanta, GA: Whitman Publishing, 2005).

Lange, David W. *The Complete Guide to Lincoln Cents.* (Wolfeboro, NH: Bowers & Merena, 1996).

Lange, David W. *The Complete Guide to Buffalo Nickels.* (Virginia Beach, VA: DLRC Press, 2003).

Lange, David W. *The Complete Guide to Mercury Dimes.* (Virginia Beach, VA: DLRC Press, 1993).

Lawrence, David. *The Complete Guide to Barber Dimes.* (Virginia Beach, VA: DLRC Press, 1991).

Lawrence, David. *The Complete Guide to Barber Halves.* (Virginia Beach, VA: DLRC Press, 1992).

Lawrence, David. *The Complete Guide to Barber Quarters 2nd Ed.* (Virginia Beach, VA: DLRC Press, 1994).

Logan, Russell, with McClosky, John. *Federal Half Dimes 1792–1837.* (Manchester, MI: John Reich Collectors Society,1998).

Maris, Edward. *A Historic Sketch of the Coins of New Jersey.* (Philadelphia: Kenneth Morrison, 1881, three reprints since).

Miller, Henry C., and Hillyer, Ryder. *The State Coinages of New England.* (New York: 1920).

Nelson, Philip. *The Coinage of William Wood 1722–1733.* (London, England: 1903, reprinted 1959). Reprint New York: S.J. Durst, 1978.

Newcomb, H.R. *United States Copper Cents 1816–1857.* (New York: Quarterman Publications, 1944, reprinted in 1983).

Newman, Eric P. *Coinage for Colonial Virginia.* (New York: American Numismatic Society, 1957).

Newman, Eric P., and Doty, Richard G. *Studies on Money in Early America.* (New York: American Numismatic Society, 1976).

Noe, Sydney P. *The New England and Willow Tree Coinage of Massachusetts.* (New York: American Numismatic Society, 1943, reprinted in 1973).

Noe, Sydney P. *The Pine Tree Coinage of Massachusetts.* (New York: American Numismatic Society, 1952, reprinted in 1973).

Noe, Sydney P. *The Oak Tree Coinage of Massachusetts.* (New York: American Numismatic Society, 1947, reprinted in 1973).

Noyes, William C. *United States Large Cents 1793–1814.* (Bloomington, MN: Litho Tech Services, 1991).

Noyes, William C. *United States Large Cents 1816–1839.* (Bloomington, MN: Litho Tech Services, 1991).

Overton, Al C. *Early Half Dollar Die Varieties 1794–1836.* (Colorado Springs, CO: Al C. Overton, 1967, reprinted in 1990).

Pick, Albert. *Standard Catalog of World Paper Money.* (Iola, WI: Krause Publications, 2003).

Rulau, Russell, and Fuld, George. *Medallic Portraits of Washington.* (Iola, WI: Krause Publications, 1999).

Sear, David R. *Byzantine Coins and Their Values.* (London, England: Seaby Publications, 1987).

Sear, David R. *Greek Coins and Their Values.* (London, England: Seaby Publications, 1978).

Sear, David R. *Roman Coins and Their Values.* (London, England: Seaby Publications, 2000).

Sheldon, William H. *Penny Whimsy (1793–1814).* (Lawrence, MA: Quarterman Publications, 1981).

Snow, Richard. *Flying Eagle and Indian Cents.* (Tucson, AZ: Eagle Eye Press, 1992).

Spink & Co. Ltd. *Standard Catalogue of British Coins. Coins of England and the United Kingdom.* (London, England: Spink & Sons Ltd., 2005).

Swiatek, Anthony, and Breen, Walter. *The Encyclopedia of United States Silver and Gold Commemorative Coins 1892–1954.* (New York: ARCO/F.C.I. Press, 1981).

Travers, Scott A. *The Coin Collector's Survival Manual.* (New York: Random House, 2006).

Travers, Scott A. *Official Guide to Grading and Counterfeit Detection.* (New York: The Ballantine Publishing Group, 2004).

Valentine, D.W. *The United States Half Dimes.* (New York: American Numismatic Society, 1931, reprinted Lawrence, MA: Quarterman Publications, 1975).

Van Allen, Leroy C., and Mallis, A. George. *Comprehensive Catalogue and Encyclopedia of U.S. Morgan and Peace Silver Dollars.* (New York: WorldWide Ventures, Inc., 1997).

Wescott, Michael. *The United States Nickel Five-Cent Piece.* (Wolfeboro, NH: Bowers & Merena, 1991).

Wurtzbach, Carl. *Complete Set of Massachusetts Colonial Silver Money.* (Sun Printing Co., 1937).

Yeoman, Richard S. *A Guide Book of United States Coins.* (Atlanta, GA: Whitman Publications, 2006).

Weekly and Monthly Trade Publications

In weekly and monthly coin collecting publications, you can find information about coins and coin collecting and also about the social aspects of the hobby. Here are some of the more widely circulated publications specializing in numismatics.

Bank Note Reporter
Krause Publications, Inc.
700 East State Street
Iola, WI 54990

Canadian Numismatic News
Trajan Publishing Corporation
103 Lakeshore Road, Suite 202
St. Catherines, Ontario, Canada L2N 2T6

The Celator
P.O. Box 839
Lancaster, PA 17608
Coin Dealer Newsletter

CDN Inc.
18807 Crenshaw Place
Torrance, CA 90504-5923

Coin World
Amos Press Inc.
911 Vandemark Road
Sidney, OH 45365

COINage Magazine
Miller Publications Inc.
4880 Market Street
Ventura, CA 93003

MRI Bankers' Guide to Foreign Currency
Monetary Research Institute
P.O. Box 3174
Houston, TX 77253-3174

Numismatic News
Krause Publications, Inc.
700 East State Street
Iola, WI 54990

The Numismatist
American Numismatic Association
818 Cascade Avenue
Colorado Springs, CO 80903-3279

World Coin News
Krause Publications, Inc.
700 East State Street
Iola, WI 54990

Munzen Review
Blotzheimerstrasse 40, 4055
Basel, Switzerland
Coin News

Token Publishing
Orchard House, Duchy Road, Heathpark
Honiton, Devon EX14 1YD
United Kingdom

appendix c

Groups and Organizations

Here are the major organizations within the hobby through which you can gain the knowledge necessary to participate in a meaningful way. The American Numismatic Association provides its members with a free list of its member clubs and associations.

National Organizations

American Numismatic Association
www.money.org
818 North Cascade Avenue
Colorado Springs, CO 80903

American Numismatic Society
www.numismatics.org
96 Fulton Street
New York, NY 10038

Canadian Numismatic Association
www.canadian-numismatic.org
4936 Yonge Street, Suite 601
North York, Ontario M2N 6S3
Canada

Other Major Domestic Coin Clubs

Inquire through local coin dealers, other collectors, and the local chamber of commerce to learn where clubs exist in your local area.

Chicago Coin Club
www.chicagocoinclub.org
P.O. Box 2301
Chicago, IL 60690

New Jersey Numismatic Association
c/o Ray Flanigan
Madison Public Library
39 Keep Street
Madison, NJ 07940

Central States Numismatic Society
www.centralstates.info
P.O. Box 841
Logansport, IN 46947

Other Specialized Coin Clubs

There is likely a club focused on almost any aspect of coin collecting that may interest you.

American Israel Numismatic Association
www.amerisrael.com
12555 Biscayne Boulevard, No. 733
North Miami, FL 33181

Bust Half Nut Club
www.busthalfprices.com
c/o Glen R. Peterson
9301 Park West Boulevard
Knoxville, TN 37923

Early American Coppers
www.eacs.org
P.O. Box 15782
Cincinnati, OH 45215

Numismatic Literary Guild
www.numismaticliteraryguild.org
P.O. Box 6909
San Diego, CA 92166

Polish American Numismatic Association
P.O. Box 46829
Chicago, IL 60656

Russian Numismatic Society
www.russiannumismaticsociety.org
P.O. Box 3684
Santa Rosa, CA 95402

Silver Dollar Roundtable
P.O. Box 913
Bowie, MD 20715

Index

HOME IMPROVEMENT

Everything® Feng Shui Book
Everything® Feng Shui Decluttering Book, $9.95
Everything® Fix-It Book
Everything® Home Decorating Book
Everything® Home Storage Solutions Book
Everything® Homebuilding Book
Everything® Lawn Care Book
Everything® Organize Your Home Book

KIDS' BOOKS

All titles are $7.95

Everything® Kids' Animal Puzzle & Activity Book
Everything® Kids' Baseball Book, 4th Ed.
Everything® Kids' Bible Trivia Book
Everything® Kids' Bugs Book
Everything® Kids' Cars and Trucks Puzzle & Activity Book
Everything® Kids' Christmas Puzzle & Activity Book
Everything® Kids' Cookbook
Everything® Kids' Crazy Puzzles Book
Everything® Kids' Dinosaurs Book
Everything® Kids' First Spanish Puzzle and Activity Book
Everything® Kids' Gross Hidden Pictures Book
Everything® Kids' Gross Jokes Book
Everything® Kids' Gross Mazes Book
Everything® Kids' Gross Puzzle and Activity Book
Everything® Kids' Halloween Puzzle & Activity Book
Everything® Kids' Hidden Pictures Book
Everything® Kids' Horses Book
Everything® Kids' Joke Book
Everything® Kids' Knock Knock Book
Everything® Kids' Learning Spanish Book
Everything® Kids' Math Puzzles Book
Everything® Kids' Mazes Book
Everything® Kids' Money Book
Everything® Kids' Nature Book
Everything® Kids' Pirates Puzzle and Activity Book
Everything® Kids' Princess Puzzle and Activity Book
Everything® Kids' Puzzle Book
Everything® Kids' Riddles & Brain Teasers Book
Everything® Kids' Science Experiments Book
Everything® Kids' Sharks Book
Everything® Kids' Soccer Book
Everything® Kids' Travel Activity Book

KIDS' STORY BOOKS

Everything® Fairy Tales Book

LANGUAGE

Everything® Conversational Chinese Book with CD, $19.95
Everything® Conversational Japanese Book with CD, $19.95
Everything® French Grammar Book
Everything® French Phrase Book, $9.95
Everything® French Verb Book, $9.95
Everything® German Practice Book with CD, $19.95
Everything® Inglés Book
Everything® Learning French Book
Everything® Learning German Book
Everything® Learning Italian Book
Everything® Learning Latin Book
Everything® Learning Spanish Book
Everything® Russian Practice Book with CD, $19.95
Everything® Sign Language Book
Everything® Spanish Grammar Book
Everything® Spanish Phrase Book, $9.95
Everything® Spanish Practice Book with CD, $19.95
Everything® Spanish Verb Book, $9.95

MUSIC

Everything® Drums Book with CD, $19.95
Everything® Guitar Book
Everything® Guitar Chords Book with CD, $19.95
Everything® Home Recording Book
Everything® Music Theory Book with CD, $19.95
Everything® Reading Music Book with CD, $19.95
Everything® Rock & Blues Guitar Book (with CD), $19.95
Everything® Songwriting Book

NEW AGE

Everything® Astrology Book, 2nd Ed.
Everything® Birthday Personology Book
Everything® Dreams Book, 2nd Ed.
Everything® Love Signs Book, $9.95
Everything® Numerology Book
Everything® Paganism Book
Everything® Palmistry Book
Everything® Psychic Book
Everything® Reiki Book
Everything® Sex Signs Book, $9.95
Everything® Tarot Book, 2nd Ed.
Everything® Wicca and Witchcraft Book

PARENTING

Everything® Baby Names Book, 2nd Ed.
Everything® Baby Shower Book
Everything® Baby's First Food Book
Everything® Baby's First Year Book
Everything® Birthing Book
Everything® Breastfeeding Book
Everything® Father-to-Be Book
Everything® Father's First Year Book
Everything® Get Ready for Baby Book
Everything® Get Your Baby to Sleep Book, $9.95
Everything® Getting Pregnant Book
Everything® Guide to Raising a One-Year-Old
Everything® Guide to Raising a Two-Year-Old
Everything® Homeschooling Book
Everything® Mother's First Year Book
Everything® Parent's Guide to Children and Divorce
Everything® Parent's Guide to Children with ADD/ADHD
Everything® Parent's Guide to Children with Asperger's Syndrome
Everything® Parent's Guide to Children with Autism
Everything® Parent's Guide to Children with Bipolar Disorder
Everything® Parent's Guide to Children with Dyslexia
Everything® Parent's Guide to Positive Discipline
Everything® Parent's Guide to Raising a Successful Child
Everything® Parent's Guide to Raising Boys
Everything® Parent's Guide to Raising Siblings
Everything® Parent's Guide to Sensory Integration Disorder
Everything® Parent's Guide to Tantrums
Everything® Parent's Guide to the Overweight Child
Everything® Parent's Guide to the Strong-Willed Child
Everything® Parenting a Teenager Book
Everything® Potty Training Book, $9.95
Everything® Pregnancy Book, 2nd Ed.
Everything® Pregnancy Fitness Book
Everything® Pregnancy Nutrition Book
Everything® Pregnancy Organizer, 2nd Ed., $16.95
Everything® Toddler Activities Book
Everything® Toddler Book
Everything® Tween Book
Everything® Twins, Triplets, and More Book